The arc and the machine

MANCHESTER
1824
Manchester University Press

The arc and the machine
Narrative and new media

Caroline Bassett

Manchester University Press
Manchester and New York
distributed exclusively in the USA by Palgrave

Published by Manchester University Press
Oxford Road, Manchester M13 9NR, UK
and Room 400, 175 Fifth Avenue, New York, NY 10010, USA
www.manchesteruniversitypress.co.uk

Distributed in the United States exclusively by
Palgrave Macmillan, 175 Fifth Avenue,
New York, NY 10010, USA

Distributed in Canada exclusively by
UBC Press, University of British Columbia, 2029 West Mall,
Vancouver, BC, Canada V6T 1Z2

British Library Cataloguing-in-Publication Data is available

Library of Congress Cataloging-in-Publication Data is available

ISBN 978 0 7190 7343 4 paperback

First published by Manchester University Press in hardback 2007

This paperback edition first published 2014

Printed by Lightning Source

For A. M. B.

Contents

Acknowledgements

Many people offered advice, support and friendship during the writing of this book. As is usual in these cases, none of them are to blame.

Thanks go to current and past colleagues at the University of Sussex including Roger Silverstone, Mandy Merck, Alan Cawson, Kate Lacey, Michael Bull, Mary-Agnes Krell, Jenny Alexander, Thomas Austin, Lizzie Thynne, Mel Friend, Dolores Tierney, Andy Medhurst, Janice Winship, Wilma de Jong, Lee Gooding and Sue Thornham. Gratitude is also due to my D.Phil. students: I'd especially like to mention Dave Berry, Giota Alevizou and Alison Bambridge, thanks to them for many energetic discussions and arguments. Thanks to Jane Bassett and Kate O'Riordan for reading drafts early and late, to Julie Doyle and Irmi Karl for reading chapters (and for elephant jokes), to Ben Morgan for coffee, and to Joanne Hurley, Chris Wilbert and Hilary Baker for many forms of collaboration, interaction, provocation, friendship and love.

Introduction

All you need is a different notebook, and the words will start flowing again. (Paul Auster, *Oracle Night*, 2003, 229)

New Engine, Same Soul. (Advertisement for a Macbook Pro, AppleStore, 2006)

Once, even recently, narrative was widely accepted as a dominant cultural logic and it did not seem controversial to suggest that lives, histories and cultures could be understood within its grounds. These days, in the first decade of the twenty-first century, global information systems of all kinds have come to pervade every aspect of life in the North and to redefine the terms of its inequality with the South, so that information systems cast a shadow there too, even as they are held out of the reach of many. And these days narrative's centrality seems less certain.

Standing on the threshold of the age of mass communication Walter Benjamin argued that narrative could not survive the moment of information (Benjamin, 1992: 73–89). Today these words may have a new resonance as they are rehearsed in relation to immeasurably complex information systems operating at scales at once grander and more intimate that Benjamin could ever have dreamed of.

Narrative has been understood as something that can encompass vast landscapes and single atoms, the life span of individuals and the rise and fall of empires, but its place looks less sure in a world where information is pervasive, so that more and more cultural forms and practices of more and more kinds can be included under its banner. In doing so they change their shape, take on another logic, become more or less significant, or fade away. The question is whether narrative can survive this remediation of the world through information.

At one level these doubts about the future of narrative cohere around specific cultural forms. Contemporary culture is marked by the database query, the fragment of talk, the evanescent shred of the news item exhausted in the moment of its delivery, the oscillating activity and stasis – Game On or Game Over – of the player. These cultural forms find their corollaries in what is characterized as an increasingly immaterial economy, which reorganizes work so that it is now experienced as a series of temporal and spatial discontinuities and ruptures, operating both at micro- and macro-levels: the call/hold of the phone call, the on/off of the job itself.

The forms of temporal resolution, and with them the forms of continuity, that narrative offers as it binds up experiences in time may seem inimical to these new cultural forms and practices. These gestures of automated labour and computerized leisure[1] may seem too fast and too fragmented for meaning to take hold, and they may also seem to be understandable within their own horizons, to need no other form of interpretation.

Within this world-view the logic of information is offered *in the place of* the logic of the tale. Through this logic, it is said, we are constituted as individuals, through this logic we are said to act and speak, to be entertained, informed and controlled. Within this logic everyday life is conducted. Responding to the rise of information Jean-François Lyotard famously argued that the databases should be opened to the people; today many would argue that we have moved inside the machines, taken on board their mode of operation, aligned our sensory perception to their outputs. Perhaps even our desires have become machinic.

These arguments are seductive. For some the end of narrative, and with it the end of a particular form of interpretation, seems to usher in new possibilities: new forms of pleasure and sensation and indeed new forms of freedom. At the very least, what is lost, or so it is said, is a clinging to the past, an irrational refusal to consider the post-human future. The apocalyptic predictions of writers such as Paul Virilio, who fears that we lost the ontological grounds for narrative when we punctured the sheltering horizon of the sky with space travel on the one hand and with virtual space on the other, also have a stark glamour and are certainly performed with mordant brio (Virilio, 1997). Finally the systematic and rigorous arguments of thinkers such as Lev Manovich, working around particular cultural forms, have a real allure; and if this is in part because they offer brand new theoretical frameworks to match brand new machines, it is also because they grapple with the remediation of existing cultural forms in penetrating ways. Whatever position on narrative is to be taken, it is undoubtedly the case that databases, archives, algorithms, the visible forms of information, are crucial elements of contemporary cultural forms and practices. The case against narrative seems to be made.

The Arc and the Machine refuses to be seduced. This book comes to the defence of narrative, arguing that it is a vital element of contemporary culture, lying at the heart of the processes through which humans make sense of their experiences in everyday lives that are, by virtue of their mediation through and across information, increasingly multi-layered and complex both temporally and spatially. Narrative, understood as an extensive arc constituted by a process of emplotment that both reaches back into the horizon of the event and forwards into the horizon of the reader, can make sense of these experiences through a form of assembly that is not retrospective but in process, not necessarily linear but rather expansive, and that is certainly open and indeed *generative*.

The point here is not to make comparisons between linear narrative as a fixed form whose moment has passed and the database as form whose moment has come (and nor is it useful to posit narrative as a transcendental floating above all the tumult). Rather I argue that narrative is an intrinsic part of a new informational economy which becomes its material and which it holds and articulates. Narrative *lives* because it is contingent and mutable, because it is changing and transforming rather than fading in response to alterations in the material conditions under which we live, which are themselves articulations of a social totality.

Fredric Jameson argued that the cultural object, 'as though for the first time, brings into being that very situation to which it is also at one and the same time, a reaction' (Jameson, 1981: 82). It is thus socially symbolic, the *bearer* of the time in which it was made. Narrative, a continuous reaction to information and its discontinuity, might in this sense also be understood to bring information into being *as* a material cultural form. Or if we switch this around, we could say that narrative can produce information's and information technology's *concept*.

The book itself traverses a narrative arc. The first section explores narrative theories in relation to questions of technology and text, and then turns to consider the claims made for new media when they are understood within a longer history of innovation marked by swings between technological and culturally deterministic approaches. In particular here I focus on questions of the interface, understood as an extension of automation rather than in terms of simulation. This leads to a reconsideration of technoculture, and in particular to an exploration of the divisions between more or less Marxist and post-human approaches to thinking about information, as they have emerged out of this history.

Bringing these two chapters together produces new grounds for thinking about questions of narrative and new media, and it is from these grounds, or within them, that the second section of the book sets out to explore a series of new media forms and practices, each of which are considered through the optic of narrative.

The first of these chapters considers digital identity in narrative terms through an exploration of *Rehearsal of Memory*, an early digital artwork which helped to constitute contemporary forms of speculative software. In part this is also a dialogue with performative accounts of identity, as they have been widely explored in relation to informational culture.

This is followed by a chapter that traces the history of a long-standing virtual community, read here as the history of a change in narrative space. At issue is the degree to which narrative itself may be something that is recuperated and commoditized within the new economy of the Internet.

Finally I turn to *Elephant*, Gus Van Sant's film about the Columbine killings, which may be regarded as interactive and which provokes consideration of non-linearity as a new form of composition, rather than as a form of decomposition or simple disruption. This opens the way to a broader consideration of the cultural forms and practices of everyday life within informational culture. The logic of narrative as an ongoing response to information may be generalized: there is an elephant called narrative in the room.

Notes

1   '[The everyday is] made of recurrences: gestures of labour and leisure, mechanical movements both human and properly machinic . . . cyclical repetitions'. (Henri Lefebvre, cited in Clucas, 2000: 19)

1

Narrative machines

Preface: 'like life itself'
The narratives of the world are numberless ... Able to be carried by
articulated language, spoken or written, fixed or moving images, gestures
and the ordered mixture of all these substances; narrative is present in
myth, legend, fable, tale, novella, epic, history, tragedy ... comics, news
items, conversation ... [U]nder this almost infinite diversity of forms,
narrative is present in every age, in every place, in every society ... Caring
nothing for the division between good and bad literature, narrative is
international, transhistorical, transcultural: it is simply there, like life itself.
(Barthes, 1982: 79)

There is a long-standing popular conviction that narrative is natural,
found in all societies, carried across many different kinds of delivery
channel, infinitely variable because all stories are different but also always
the same. Understood in this way, narrative is part of what it is to be
human, it *wells up* 'like life itself', something independent of historical and
cultural forces and also of technological ones. However, as biotechnology
advances, it is clear that 'life itself', the guarantor of narrative's constancy,
isn't quite what it was; certainly it is impossible to regard it as unproblem-
atically natural, as legions of feminists, amongst others, have pointed
out (Waldby, 2000; Davis, 2000). In these contexts, perhaps, we are
authorized to twist Barthes's famous phrase around. If 'life itself' is
understood as socially, culturally and historically defined, then comparing
narrative to life would suggest that narrative too needs to be considered
as a product of history rather than as a transhistorical necessity. That is,
narrative, as it comes to shape fiction and also life, can be understood as
mutable. This mutability opens up the possibility that narrative can reflect,
in its forms and its contents, the technologies of which it itself is partly
made, the more general technological conditions of the societies which
make it and the historical conditions in which those technologies are
developed.

To assert that particular narratives can be revealing of the historical conditions in which they were made is not contentious. Nor is it unusual to suggest that many narratives have something to say about technology. Science fiction and social prophecy of all kinds operate at the interchange between information technology, culture and society, exploring possible worlds and thereby this one. 'If you want a picture of the future' of a society based on information systems, George Orwell and many others provide it (Orwell, 1989: 234). Here, the focus is not on the tales that take as their subject future technologies and future cultures. It is narrative 'itself' that is under discussion here, and I explore it neither as a fixed form nor as a contingent content but rather as a formation emerging out of the contemporary interchange between information technology, culture and society. If narrative is socially symbolic then the materials of which it is made, the conditions within which it is read, as well as the forms in which it is written or practised and the tales that it gathers up within itself, *matter*. They are a part of *what* gets symbolized, and *how*. To explore changing narrative formations developing in relation to new media might thus offer insights into the cultural significance of contemporary processes of automation transforming the temporal and spatial dimensions of everyday life.

Narrative doubts

What previously was a representational culture of narrative, discourse and the image which the reader, viewer or audience encountered in a dualistic relation, now becomes a technological culture. Culture is comprised no longer primarily of such representations but instead of cultural objects as technologies that are in the same space with what is now less the reader, viewer, spectator or audience than the user, the player. (Lash, 2002: x)

When did 'technological culture' begin? The timing, and even the tense, of the technological event that supposedly ended representational culture, and within it narrative, are left decidedly vague in accounts like the one above, which are marked by a tendency to slip between the present and the near future. As it is for the Jehovah's Witnesses, so it is for the information theorists: those in the know can feel the heat, but the fire itself (or at least the purgation to be provided by salvational technology) is always next time. This allows for continued prophesying, but means that information theorists can run the risk that, like Belloc's Matilda, they may not be believed when the real fire comes.[1] In this case repetition produces incredulity towards (another) metanarrative about information technology; there is reasonable doubt about the exact arrival-time of the information society. Out of this a question arises: what is meant by 'narrative' here? For Scott Lash, what narrative is, or does, isn't crucial, because, in his view, narrative has been superseded so that the 'axial principle of culture' is not the unit of narrative but the unit of communication (Lash, 2002: viii). Still, it seems important to me to ask what form of narrative the coming, or arrived, 'technological culture' will override.

Lash's views, shared by many, are indicative of a new stage in a period of narrative doubt that began in the 1980s, and that famously found a focus in Jameson's account of postmodernism/late capitalism, which bound up narrative's demise within an account of the cultural and political logics of post-industrial or late capitalist society (Jameson, 1991). For Jameson, the cultural logic of late capitalism is such that it all but eliminates the possibility of achieving critical distance, fracturing vision, texts and meaning itself. Jameson is articulating what has become a more-or-less standard understanding of postmodernity as the eclipse of meaning. As a part of this eclipse, Jameson predicted the loss of narrative resolution and the descent into cultural schizophrenia at the hands of highly informated capital.

Today these narrative doubts, re-emerging in the contemporary era of digital capitalism, are worn with a difference. For Jameson, technology is not ultimately determining, rather it *seems* to be so; it is, as he describes it, a 'distorted figuration of something deeper, namely the whole world system of present day multinational capitalism (Jameson, 1984: 79).[2] For Lash, the differentiated but materially indifferent plane of information is what there is; nothing remains to be revealed; there is no place for a hermeneutics of suspicion. So, where the Jameson of the *Cultural Logic* calls for cognitive mapping as a response to disorientation, Lash calls for a melancholic form of *flânerie* amidst the immanent planes of information. This time around even the *desire* to re-establish 'older' modes of interpretation (possible or not), or to find new ones, has often disappeared. Lash's bid is to develop a critique appropriate to the condition of information, which is, as he views it, a condition of more or less absolute immanence within which the possibility of interpretation is lost. I respect his attempt. However, given his sense of what is no longer possible in these new conditions, it doesn't surprise me that in the end the form of critique he offers operates as melancholia. In a sense, indeed, the *Critique of Information* is an elegy for times past. Lash, now in the endless bittersweet hereafter, is left mourning for the time of the tale.

To me mourning seems premature. Such claims for the death of narrative at the hands of information are widespread, but I believe they are, in the end, unsustainable. I read them as contemporary symptoms of a pervasive and recurrent, but transient, cultural anxiety evident around processes of technological innovation involving information. Jameson's famous essay marks one moment in this cycle, but this is an anxiety that might be said to have begun with Plato and his fears that writing would be deleterious to memory (Plato, 1973), and which was certainly present, and specifically located as an anxiety about narrative, in the early years of the development of mass communication systems (see Benjamin, 1992: 83).

In this chapter I shall begin to make the twin argument that narrative remains, and that it remains important: the point is not to look for bodies, or for tenacious narrative survivors, in Jameson's rubble of empty signifiers, nor is it to dwell on the memory of tales once told that might persist in Lash's new order. The point is to argue that narrative remains *central* to what we do in an information-saturated world. Narrative is at the heart of the operations of everyday life and everyday culture within a world where digital technology is becoming pervasive. To consider contemporary narrative formations *is* to engage with contemporary techno-culture.

This is to assert that the relationship between narrative and information technology 'naturalized' since being set out by Jameson, and others writing in a similar vein, in the 1980s and early 1990s – so that it now seems to be common sense to assert that the rise of information entails the demise of narrative – needs to be reconsidered, as does the vague but pervasive assumption that the forms of information are automatically postmodern forms, which comes with it. In this work of disturbance, I go behind and around some of ways of thinking about narrative that the *Cultural Logic* articulates and produces (including forms of thinking that Jameson himself would perhaps not recognize, but which are nonetheless part of the legacy of his work), considering earlier theories of narrative and looking in particular at whether the place accorded (implicitly or explicitly) to the technological within these theories might allow 'broken narratives of possibility' (Pollock, 2003) for narrative itself to be revived and developed.

At best this move clears the way for redefining narrative in relation to information, exposing the theoretical contradictions of contemporary expositions of their relationship where they rest on contradictory senses of the determinations of culture on the one hand, and of technology on the other. At the least, it raises the prospect that the relationship between a particular cultural form (narrative today), a particular set of technologies (networked new media) and a particular historical moment can be *explored* rather than assumed. If narrative is dead, we will at least have exhumed and named the corpse rather than jumped up and down on a grave whose legend is clear but whose contents are obscure.

A return to structural narratology provides a suitable starting point in this process, partly because it marks a point of origin for contemporary theorizations of narrative and continues to influence later theorizations in various ways. In fact, structuralist theories of narrative remain *operational* despite shifts in the field of cultural theory in general – and this is both the marker and the result of a certain theoretical neglect of narrative in recent years. Certainly versions of structural narratology continued to be deployed well into the era in which post-structuralism came to dominate as a general analysis of cultural production – and they continue to be deployed today when this domination is less certain. Indeed accounts of narrative labelled 'post-structuralist' may be closer to revisionist forms of structural narratology than anything else, as Andrew Gibson has pointed out (Gibson, 1996a). This theoretical conflation/confusion accelerates in relation to techno-cultural writing, which has done very little theorizing of narrative. In some cases, the kind of reliance on older structural models described above is evident. In others, narrative is unexamined as a category even while it is set aside, declared fatally wounded by informatics. Here is one justification for demanding which 'narrative', which 'narrative culture', it is that is superseded?

It would be possible to speculate on why this narrative neglect occurs. It is a characteristic of much techno-cultural critique (and of many accounts of new technologies) that the old is hypostatized in the attempt to define more sharply the outline of the new, and this may have a bearing here; certainly many modernists would fail to recognize in their writing the narrative that techno-cultural theorists declare to be dead; and chemical photography was never so *indexical* as in the time just preceding the pixel, as Martin Lister points out (Lister, 1995). Less speculatively, it is clear that in the case of narrative this neglect (or reversion) produces some convoluted theoretical twists and turns. It is striking, for instance, that arguments made for narrative's decline couched in terms of nature/culture dualisms – so that narrative is put on the side of 'the human' (as nature) and technology on the side of 'progress' (as culture) – emerge in techno-cultural writing grounded in forms of thinking that vehemently oppose such distinctions. A certain theoretical exceptionalism is evident here; within a world-view which places humans and technology on the same plane, in which actions and practices may be understood as in a continuum with technology and sensation may be felt between human and machine, narrative is set apart. In this rush of transformation it alone has not changed and is, therefore, irrelevant to technoculture – oddly enough, impossibly enough within the terms of the argument, standing above it. The narrative/information dichotomy produced here thus stands as a startling exception to post-humanism's vigorously asserted sense of *continuity* between the human and the machine.

A final reason to make the detour through structural narratology in a bid to explore contemporary new media is found in the connections between structuralism and cybernetics. Structuralism flowered in an era when cybernetics and information theory were highly influential as components for critically thinking about earlier forms of the 'information revolution' (see Heims, 1991), and the rigorous exclusions upon which structuralism is founded resonate with the bid to make narrative more scientific, which is also, as Eco might put it, a bid to make it *computational*. Structuralism, as it developed in these years, thus owes a debt to cybernetics and information theory; we might say that it not only haunts later forms of narratology, but that it is itself haunted – and that this time the ghost in the system is information technology. Another way to put this is to suggest that structuralism was never as *hygienic* as its adherents thought it could be. Further, we can note that the extension of structuralism, its study of secondary systems, has largely been predicated on, and has certainly been theorized through, media systems (the oral, the chirographical/typological, the cinematic, the televisual/video and now the digital). Intended to operate as a closed system, independent of material substrates, it turns out to have been infected from the start.

Engaging with structural narratology leads to a brief consideration of various post-structural accounts emerging in response to these closures and tending to deprioritize structure and interpretation in favour of force or affect so that narrative itself is deprioritized as a mode of experience, becoming one possibility amongst many for thinking the text, or the artefact, or life itself in so far as it is understood as a narrative construction.

The final sections of the chapter begin with another return, since here I reach behind Jameson's *Cultural Logic* to explore the *Political Unconscious*, an earlier work on narrative and a 'reckoning with structuralism' (LaCapra, 1983: 235) that seeks to exceed it through its own deployment as much as to attack or defend it (Jameson, 1991: 297). In this work Jameson argues that narrative is a resolution in *poesis* of the contradictions of the society in which it is made so that, opened in the right way, narrative can reveal the logic of that society, and beneath it the repressed logic of history itself (Jameson, 1991). Jameson's work is read in tandem with the post-structural hermeneutics of the French philosopher and cultural theorist Paul Ricoeur. Reading narrative as a central act of configuration, the way in which human experience is made meaningful, Ricoeur reconnects narrative with event and experience, extending the scope of its formal operations to encompass the act of reading or interpretation alongside the act of production and the moment of the text, thereby extending the narrative arc from the text into the world. Both of these accounts extend the horizons of narrative beyond the limits dreamed of by structuralism; in Jameson's case the trajectory is shaped by a properly Utopian desire for emancipation, and in Ricoeur's by a form of eschatology.

'No sharing of motives': structural narratology
For narratology, geometry is a kind of universal law. (Gibson, 1996a: 5)

Narratology,[3] understood in its strict sense, is the study of narrative rooted in Saussurean structural linguistics. This is a conception of narrative that accepts the Saussurean imperative: a demand that the study of language is understood as the study of its formal structures. At the heart of structural linguistics is the insight that the nature of the sign is arbitrary – that is, the link between signifier and signified is an arbitrary relation. Two crucial conclusions flow from this insight: the first is the observation that language is not to be understood as a set of descriptions but as a system of differences (Saussure, 1983), so that signs can only be understood to gain their meaning in relation to other signs. This is the reification of the text at the heart of structuralism, aptly summed up by the Russian linguist Voloshinov in his critique of structuralism in *Marxism and the Philosophy of Language*. Voloshinov suggests that structuralism amounts to

> [A] stable immutable system of normatively identical linguistic forms which the individual consciousness finds ready made and which is incontestable for that consciousness . . . the laws of language are the specifically linguistic laws of connection between linguistic signs within a given, closed linguistic system . . . (Voloshinov, 1973: 57)

The second conclusion flowing from the insight that the nature of the sign is arbitrary is that in this closure inheres the necessity for structure. That is, given that signifiers and signifieds are not in a natural relationship, without a shared linguistic structure humans would have no means of understanding each other. As Derrida has pointed out, here is the rationale not only for the erection of a formal structure (*langue*) but also for Saussure's concomitant belief that the proper study of linguistics is the study of that structure (Derrida, 1972: 60–76). This is a structure Saussure understood both as the condition for the possibility of comprehension and as standing outside language in its lived everyday use (*parole*).

Saussure's system does not rule out shifts in linguistic form; on the contrary, they are assumed. Voloshinov points out that within Saussure's system acts of refraction, variation and distortion of normative forms take place and 'explain the historical changeability of linguistic forms' (Voloshinov, 1973: 57). However this constant insubordination of *parole* in its relation to the rule of language is precisely what Saussure believes should not be studied.[4] As the former puts it (and this is the root of Voloshinov's critique of Saussure), from the language point of view (de Saussure's) this changeability 'is irrational and senseless. There is no connection, *no sharing of motives*, between the system of language and its history. They are alien to one another' (Voloshinov, 1973: 57, my italics). For Saussurean structuralism the relationship between the overarching structure of a language (*la langue*) and language in its living use (*le parole*) is occluded. There can be no consideration of 'shared motives' within this model between abstracted linguistic models (essentially synchronic), and diachronic approaches. In this synchronic analysis, what Voloshinov calls history, what Ricoeur and Derrida (differently) might understand as temporality, and what all three might consider to be the implications of the contexts of language, cannot be considered. They lie outside of a closed system and it is precisely on this closure or systematicity that the authority of structuralist linguistics, which is based on its claims to scientificity, rest. For Saussure the proper study of language is therefore to be understood as the study of a closed system that is frozen in a perpetual present (this latter being understandable as the structure of language at the time of inquiry).

Structural narratology emerges directly from the Saussurean tradition and is also influenced by Russian formalism.[5] For the structuralists, narrative, like language, may be understood in terms of underlying structures that are not themselves narratives, but are rather the conditions of possibility for all narratives. Structural narratology extends into meta-structures what structural linguistics confined to smaller units,[6] which implies to varying degrees a shift from a focus on semiotics to one on semantics. Narrative structures, as envisaged by various narratologists, might thus be said to have semantic trajectories (see for instance Greimas, 1987: 63–84). Narrative then becomes, in various ways, a secondary articulation of a primary or founding linguistic model, or a form of discourse forming 'the object of a second linguistics' (Barthes, 1982: 83). Barthes's formulation points to the inescapably linguistic nature of this form of analysis, which is retained despite its later extensions.

The giant works of formalist and structuralist narratology produced by theorists such as Propp, Greimas, Bremond and Genette still cast their shadows over contemporary theories of narrative. There are important distinctions between these accounts – the temporally based analysis of Genette contrasts with the systemic analysis of Greimas and Lévi-Strauss, for instance (see Silverstone, 1981: 9) – but these works are largely not competitive but concurrent, as Barthes, who was certainly one of the most influential theorists attempting to bring them together, points out (1982: 100). All were stabs at a general theory of the structure of narrative, bids to produce a grand explication of a completed narrative model, a model standing behind every story ever told and every story that is yet to be told. Taking their cue from structuralism itself, these models share a preoccupation with form, and are widely characterized as geometric: 'neatly segmented, symmetrically mapped, closed in and closed down by the geometric mode of description' (Gibson, 1986: 81). These models also had what the French narratologist A. J. Greimas called a certain 'operational facility' (Greimas, 1996: 87–98), which is to say they were intended for use. Greimas's own model was operationalized through the deployment of 'actants', ambiguous figures at once pointing to and withdrawing from real-world engagement. (Actor Network Theorists explored the constitution of scientific and technical networks through the extensive use of a theory of actants, and I briefly explore ANT's narrative adaptations below.)

The proliferation of detail, the parallels, divergences, shifting typologies, overlaps, conflicts and agreements found in these accounts make them tough to look back upon. However some key elements of the analysis, as they pertain to this discussion, emerge in Barthes extraordinary 1966 'Introduction to the Structural Analysis of Narratives' (Barthes, 1982), which synthesizes the ongoing work of many of these theorists, using the categories of function, action and narration culled from Bremond, Greimas and Todorov. Here I draw out five points. The first concerns questions of induction/deduction. For Barthes, the vast universe of narratives means that models are deductive first: a pre-built model is subsequently taken back to the specific instance of narrative. Second, they are characterized by multi-layered levels of meaning and scale; not only is there an initial elaboration of a relationship between primary and secondary systems but also 'a hierarchy of instances' within the system itself (Barthes, 1984: 87). Third, this system is dense and irregular: 'narrative integration . . . does not present itself in a serenely regular manner like some fine architectural style leading by symmetrical chicaneries from an infinite variety of simple elements to a few complex masses' (Barthes, 1982: 122). Rather, narrative is like a fugue; each part 'radiates in several directions at once' so that that narrative only ' "holds" by the distortion and irradiation of its units' (Barthes, 1982: 118–119). Barthes can thus assert that meaning is not found at the end of a narrative but runs across it (Barthes, 1982: 87), suggesting that the structures under investigation are far more complex than caricatured versions of narratology ('structuralism equals linear narrative') might suggest. Fourth, temporality is viewed as *only* a structural category, an element of a semiotic system operating a law of immanence. And fifth, following the logic of the same law, the narrational code is the final level attainable and the end point of analysis: we do not step outside. For Barthes, *narration* gives on to the world and closes the analysis. Here narrative is not made but consumed and in that consumption it is *undone*.

These are highly abstracted models, closed economies from which the particular, the lived and the material, are always carefully expelled. At the same time, however, the story model that structural narratology defines presumes a second space. Particular manifestations of narrative are assumed to be 'instances of a larger geometry [that is also] implicit in the human, narrative mind' (Gibson, 1996: 5). Or, as Barthes put it somewhat differently, there is a narrative language within us, one which we use to *construct* the narrative offered to us *as* narrative so that 'to listen is not only to perceive a language, it is also to construct it' (Barthes, 1982: 102, my italics). The presumption that narrative is already 'out there' conditions the ways in which structural narratologists approach questions of the operationalization of their narrative models in general, not only in relation to the question of primary and secondary articulations but also in relation to the *technological* articulation of narrative. So, what can structuralism say about the material substrate, which clearly plays a role in the effecting of this required conjunction? Can it too be a system? Does narrative resound 'in' machines as Barthes says that it resounds in man? Given that, despite claims that it adopts a purely deductive approach, the elaboration of various forms of semiology has been driven by the development of particular media systems (the cinematic, televisual/video and now the digital), narrative can be understood to be partly *formed* through its instantiation in media technologies of various kinds, even as it maintains its claim to be immune from infection by its carriers. It was perhaps with the question of materiality in mind (as well as with reference to cinema as a locus for elaborations of narrative theory as it might be more broadly conceived) that de Lauretis could argue that '*any* theory of narrative should be informed by the critical discourse on narrative that has been elaborated in film theory' (de Lauretis, 1984: 10, my italics). Faced with the insistent presence of the cinematic apparatus, these questions demand elaboration.

Apparatus: holodectual and cinematical

In the days when the cinema was a novel and astonishing thing and its very existence seemed problematical, the literature of cinematography tended to be theoretical and fundamental . . . Today we tend to smile at this attitude; at any rate we believe . . . that the criticism of individual films states all there is to be said about film in general. (Metz, 1974: 1)

Consideration of the *technological* expression of narrative became the project of the apparatus theorists of the 1970s/1980s, as they set out to explore what Philip Rosen characterizes as the articulation between the technological apparatus of cinema and a particular regime of signification or cultural form that might be enabled by it in specific ways (Rosen, 1985: 282). Integral to the project was a desire to explore the operations of ideology within new kinds of media apparatus, and a concern expressed by Rosen was that the technology of cinema, or what he calls its funda-mental machinery, might determine this system, leaving no space for the operations of ideology. This concern was consistent with the priorities of these essentially literary theorists, for whom it was perhaps inconceivable that ideology might operate also through the medium, that a technology itself might 'hold' an ideological message. Here, however, the question of determination might usefully be turned on its head: suppose we do not ask if technology is a determinant here, but if *narrative* is? At this point, not only does the prospect of a different kind of determination emerge but also a different trajectory of co-determinations can be envisaged, raising questions about the relationship between narrative and technology that are central to my own inquiry. At issue here is the degree to which particular narrative formulations allow an engagement with the force and signification of *technology*: to what degree, that is, do these models allow technology to figure within an account of cultural forms and practices involving narrative?

Christian Metz's account of cinema as a 'narrative machine' in *Film Language* (1974), a classic analysis of narrative and the cinematic apparatus, provides a site to perform this up-ending. In *Film Language* Metz explores the phenomenology of the cinema audience, working to develop a sense of cinema itself as a visual technology (apparatus) while bringing this into conjunction with a model for narrative. At the core of this exploration is the recognition that something corresponding to the narrative model that structural narratology describes can be found in the world, and in particular can be found in the consciousness of the spectator. Structural accounts of narrative can thus be said to produce models that account 'with more precision for what a naïve consciousness had picked up without analysis' (Metz, 1974: 17). Metz can thus argue that cinematic signification 'renders explicit what had first been experienced as . . . perception' (1974: 17), assuming 'by virtue of an implicit or prior stage, something like a phenomenology of its subject' (1974: 17). In other words the cinematic apparatus, viewed as a narrative machine, here becomes something that *enables an already existing narrative*.

This has implications for the way in which the spectator is said to experience narrative as it is offered by the cinematic apparatus, and for the way the apparatus itself is conceived as a narrative machine. Metz's psychoanalytic account of cinematic signification is based on identification and begins with the space of the cinema itself, which renders the audience immobile as it sits in the dark facing the screen, an arrangement that resembles the subject facing the Lacanian mirror, except that in this case the mirror does not reflect the body of the spectator, who, by virtue of this missing body, is left free to transfer his (always problematic and partial) identifications elsewhere (on to the camera). The missing body on screen and the viewer's own disregarded body help produce kind of a 'vacuum . . . which dreams readily fill' (Jean Leirens, cited in Metz, 1974: 10). These, of course, are narrative dreams, and Metz can thus define *narrative* itself, *as the cinema reveals it*, as 'a closed discourse that proceeds by un-realizing a temporal sequence of events' (Metz, 1974: 28).

It is striking that the cinematic apparatus, as Metz describes it, leaves 'what narrative is' almost entirely untouched by 'what technology does'. Instead, the cinematic apparatus is viewed as a powerful 'vacuum', and the implosive pull of this emptied out space, forcing together narrative expectation and narrative offering, produces a dreamscape that may be experienced with a particular intensity. It may be in the sense that it compels action that de Lauretis can conceive of film narrative as sadistic (1984: 103); the sense of violence also connects with Barthes's comment that 'however casual . . . the act [of using media] . . . nothing can prevent that humble act from *installing in us*, all at once and in its entirety, the narrative code we are going to need' (Barthes, 1982: 116–117).

My question is not where does that leave ideology (let alone psychoanalysis) but where does that leave technology? In the end, Metz's conception of the cinematic apparatus as a narrative machine places media technology on the outside of the narrative system as he defines it. Indeed, the only way technology could find a way inside narrative within Metz's account would be if it figured in one of the dreams cinema enables (*Metropolis, Blade Runner, Terminator, The Matrix*).[7] That is, it would involve a retreat from a consideration of the cinematic, the project of apparatus theory, and a return to textual (on-screen) analysis. For Metz, narrative stands before its technological iteration as cinema, even while cinema stands in advance of the individual film. So, here it is not technology that determines, as theorists such as Rosen feared, rather it is the narrative system that operates *as* a closed and complete economy. The apparatus theorists produced a hugely powerful analysis of the ideological effects of film, but they operated with a narrative model that in the end excludes the technological in particular ways. (Once again the irony here is that these accounts are inflected by the general climate of the time, which was one in which cybernetics was highly influential.) This general framework enables particular kinds of investigation but forecloses others. It *is* possible to ask if something is a more or less powerful *transmitter* of narrative (is the large screen a better 'dream machine' than a small one, for instance). However, what can't be explored are the specific differences between the narrative *formations* that technological apparatus might not only enable but also partially constitute.

At risk of chronological violations, but in the hope of finding useful parallels, here I briefly fast forward to two accounts of new media. The first is offered by Janet Murray in *Hamlet on the Holodeck*, which is a sustained exploration of narrative and new media characterized by an ambiguous theorization of narrative. *Hamlet on the Holodeck* often works with structural narratology (the measure against which the 'incunabula' of existing experiments in online fiction are compared) but also diverges from it at various points. Murray is optimistic about the prospect of new forms of literary work on the web, but I want to suggest that her avowedly technophile account can also be read as hostile to information technology. Murray argues that 'characteristic pleasures' the new medium offers (defined here through its aesthetics) might be described as procedural, participatory, spatial and encyclopedic (1999, 71). Her sense is that these can successfully translate narrative into a new sphere. The new media of the future might work to manipulate texts and organize users' perceptions and reactions in order to produce satisfying experiences that we can now only glimpse. In particular, immersive experiences would work by giving interactors a sense of control, while at the same time allowing for a structured engagement with the text, the latter being viewed here as necessary to story. It is striking that in *Hamlet on the Holodeck*, the terms of interrogation become a means by which to explore the implications of this medium for the 'traditional' satisfactions of narrative and for its 'traditional' forms. In this sense narrative is not only indifferent to but works *against* the machine. At the height of narrative, technology fades away and only 'story' remains evident to the reader – who at this point recognizes it *as* full blown narrative. Murray's analysis is thus based on a sense of narrative as a resilient force able to 'route around' impediments which seem to threaten its *internal* coherence. This coherence will emerge unchanged in its essentials, a signal that, amidst all the noise, what it is to be human remains constant. The essentially conservative nature[8] of this account is made clear. If the difference between old modes of storytelling and new ones is 'so little but technology', as Roger Silverstone has put it in an argument for the persistence of the mythic in contemporary cultural formations, then the best that can be hoped for is for is the *preservation* of existing forms of cultural experience within increasingly technologized worlds (Silverstone, 1981: 1).

Hamlet on the Holodeck can be read as a confident appeal, from the guardians of the old order (that of the book) to the custodians of the new (that of information). This appeal amounts to a demand for the reinscription of the values of the literary tradition into a new technological regime.[9] The setting aside of technology within this account, which emerges in part from the adoption of the structural narratological model as an operational model, thus has ideological consequences and produces certain ideological closures.

There are other ways that contemporary work draws on structuralist or formalist narratology to engage with new media technology. Marie-Laure Ryan's 1990s work increases structural narratology's original emphasis on tight spatial models, while extending the geometrics of narratology into the field of AI computing, finding homologies between code structures and story architectures in a bid to reinvigorate formalism within a new technological context (Ryan, 1991). Once again a narrative geometry finds its echo, but this time narrative meets narrative within a technological 'intelligence' rather than in the human mind. System once again meets system, but this time more perfectly than before, since code has none of the vagaries of the human psyche.

The rigidities of the structural geometries that produce this model of narrative (which is also in a significant sense claimed as an actually existing or pre-existing narrative form), are thus *extended* in this account, which involves a dual process of reduction: in the first place narratology is reduced to machine architecture, and in the second machine architecture is reduced to narratology. What is offered here, in the place of Metz's sense of correspondence in which narrative encounters what has already been dimly perceived as narrative, is a more or less total isomorphism between (narrative) code and machine code or intelligence. The user has little to do or say in this account.

As Gibson puts it, Ryan's work represents a 'massive consolidation and extension of narratological geometrics . . . one of the fiercest exclusions yet from the field of narratology of forms of narrative that are not obviously reducible to the geometric diagram' (Gibson, 1996: 83). In Ryan's hands narrative in 'use' and as it is modelled becomes, in an echo of a curious comment in Barthes, who defined *structural analysis* as an 'art without noise (as that term is employed in information theory)' (Barthes, 1982: 89).

Structuralist narratology emerges here as a theory ill-equipped to grapple with digital media as an emerging form, since it operates through a series of fierce and rigid exclusions – of the material, the lived and the specific. It is not only in the particular case of AI that exclusions of all kinds (of the material, of practice and of the specific iteration) are necessary if a case is to be made for structural narratology as a general organizing principle for new media narratives. Murray's account, for all its optimism, also brings the unruly technological back under control by way of a process of theoretical acculturation that amounts to a process of exclusion. And this becomes more marked in less optimistic accounts. Reverting to the saved version of structural narratology as a mode of media analysis means that digital media are not explored as something that might remediate narrative, and in doing so redefine the relationship between the text and the user, between use and the constitution of the object. Rather, conformed to the original model through a process of pruning and selection, new media narratives become *like* old media narratives, and *do* narrative like old media but often not as well. This approach underpins various critical accounts: those that suggested that CD-ROM content and/or computer gaming were disappointing as 'narrative' experiments, for instance (see Cameron, 1995). It tends to produce a model of the artefact that neglects or reallocates questions of use.

Finally, I note that particular conceptions of 'what information is' are also involved in these accounts. If the intention is to look at new media as a technology, then structural narratology is problematic, not only because it assumes that narrative is a closed and completed model but also because it is predicated, in largely unacknowledged ways, on a particular understanding of information itself, one that cannot easily take in or acknowledge specific and material forms of user interaction beyond the abstractions of a feedback system. Breaking from structural narratology allows technology to be conceived of as more than a system that tends to produce unwanted noise in the narrative machine.

In pursuit of this, two routes out of structuralist linguistics and structural narratology, each opening the way for very different accounts of narrative, are now taken up. The first route goes by way of Derrida, the second comes through Voloshinov/Bakhtin and, despite their very obvious differences, they are related. Both the Bakhtin/Voloshinov axis, on the one hand, and Derrida (and the Derridean/Foucaultian/Barthesian axis), on the other, pierce the formal abstractions, the bubble, in which structural theory held language and metalinguistic narrative structures. In this process the ghost in the machine is made substantial, or at least is acknowledged, technology being central to Derrida's thinking of language as writing and to the tradition of historical materialism to which Bakhtin and Voloshinov belong.

Becoming time: the post-structural différance

With every sign already, every mark or trait, there is distancing, the post, what there has to be so that it is legible for another. (Derrida, 1987: 29, cited in Luckhurst, 1996: 179)

The deconstructive movement against structuralism set out to break the barriers between discrete texts, introducing in the place of bounded narrative worlds the infinite universe of the intertextual. It was in 'Différance', an important text within deconstruction, that Derrida, writing against structuralism's stress on the synchronic, first coined the neologism *différance*, from 'to differ' and 'to defer' (Derrida, 1972). *Différance* is used to rethink the relationships between signifiers, and in particular to rethink the contexts within which signifiers differ from/ towards each other but also relate to/from each other. Chains of signifiers, each in the context of the others, are understood by Derrida to be both referring back (bearing the mark of past signifiers) and referring towards – being 'vitiated' by – the mark of the future. The process produces a structure of delay in which the closure of the text or the attribution of a final meaning is always deferred. Equally the past can never be returned to, since there is no arrived present from which to view it, and texts thus remain always open, always unbounded, and always to be read in contexts which are never entirely to be determined. It is in this way that *différance* may be understood as the 'becoming space' and the 'becoming time' of language: not language itself, but the conditions for the possibility of language. Derrida's formulations ruptured the unified and closed linguistic models of the structural theorists upon which structural narratology drew and, indeed, the structural narrative model, and in particular what Derrida calls 'geometrical metaphorisation', are pushed aside in his thinking (1978: 20). The 'force of the work' is read here as cohering around that part of a text that resists final codification in structural terms, and which, therefore, disrupts the closed structures narratology offers – and demands (Gibson, 1996a: 33).

This is a technological as well as a textual analysis since it is the distinction between speech and writing, and arising from it the current priority accorded to speech over writing, that Derrida deconstructs in 'Différance', arguing that all speech is in a sense already writing in that there is always distance, even if only 'the distance of a breath', between thought and self. And if all language is already a species of writing (Derrida, 1976) then all language is also always technological. At this point the opposition between the human as primary and the merely technological as supplemental or secondary also falls (see Coyne, 1999: 235–237).

The priority accorded to speech over writing, to immediacy over delay, and to absolute self-presence over absence, has, according to Derrida, produced a conception of technology itself as secondary. Thus, until recently at least, technology has only been allowed to be instrumental – again secondary – rather than being in any way regarded as a constitutive.

Derrida's claim is that that the status of writing may be changing, something signalled by the emergence of new forms of inscription technology that disturb the barriers between speech and writing. Given the links already made between writing and technology, the inauguration of a new kind of writing, heralded by Derrida and found, he says, within new technological forms, can thus be understood as the inauguration also of a new sense of technology as constitutive inscription, or force.

Two points are picked up here: the first about technology, the second about (hyper)textuality and the intertextual. First, in the realm of *différance*, how do we think about distinctions between different kinds of technologies, different kinds of inscriptions, different kinds of narratives? Richard Coyne offers one articulation of this problem in a different register in *Technoromanticism* (1999). Here he points out that Derrida actually has very little to say about the specific shifts that digital media are supposed to be producing and/or the specific processes of 'cyborgization' currently taking place. This is because, for Derrida, the oppositions which digital media have allegedly overcome (those between speaking and writing; technology as supplemental and the properly human) have never been oppositions. We have merely thought them to be so (Coyne, 1999: 235–237). The discussion of the force of the archive in *Archive Fever*, an investigation conducted with (loose) reference to e-mail (1995) is an example here. Derrida's point is that the contents of the archive are reshaped by the form in that the archive is takes, producing a form of 'archival violence' (1995: 7). This is a sharp characterization of the electronic archive, but what emerges through this account of e-mail (or more obviously of search engines) is the nature of 'the archive', not an account of any specific form of archiving. The conflation between *techne* and technology at the root of this lack of distinction between specific technologies is an element in the paradeictic[10] tendencies of some of the extant writing on new media working within the tradition of post-structuralism/postmodernism.

A parallel form of this *techne*/technology blindness can arise in relation to other text and technologies, and here I reference my own attempts to consider the performative production of virtual spaces (Bassett, 1997a). Material heterogeneity (embodiment or technological specificity, for instance) becomes slippery within an act that understands everything as language and everything also as *techne* but not technology, a world-text refracted into multiple fragments (Idhe, 1993: 7) rather than a materially heterogeneous world. Indeed it may be surprisingly easy to understand the technological simply as text and, as an example of how this spins out, let me skip forwards momentarily to the celebratory – if weightless – moment of the hypertext theorists, who celebrated the end of the narrative line in their analysis of various forms of literary hypertext emerging from the early 1990s onwards.

Working on the basis that digital media fragment the geometrical model of narrative and prevent narrative closure, producing a form of instantiated intertextuality, a group of postmodern literary theorists – hypertext theorists – have long claimed digital media in general and hypertext in particular as their own. Theorists such as Landow, Lanham and, to some extent, Bolter have declared hypertext to be the instantiation of the 'classic' postmodern text (Landow, 1994; Lanham, 1993; Bolter, 1991), the text, perhaps, that could not find its form in print. Hypertext stacks, and later multi-user domains, chat-rooms and other Internet sites have all been considered by hypertext theorists, and they have found in the architectures of the machine a new sphere within which the topo-graphic novel can be instantiated, sometimes with the peculiar result that what was non-linear and open (indeterminate) as a printed text becomes increasingly fixed and complete. This writing, however, is remarkable for the degree to which it takes on the textual mores of deconstruction but sets aside questions of inscription (of writing as inscription) almost entirely; the new media technologies it works with are conceived of as hyper*texts* in a sense that precedes Derrida's understanding of the text itself (writing) as an inscription. In this sense hypertext theory stands in an oblique relation to the influential medium theory of Kittler, since this focuses on the discourse networks that *materiality* produces (Kittler, 1997). It is with some justification that those who set out to critique deconstruction and the textual approach in new media circles argue that it tends to dissolve the technological into discourse.

Form, force and passion: beyond the signifier

Deconstruction brings about a change in focus within narrative inves-tigation, opening closed texts and instantiating particular forms of indeterminacy. However it also focuses attention on what exceeds formal structural features. Thus Lyotard's consideration of the the 'libidinal economy' of the text is focused on those moments when the libidinal erupts into the system and disrupts it. In Lyotard the passion for meaning that Barthes found in the signifier becomes a desire for sensation and affect that might be beyond signification, or that overwhelms it (see de Lauretis, 1982 and Barthes, 1982: 124). Lyotard thus works not through a search for meaning within a text, insisting there is no clear semantic trajectory to be had, but is rather motivated by the desire 'to be put in motion' by the force of a text or narrative (Gibson, 1996a: 59).

If form and force oppose each other here, at least to some extent, there are also some notable fusions. Lyotard's sense of the 'figural', a 'semiotic regime where the ontological distinction between linguistic and plastic representations breaks down' (David Rodowick, cited in Bal, 2003: 10) represents one of these and is deployed by David Rodowick in his account of the new media as a system of simulacra (Rodowick, 2001).

Deleuze and Guatarri also seek a way of thinking that is able to prioritize force or energetics over form. Unlike Lyotard, however, they remain within a form/force *relation*, understanding force as acting to deform form (Gibson, 1996a: 49) even while dividing affect from sensation (Rajchman, 2001). The trope of rhizomatics, taken up in cyber-cultural writings, grapples with the force/form relation (see Watson, 1998: 170–171; Deleuze and Guattari, 1987; Malik, 1997) and is one of a series of tropes used to describe forms which express the prioritization of force within a cultural production where diachrony rather than synchrony, multiplicity rather than closure, and force (affect) rather than signification (meaning) are the key principles.

To invoke Deleuze and Guattari is to turn decisively away from the linguistic field, since what is at issue in their world-view is not representation but rather culture as a material force, a field across which various actions and objects intersect and assemble. For Deleuze and Guattari the *material* form of a work and its *textual* form and content are not to be divided the one from the other, but neither do they unite in discourse. Rather, texts are made of 'variously formed matters, and very different dates and speeds' (Deleuze and Guattari, cited in Gibson, 1996a: 48). There is very little space for representation here. Indeed, as Deleuze put it in relation to cinema 'the brain *is* the screen' (Flaxman, 2000: 92, my italics). Questions of form and force are thus reinscribed in accounts based on Deleuze and Guattari, since here the cultural text itself, the narrative, is not to be explored in terms of representation but in terms of how it performs, acts upon us, or materially produces an effect – how it *galvanizes* us, as Brian Massumi has put it, describing how the skin is faster than the word in responding to various narrations of a tale (Massumi, 1995a).

The Deleuze/Guattari route out of the textual lock-in of the world in language has been popular amongst techno-cultural theorists attempting to grapple with the advent of a new cultural form, which is delivered *as* a new technology. Difficulties emerge here when Deleuze's and Guattari's essentially abstract insistence on the importance of the concrete impact rather than the ideological effect (Spivak, 1988) of a cultural production is 'applied' to a specific assemblage, such as a new media production, or a new media narrative. This produces a problem of differentiation, since although the force/form relation and the prioritization over force over form do not *have* to be understood in terms of a division between the technical and the textual (or indeed between the technical and the human) aspects of an assembly, they often are, in practice (in the practice of theory). When this occurs the distinction between (new) technology and (old) narrative is remade, so that new media in general come to stand in opposition to narrative as attenuated. Here then *technological* force, read as irruption, chaos, speed, multiplicity, vitality, comes to be understood as that which disrupts narrative. Narrative, meanwhile, is stripped of all but its formal patterning and is reduced to a mode of interpretation capable of operation only within the limited sphere of the text (narrative then becomes nothing more than the old content of a new form).

The import of this is that a division is drawn between narrative (that which concerns something very like good old interpretation) and new media (invested with a form of energetic emergence), producing two incommensurable horizons: a technological horizon and a cultural horizon. Within the cultural horizon we find narrative deployed only in relation to a notion of significance as meaning, rather than one that might involve (for instance) value, taking the latter as something that may involve engagement and affect as well as ratiocination. It is, in both of these senses, *attenuated*. Which raises the question of whether it would be possible to consider narrative as a process engaging with all of these elements. More, what would the resulting cultural formations involving a play of force and form signify?

My questions arise because I would like to slip between Lyotard, who wanted to be 'put in motion' by a text, and the structural narratologists, who wanted to map the pure code at the heart of narrative. I am interested in how the force of narrative contributes to a more general or overarching process of signification involving form *and* force. What *meaning* do I take from being moved by a narrative in a particular way? A response here requires consideration of narrative affect as part of a series of questions about signification, value, meaning and ideology, rather than as that which simply overwhelms signification (Lyotard's position), or perhaps as something that precedes it (and that precedes the judgement that might come with signification), as Deleuze might insist. To make this move might be to restore to narrative a sense of fullness, a sense that it can model 'desire, communication, struggle', which was the claim made for it by Barthes (1982: 107).

A re-expanded account of narrative would certainly make it more difficult to dismiss narrative as one – and one increasingly unimportant – element amongst many contributing to a definition of new media. More, to make this move is to restore to narrative its capacity to explain the artefact in its *totality*, since this is what is stripped away in accounts that understand narrative as one element amongst many contributing to the production of a cultural artefact. It is to break with structuralism by another route from that taken by deconstruction, but it is also to break with post-structuralism's continued insistence on discourse, and in a way that is markedly different from the route out offered by Deleuze and Guattari's insistence on the concrete.

In pursuit of this break I turn to the Marxist work of Voloshinov, whose consideration of the struggle within language, when language itself is understood in terms of use and in terms of structure, and when it is understood to operate within the horizons of ideological contest, offers a distinctively different route out of structuralism. It might also act as a bridge towards the thinking of Paul Ricoeur and the early Fredric Jameson to whom I turn in the closing sections of the chapter.

Materialist deconstruction?

At a certain point, surely we must accept that material reality exists, that it continually knocks up against us, that texts are not the only thing. (Liz Stanley, cited in Cavarero, 1997: 127)

Voloshinov has been characterized as producing a materialist alternative to deconstruction (Cohen, 1996: 42) and as Derrida's attack did, Voloshinov's critique of Saussure breaks the synchronic structure of structuralism, opening language up to diachrony. In Voloshinov's case, however, this rupture is achieved by emphasizing the links between language and the material/social world rather than by focusing on the linkages between endless and endlessly extending texts. Volsinov places utterance, the dynamics of speech, at the centre of the linguistic model he develops in *Marxism and the Philosophy of Language* (1973). Later, Bakhtin considers Voloshinov's model in terms of dialogism, which might begin to be defined as 'a certain relationship between distinct voices in the narrative text . . .' (Hirschkop, 1989: 6).

The key to Voloshinov's conception of language is that it cannot be understood in terms of Saussure's division between structure and use. In *Marxism and the Philosophy of Language* the priority is not to place *parole* over *langue*, rather it is to explore the relationship between overarching structures of language and the river of its living use (Voloshinov, 1973). Voloshinov therefore is writing against both the 'abstract objectivism' of Saussurean linguistics[11] and its opposite, the latter being defined as individualist subjectivism, an exclusive concentration on the subjective experience of language.[12] In stressing utterance, Voloshinov is thus not reifying it, but seeking a dialectical relation between utterance and rule. Another way of seeing this is to suggest that Voloshinov is seeking a means by which to adjudicate between a form of analysis that can see only form and one that can see only force – or perhaps affect.

Above all, for Voloshinov language is a social relation, and not only because the arbitrary relations between signifiers and signifieds are of necessity shared relations (in this sense, of course, language is social also for Saussure). Language is a social relation because language is shaped – finds its structures – through dialogue (hence Bakhtin's dialogics), which is to say through its embedded use within a *history* of use. While linguistic structures may be said to endure, they may not, therefore, be understood to be trans-cultural, or universal, or permanent. Rather, they are understood to be always in process of negotiation, contestation and production (within dialogue in the novel, or outside it). As Voloshinov himself put it: 'language . . . endures as a continuous process of becoming' (Voloshinov, 1973: 81).

With this interpretation of language, Voloshinov rends the closed structure of the self-contained text and the geometric narrative model characteristic of structuralism, introducing, as Derrida has also done, the notion of language as a dynamic becoming which has always to be considered temporally as well as spatially. In the place of Derrida's concern with the infinite universe of the text, however, Voloshinov and Bakhtin work through dialogics, binding the signifier to the shared referents of social relations, but also opening up the possibility that this binding process is continuous and without closure.

Voloshinov and Bakhtin read the quality of a dialogue or the quality of the becoming of a language in relation to the degree of heteroglossia it allows, a heteroglossic text being open to, or offering multiple possibilities for, interpretation. Voloshinov describes heteroglossia in language both as normative and as an inherent quality of language when it is used 'naturally' (Hirschkop, 1989: 9). Language is not being used naturally when it is distorted and attenuated under particular conditions; the case of authoritarian regimes tends to be cited here,[13] but another example of this kind of language degradation could be 'technobabble', or the jargon of computerese (Barry, 1991). The language computers 'speak' might be regarded as monoglossic given the poverty even of newer 'natural language' interfaces, which are offered as an advance on 'machine code' or on low-level languages such as Assembler.[14] (Here what is at issue is the form of dialogue computer mediation enables between humans and computers, but it would be intriguing to explore this in relation to artificial intelligence where dialogics might constitute the measure of a form of Turing test.)

Whether Voloshinov's sense of the heteroglossic features of language is taken as normative or as descriptive, by his lights both language and narrative can be judged. Language is 'not as an indifferent medium of social exchange, but as a form of social exchange susceptible to political and moral evaluation, like any other' (Hirschkop, 1989: 6). The theory of narrative emerging out of Voloshinov's formulations is one that understands language production (and narrative production) as an ideological process. Dialogism itself can thus be more completely defined (again following Hirschkop, but this time completing his formulation) as 'a certain relation between distinct voices in a narrative text *in which each takes its shape as a conscious reaction to the ideological position of the other*' (Hirschkop, 1989: 6). Later in this book I take up the question of who – or what – might have a voice in the production of new media narrative.

Voloshinov's analysis thus points to language as a becoming, but also understands this becoming in terms of an *ideological* contest for meaning. Voloshinov's writing has much in common with hermeneutic attempts to consider narrative after structuralism, and the former indeed has (also) been described as an alternative to deconstruction 'because its dialectic orientation keeps it open ended as a dynamic process but does not sacrifice transmission' (Valdes, 1991: 25). And is to hermeneutics that I turn in the final sections of this chapter in order to consider new media and narrative in relation to interpretation.

Ricoeur's narrative hermeneutics
God could slow the spinning of the stars but for humans the day would still be the length of a day. (Augustine, 1991: 12)

Paul Ricoeur defines hermeneutics as the art of deciphering indirect meanings in the present and the past. For Ricoeur there is no access to raw experience that is not always already mediated, and the narrative act is a processes of mediation through which humans make sense of their experience of being in the world and their experience of being in time (Ricoeur, 1984: 79). Narrative is understood as a means of organizing event and experience, a way to make it meaningful (Valdes, 1991). For Ricoeur these operations are *the central* means through which humans interpret the world as they have grasped it through experience, stretching from fiction and history to lived experience. Echoing Wittgenstein, he can thus declare that the meaning of human existence is itself narrative (1984).

Temporality is at the heart of Ricoeur's theorization of narrative and the latter is the means by which humans organize their experience within temporal horizons that operate both at the cosmological and the human scale. This is effectively a metaphysics of temporality (Callinicos, 1995: 54), and in *Time and Narrative* Ricoeur draws on Aristotle and Augustine to sketch out this metaphysics, beginning with two meditations. The first explores the theory of narrative as emplotment (*muthos*) developed by Aristotle in his consideration of tragic drama as the triumph of concordance over discordance in the *Poetics*. The second explores Augustine's discussion of the *aporias* of time in the *Confessions*. Here the subjective human experience of time as finitudinous time (being towards death) is viewed in the context of cosmological time, and indeed in the context of eternity.

In the *Confessions* Augustine addresses himself to the problem of the being and non-being of time, and to the *aporia* arising around the possibility of the measurement of (subjectively experienced) human time. The core of the problem, as Ricoeur develops it in *Time and Narrative* by way of Augustine, concerns the possibility of thinking human time in terms of duration and extension. Ricoeur recounts how, against the arguments of the sceptics, Augustine, variously argumentative, resigned and obedient, struggles to comprehend the subjective experience of time. Augustine begins with a conception of time as the point-like threefold present, a formulation of time that does not allow time to be measured since it has no duration. The possibility of the extension of this moment, which offers a different way of thinking about time emerges through consideration of how the soul may secure the present in time. The point-like present, which has no extension and is measurable only as time passes can, by means of the 'soul that holds', be replaced by the conception of a newly configured dialectical threefold present. This is a distention of time, and it is within this distention that time, subjectively experienced as 'an extension of the mind itself', comes to have duration (Augustine, cited in Callinicos, 1995: 47). Thus the present of past things becomes 'memory', the present can be understood as 'attention' and the present of future things is 'expectation' (Ricoeur, 1984; Augustine, 1991).

This distention of time occurs through what is initially called 'attention' and later 'engagement'. To cite Ricoeur (himself citing Augustine), 'there would be no future which diminishes, no past that increases, without the mind (1984: 19)'.[15] Ricoeur can thus argue that the extension of time beyond the point-like present, into a form of time which can be considered to be properly human, can be understood as a gathering and a distending (1984: 21). The extension of time – or duration – is gathered, within the distention of the soul, by the act of an attentive mind, in a process that is both continuous and multi-layered, crossing and recrossing distinctions between the textual and intertextual, but also moving between text and world. The experience of time produced in this way is many-layered, so that time, thus configured, becomes a 'moving, slipping stream' (Ricoeur, 1984: 22). It is, as Augustine saw it a temporal rupturing and exploding of the present in contrast to the eternal present of God (Ricoeur, 1991: 465). It is to the tension raised in this account of time, which can be understood in terms of the dialectic of distention/intention, that Ricoeur seeks a resolution and, reading 'attention' as 'emplotment', he finds this in narrative.

Ricoeur's formulation of narrative begins with Aristotle's account of tragedy in the *Poetics*. The crux of this reading is the unity ('quasi-identification') Ricoeur finds between the concepts of *muthos* and *mimesis* as they are developed in the *Poetics*, which suggests possibilities for a general principle of narrative. Ricoeur describes the Aristotelian *muthos* in terms of emplotment, and understands it as the organization of events, an operation rather than a system. *Mimesis*, similarly, is understood as the act of representation, considered not in terms of imitation but in terms of *configuration*, and is thus read as a 'break which opens the space for fiction' (Ricoeur, 1987: 46).

The term linking *muthos* and *mimesis*, as Ricoeur develops them, is *poesis*, here understood as a poetic *act*, the act of composing plots and making representations. *Poesis*, then, stands in contrast to the dispersion and rupturing which are characteristic of the sense of time that Ricoeur develops from Augustine, since this form of *poesis* offers 'a way of unifying existence by retelling it'. Narrative can then be defined in terms of an opposition between 'the discordance of time (*temps*) and the concordance of the tale (*récit*)' (Ricoeur, 1991: 465).

Weaving together these two meditations, Ricoeur's own project emerges as a call for the privileging of narrative as the poetic act by means of which we order our world. Narrative (the triumph of concordance over discordance) becomes an act through which the *aporias* inherent in the subjective experience of time as discord can be resolved (Callinicos, 1995: 47). The problematics of time and narrative, therefore, may be intertwined to produce concordant discordance: a resolution by way of *poesis* of the *aporias* of time – and being in time – with which Augustine grappled. Narrative is thus *an act of articulating time*. As Ricoeur puts it: 'Time becomes human to the extent that it is articulated through a narrative mode, and narrative attains its full meaning when it becomes a condition of temporal existence' (Ricoeur, 1984: 52).

Ricoeur's narrative dialectics, in which narrative is at once read as an active and ongoing emplotment (narrative as a dynamic becoming), and as a form that offers resolution (narrative as an interpretation), develops out of these meditations. The narrative model emerging out of this dialectic is extensive, and is organised into three moments, or horizons: $mimesis_{1, 2}$ and $_3$. The first moment of *mimesis* reaches backwards towards the horizon of event and experience. The second is the moment of *poesis* relating to that referent and breaking with it. The third moment of *mimesis* occurs when the configured text is reconstituted within the horizon of the reader. This is the arc of narrative. It extends across these three horizons and is traversed by the reader, who takes from the work its sense of reference and who opens this same work into her or her own horizons.

Ricoeur is adamant that narrative cannot be understood outside the span of this extensive arc. In particular, the central moment of *poesis* (*mimesis*$_2$), recognized as the central moment of the model, are meaningless *except* as part of the hermeneutic process as a whole. The world of the text and the world of the reader, actively brought into relation to each other through *poesis*, constitute narrative. It is thus narrative that 'endures as a becoming' here. The narrative arc breaks from structural models of narratology since it is a trajectory based on experience rather than on formal geometries. Where these exist in Ricoeur's account, they are open elements within a larger – and surpassing – whole.

Mimesis$_1$, the first moment in Ricoeur's narrative arc, is concerned with as yet untold stories and constitutes the first hermeneutic horizon in this model. *Mimesis*$_1$ is concerned with the referent and with the referential intention of narrative works, particularly narrative works of history. At the same time it involves a process of symbolization. For Ricoeur there is no raw unmediated perception; all experience is always already symbolic, and to a degree always already mediated.[16] *Mimesis*$_1$ thus begins the process of emplotment that produces a narrative resolution and is already within narrative's arc.

The narrative break becomes marked in *mimesis*$_2$, the central moment of Ricoeur's model, whose horizons are those of the world of the text. It is within the horizon of the text that the rules of composition as Ricoeur understands them come into force. These narrative rules combine chronology (the episodic dimension of the narrative) and a concern with temporality more often understood in terms of theme. The key here for my purposes, however, is to stress that this, the central panel of Ricoeur's triptych, both links to and breaks from the prefigurative and reconfigurative moments that surround it, and that *mimesis*$_2$ thus amounts to an act of *configuration* rather than an act of transmission, but is always open ended.

At the far end of the arc Ricoeur has placed *mimesis*$_3$, where the text re-emerges into the horizon of the reader. Ricoeur formulates this movement in terms of the dialogic functioning of a language irretrievably orientated beyond itself. In other words, through a process of dialogue between the reader and the text, the text itself is reproduced in new ways as the horizons of the text are fused with the experiences the reader brings to language. What is communicated to the reader is thus '[n]ot only the sense of the work, but the sense of its reference and its temporality, that is, the experience it brings to language, and in the last analysis the world and the temporality it unfolds in the face of this experience' (Ricoeur, 1984: 79).

Clearly then it is not only the central moment of *poesis*, but also the narrative arc *as a whole* which represent the process of emplotment as an 'act that draws configuration out of simple succession' (1984: 65, my italics). Ricoeur argues that this constitutes an entire model for narrative, and is the proper study of hermeneutics. He can define this last as aiming to 'make explicit the means by which a text unfolds, as it were, a world in front of itself' (Ricoeur, 1984: 81). Thus, as the parts of *mimesis* come back together, the outlines emerge both of a particular theory of narrative, and of a particular form of hermeneutics which stresses interpretation (what narrative means) over force (how it is affective) and indeed over form (what shape it is), but which also brings these elements together.

Narrative's reach/narrative's limits

Ricoeur's model restores to narrative centrality and importance. In his hands narrative comes to be understood as an extensive operation in which experience is reconfigured into the horizon of the text and into the horizon of the reader. Narrative is a mediating act through which humans apprehend the world. The narrative operations of which he writes act on many scales to organize fictions, histories and lives; not surprisingly, therefore, they also characterize the ways in which the future may be thought.

Given this extensive definition both of narrative's operation and its spheres of operation we might be forgiven for wondering where Ricoeur's theory of narrative finds its limits One constraint might be discerned in the central arc of *mimesis*$_2$, with its more or less formalist model which might be understood and adopted as a rule for composition rather than a rule for narrative. But this would be to misunderstand the central thrust of the argument here, which is to explore narrative as a form of emplotment that is fundamentally open (orientated beyond itself) rather than seeking to prescribe its final geometry. This openness, in fact, reflects back on the inner model and redraws narrative's constraints. Narrative rules *as a whole* are thus understood by Ricoeur to be constituted *within society* through an interplay between sedimentation and innovation within a context of the shared paradigms that make narrative understandable (1984: 68). Individual narratives may be found which contest traditional or sedimented forms of narrative and these contestations may produce new forms, new elements and new orderings for narrative – and forms of new media narratives are clearly a case in point here. Eventually they would also produce new theoretical models. Viewed from this essentially historical perspective narrative is flexible and mutable.

However, there are other limits to the mutability of narrative within Ricoeur's theory. These are evident once we remind ourselves that underpinning the formal rules of narrative outlined by Ricoeur in *mimesis*$_2$ (which turn out to be mutable, or to operate in an open-ended way within the arc of narrative) lies that more extensive definition of narrative as concordant discordance. Ricoeur's deeper sense of narrative is that it offers a resolution to the *aporias* of human existence in time. The limits of narrative mutability are reached at the point where narrative's capacity to offer such a resolution is threatened. At this point what is produced goes beyond antinarrative (a response to narrative that remains within its terms) and ultimately threatens the death of narrative. Ricoeur's sense is that technology might take us to these limits, and I want to look at this, but first to switch the focus back to consider the narrative arc in relation to new media.

Ricoeur's sense of narrative as an extensive arc looks promising. This is an approach that might enable, or produce the grounds for, forms of thinking about interactive media that are disallowed when narrative is held within the screen as a self-contained text; when it is regarded as content rather than as practice, or as a text rather than as materially heterogeneous; when it is considered through static models rather than being understood as a gathering together that is always in process; or when it is regarded as transcendental rather than as mutable.

The narrative arc begins not to merge into, but to mesh with, the interactive experience. Information technology and our experiences within it and across it can be drawn up into the process of prefiguration, configuration and refiguration that constitute narrative emplotment, or the resolution of experience in time, according to shared forms that give these experiences meaning. This fit doesn't only come about because the account of narrative produced here is extensive, but because of the sense of temporal resolution that sits at its heart. As computer-clock time and world time, computer space and real space, the real world and the world of the text, are increasingly brought into relation, the experience of everyday life as something operating across a patchwork of different spaces, each operating at its own clock-speed, becomes routine. Our life is characterized by time shifts and time slips, by the demand not only to operate in many places at once, but at many different speeds.

Interaction between human and machine (the interface) can thus be conceived of not as a punctual process of exchange determined by the machine, but as a distended moment in which the experience of the different temporalities and spatial dynamics involved in computer use is taken up into an arc of narrative, where sense is given to experience through its ordering as narrative. Use then becomes understandable as part of a process of mediation, a process of temporal resolution, through which meanings are made.

Is this process of resolution infinitely extensible? Ricoeur himself sets limits on the forms of temporal resolution narrative can bear, but does not set these in relation to form, but in terms of the human experience of temporality that produces particular forms and modes of emplotment. Ricoeur's fears in this area are most clearly articulated in *Oneself as Another* (1992), in which the limits of narrative identity are considered in relation to science fiction and cloning (Ricoeur, 1994: 118): what might falter first in the age of information, Ricoeur fears, is the human.

The possibility of the disintegration of the tale, brought about through technology or through other means, figures as the negative hermeneutic in Ricoeur's account. It stands against what is generally a positive one derived from the sense that in unrolling the world of the text into the world of the reader, or in a fusion of horizons, there is always *more* than representation, there is also always an opening of possible worlds. Ricoeur's particular utopian wish is eschatological, but his narrative framework creates space to think also about other kinds of wishes for the future.[17] For Ricoeur narrative is constituted within the horizons of the social world, within the social imaginary, and within shared cultural frameworks. As such it can be understood as ideologically informed. In this sense it is socially symbolic. However, narrative's ultimate limits – its ultimate horizons – are framed by a sense of the limitations of the human experience of time in the face of cosmological time. Ricoeur's model thus works within a framework that both contains and, in his terms, exceeds, history. His conception of narrative, as an interpretation of events in the world, locates narrative within the frame of history, memory and futurity. On the other hand, the formal structures of narrative are understood within a wider framework, a metaphysics of temporality that treats the subjective human experience of time within a broader conception of time as infinity or eternity. It is in this way that this is perhaps a *theological* framework. For Ricoeur, *pace* Jameson (below), narrative is *more* than socially symbolic – and the exceeding of this limit marks the limitations of Ricoeur's analysis *as* a historical analysis. This last comment might seem gnomic. I hope that the consideration now given to Fredric Jameson's different sense of narrative's ultimate horizon, and therefore of its ultimate limits, will make what I mean clear.

Jameson and the 'socially symbolic act'
The political interpretation . . . [is] the absolute horizon of all reading and all interpretation. (Jameson, 1981: 17)

Fredric Jameson's Marxist ambitions for narrative are different, although they too have their 'theological' aspect (LaCapra, 1983: 256). In his account of narrative hermeneutics in the *Political Unconscious* Jameson sets out 'to restructure the problematics of ideology, of the unconscious and desire, of representation, of history, and of cultural production, around the all informing process of narrative . . . the central function or instance of the human mind' (Jameson, 1981: 13).

Where for Ricoeur narrative emplotment produces a resolution in *poesis* of different and incommensurable forms of temporality, Jameson claims that narrative can invent 'imaginary . . . solutions to unresolvable social contradictions'. It is in this way, as he says, that 'the aesthetic act is itself ideological, and the production of aesthetic or narrative form is to be seen as an ideological act in its own right' (1981: 79). For Jameson, narrative is thus a socially symbolic act. Narratives carry with them the conditions in which they come to be produced.

In the *Political Unconscious*, Jameson reads these conditions at different scales, each constituting different hermeneutic horizons into which the textual or cultural artefact is reopened *and in which it also is reconstituted*. At the widest possible horizon, these conditions are about history when history itself is understood to be about the rise and fall of different modes of production. Here Jameson refers directly Marx's claim that the history of all hitherto existing society is the history of a struggle between contending classes (Jameson, 1981: 20), declaring, against Ricoeur, that the '*political* interpretation . . . [is] the absolute horizon of all reading and all interpretation' (1991: 17, my italics).

Like Ricoeur, Jameson develops his account of narrative by way of a three-part model. In the place of the long traversals of Ricoeur's narrative arc, Jameson's account of narrative is based on a series of concentric rings spiralling upwards from the close view to overarching contexts[18] within which the text comes to be reconstituted. The first of these narrative – or semantic – horizons is political history 'in the narrow sense of punctual event and chronicle-like sequence of events in time' (1981: 75). The second is society in the sense of a 'constitutive tension and struggle between social classes (1981: 75), and the third 'history, now conceived of in its vastest sense of the sequence of modes of production and the succession and destiny of various human social formations . . .' (1981: 75). Each of these horizons recomposes the cultural text or object, which is progressively remade within the interpretive framework Jameson offers.

Concentric horizons

The literary work or cultural object, as though for the first time, brings into being that very situation to which it is also, at one and the same time, a reaction. It articulates its own situation and textualizes it . . . (Jameson, 1981: 82)

The innermost ring of this model comes closest to offering a close reading of the text itself, as a discrete object or individual literary work. Already, however, this text is understood as a cultural artefact so that it does not *represent* the contexts in which it was made, but rather draws the fabric of the real up into the web it weaves.[19] Narrative, says Jameson, might map the world as dream, as prayer, as chart (1981: 81). The process of 'drawing in' distances the contexts of production at the same time as bringing them 'in' to the narrative. The world is made anew 'as though for the first time' in the text so that the text is itself productive and in this way it can be understood, not as informed by ideology, but as itself ideological.

How is this process of 'drawing in' the real to be modelled? Jameson is at pains to avoid slipping either into what he understands as vulgar materialism, or into structural ideology. His sense of this operation is that it will reveal social complexity and, above all, contradiction. There is no assumption that opening narrative into this horizon will simply function to reveal characters within texts as 'working class' or 'ruling class', for instance, nor that texts might be similarly categorized in the way that Bourdieu's taste codes reveal a text as barbarous or pure, for instance (Bourdieu, 1984). This deals with the question of vulgar materalism perhaps.

The question of structuralism and its attendant ideology is more complicated. Arguably Jameson does less to let himself off the charge of succumbing to structural ideology than he might do; not least because, at this layer of his model, he deploys a model of narrative based on Greimas' work. His argument here is that narrative, as it is construed in this circuit, models the social contradictions that form its horizons at the level of *aporia* or antinomy.[20] That is, as would be expected perhaps, the real is modelled in narrative terms. What we are offered is a resolution in narrative of contradictions that could only be worked out 'for real' by way of praxis. Jameson argues that structural narratology (the Greimasian square in particular) can usefully be deployed within his dialectical model to investigate the workings of this resolution – so long as its findings are then diverted towards Jameson's greater dialectical model, of which this particular circuit is only the first stage. I return to this below, since there is to me a real contradiction between this approach and the sense Jameson gives us of narrative as something that is made, rather than found as a ready-made model – *made* through that process of drawing up the real that both breaks with, and connects the text to, the world.

In the second hermeneutic circuit, the line is crossed into the horizon of social conflict, and the text is refocused as 'an utterance in a collective discourse' about class tensions (1981: 80). Drawing on Bakhtin, this

discourse is characterized as dialogic, with the proviso that it is antagonistic rather than carnival-like (Jameson, 1981: 84). Given that dialogics
has already been defined here as 'a certain relation between distinct voices
. . . in which each takes its shape as a conscious reaction to the ideological
position of the other' (Hirschkop, 1989: 6, see above), then it is to be
expected that the first key to opening the text into the wider interpretative
framework of the second circuit is to restore or reconstruct the voice to
which it was originally opposed, and this is Jameson's move.

In this case too, where what is being considered is a form of restitution,
the relationship between the specificity of the text as a narrative, and its
opening into a broader context, which in this way rewrites it as a text is
troublesome. The peril once again is that the narrative simply becomes
a reflection of social conflict (vulgar Marxism), or that it is regarded as
having a separate and abstract logic that always surpasses particular
contexts (structural narratology). It is in an attempt to think this through
that Jameson introduces the notion of ideologemes, units of description
that can move between conceptual description and narrative manifesta-
tion. The aim of ideologemes, as Jameson describes them, is thus to
mediate between ideology as 'abstract opinion' and what he calls narrative
materials. To unmask the ideologeme is then to find the ideological theme
in a text that relates to the context. It is also to understand how this theme
is produced as narrative.

The outer layer of Jameson's circuit, forming the ultimate horizon in his
world-view, is concerned with the mode of production understood in
terms of the long *durée*, as a historically antagonistic process, actually as
history. The cultural text or object specific to this final interpretative
horizon is designated by Jameson as cultural revolution, understood as a
process not limited to transitional periods between dominant modes of
production, but instead relating to a sense of perpetual contestation,
perhaps to the famous sense that, in capitalism at least, 'all that is solid
melts into the air' and all that appears fixed, fast and frozen, is contestable,
dissolvable and changeable (Marx: 1954). The form that the cultural
artefact re-emerging into this horizon takes is no longer properly textual
at all, becoming what Jameson calls a 'field of force in which the dynamic
sign systems of several distinct modes of production can be registered and
apprehended'. These dynamics produce an ideology of form, which is
actually to be apprehended as content (1981: 98–99). At this level the
problematic relationship between text and context, the problem of
retaining – or recognizing – the distinctiveness of a narrative production,
is thus addressed by way of an insistence on form, of what Jameson, citing
Hjelmslev's formulation, calls 'the content of form' (1981: 101).

Pulling these concentric rings back together, the bare outlines of Jameson's bid to understand narrative as socially symbolic emerge. One way to think through Jameson's account of narrative is as building Voloshinov's sense of language as a social becoming into a sustained narrative model. Within this model language, in and of itself, cannot be understood to be ideologically neutral. It becomes a site of contestation. In addition, because meanings are achieved dialogically, language reaches towards the world. Like Voloshinov, Jameson argues that narrative does not simply reflect particular aspects of the ideological context in which it was made but can be understood to *articulate* the totality of social relations pertaining at a particular historical conjunction. For Jameson, this historical moment is one in which a particular mode of production is dominant, but is never exclusively present, and nor is it ever entirely uncontested – history, like language, reaches before and behind. It is because narrative holds the contradictions inherent in social organiza- tion – and ultimately in history – in the form of a contingent resolution in itself, that narrative itself can be understood to function as the political unconscious. It is clear then, that no rigid distinction between narrative considered as a theory of language and Marxism as a theory of history can be drawn in Jameson's account, and in this way Jameson can claim to locate narrative between text and world while at the same time retaining narrative's specificity at each level of his analysis.

I here return to the question of sectoral validity raised earlier, since it is when the significance of the movement of the text between language and history is realized within Jameson's account that it becomes the more remarkable that Jameson builds into his model structuralist accounts of narrative based precisely on disallowing this link, claiming that these accounts have sectoral validity. The question that arises here is whether the consistency of Jameson's own model, his attention to history, can be maintained while it expands to include other models whose trajectories tend in other, very different directions, from his own.

There are those who feel Jameson's synthesis cannot work. Lyotard claims it undermines the validity of small narratives (1984: 60), while Samuel Weber, drawing on this argument, claims that Jameson's analysis is contradictory since while Jameson accuses other theories of practising 'strategies of containment' which reflect their ideological position, he adopts the same tactics himself. As Weber puts it:

> Jameson's defence of Marxism is caught in a double bind: it criticizes its competitors for being ideological in the sense of practicing 'strategies of containment' . . . of drawing lines . . . that ultimately reflect the particularities – the partiality and partisanship – of special interests seeking to present themselves as a whole. But at the same time its own claims to offer an

alternative to such ideological containment is itself based on a strategy of containment, one which seeks to identify with a whole more comprehensive than its rivals. (Weber, 1983: 22, cited in Currie, 1998: 87)

This is accurate enough as a description of what Jameson is doing – criticism of it on this basis, however, seems to me to be misplaced. In *The Political Unconscious* Jameson is looking at the interpretative categories or codes through which we read and receive a text and his (declared) assumption is that no text comes to us fresh (we read through earlier interpretations or through interpretative traditions). Part of his project therefore involves looking at ways in which texts have been read according to particular codes (for instance according to particular critical codes), and comparing these to Marxism. The latter is also of course, a code – and also one that is totalizing given that it claims as an absolute horizon the totality of society. More, Jameson never denies that his own model seeks to function precisely by operating 'strategies of containment' on these other narrative models. Structuralism, as we have seen, is given sectoral validity in ring one of Jameson's hermeneutic circles model. And, if we believe Jameson, being thus placed, structuralism's own claim to universality is lost.

Jameson's claim is that the structural model, introduced into the appropriate sector, comes to model the *limits* of a particular way of thinking about narrative, and thus models also a particular form of ideological closure. In other words, using these models serves the purpose of the greater whole, but does so partly by exposing their ideological closures, and showing them off as forms of narrative hermeneutics that can be understood as being socially symbolic in and of themselves. The models themselves therefore speak in this argument. In this sense then, for Jameson, the struggle between force and form, between structural and post-structural accounts, is translated into a struggle between his own and other interpretative models (1991: 13). Indeed, if Jameson's concentric circles are thought diagrammatically it becomes clear that the basic conceptions of narrative at each level reflect the broad sweep of narrative theory – and even that each theory is attached to a particular 'kind' of text which seems to exemplify its characteristics. Thus moving from ideological, to social, to historical horizons we also move from thinking the text as text, as intertext, and as field of force, (structuralism, post-structuralism, energetics) – a recapitulation of the field of narrative theory as it has developed. The subsuming move is thus more deadly than Weber suggests, since Jameson's charge against these models is not that they are ideological, while his model is not, but that their sense of the limitations of interpretation is also ideological. Finally, Jameson's answer to the charge of over-totalizing is that totality is not primarily a theoretical concept at all; rather it is a social reality. In this sense the validity of small narratives remains in Jameson's account; they explore minutiae which are to be understood, in their details, as part of an increasingly integrated whole.

A strength of Jameson's account of narrative's function is that it finds a way to relocate narrative between the world and the text while still retaining a sense of narratives as a particular kind of cultural formation; the problem that is emerging here coheres around the way that this is done. Structural narratology, inserted as a local truth precisely to provide this kind of specificity, actually threatens to dehistoricize Jameson's account from the inside. This is not because of structuralism's own claims to the 'naturality' and universality of narrative form (these have been redirected) but because in claiming a fixed form for narrative, even at this particular point in the concentric structure he builds, Jameson himself *reimports this universality and this fixity*. If narratives are historically contingent (and this is why and how they are socially symbolic), then narrative *models* surely need to be considered to be the same at all the levels, or horizons, of the tale.

Old fashioned ideological critique?

[D]istance in general (including critical distance in particular) has very precisely been abolished in the new space of postmodernism. We are submerged in its henceforth filled and suffused volumes to the point where our now postmodern bodies are bereft of spatial co-ordinates and practically (let alone theoretically) incapable of distanciation. (Jameson, 1991: 48, cited in Gaggi, 1997: 99)

Suggesting that Jameson's sense of narrative as the political unconscious could be reopened into the horizons of the contemporary world, I was aware that this horizon includes Jameson's own later works. Jameson himself entertains narrative doubts – at least if narrative's success or failure, or possibility or impossibility, is understood, as it is for Ricoeur (above), to relate to the very possibility of interpretation. I have already noted that, for Jameson, the cultural logic of late capitalism (Jameson, 1991), is such that it all but eliminates the possibility of achieving critical distance, fracturing vision, texts and meaning itself. The result is that it is impossible to find a place from which to evaluate or analyze, 'a place from which "old fashioned ideological critique"' (Gaggi, 1998: 99) might emerge. Jameson thus articulates what has become a more or less standard understanding of postmodernity as the eclipse of meaning.

Despite Jameson's own later doubts, I want to suggest here that a narrative analysis of new media can draw on Jameson's own earlier hermeneutic methodology (if not on his particular, or rather borrowed, sense of narrative form). A Marxist sense of hermeneutics is concerned with what it regards as the necessary unmasking of cultural artifacts 'as socially symbolic acts' (1981: 20). It is on this basis that Jameson can characterize narrative (that which is to be unmasked, and/or that which can reveal) as the political unconscious. For Jameson, writing of literature, this unmasking is central to the project of producing an analysis of forms of culture. It is necessary because humans are alienated from the real relations organizing society. These are relations in which we are embedded and so we find them difficult to see. In this case, where new media are being considered, what is being asked is how narrative might be used to explore (or unmask) new media.

Deploying narrative I am not seeking to produce a(nother) simulacrum of digital media for theoretical consumption, this time using narrative rather than 'community' or 'cyberspace' or 'theatre', for instance, as the leading metaphor. To paraphrase Jameson, who used the expression in terms of literary history, I want to use narrative to produce digital media's concept (Jameson, 1981: 12). It is my contention that the concept of new media technology can be unmasked within a series of hermeneutic horizons. Following Jameson, these horizons might be understood at the level of the individual work, at the level of the immediate context, and in terms of history. The new media work itself can be understood as something reconfigured in different ways within each of these theoretical horizons.

At all these levels, however, a narrative examination can reveal that, while the primary materialization of narrative involves digital technology, the concept of new media, in each case, at each level, is not technology 'itself'. It is by using narrative as a tool of analysis in this way that a case against the information revolution can begin to be made; that the ascendancy of information as the new prime mover, obliterating what was narrative form, what was politics and what was history, can be challenged.

To claim that the concept of technology is not technological but historical does not mean that the problem of how to think about technology and narrative here is solved. On the contrary, it is only by retaining the distinctiveness and particularity of the kinds of operations digital technology might afford that it becomes possible to reach some understanding of the role that technology plays in the way in which narrative symbolizes.

The twin understanding of technology as eventually symbolizing beyond itself, but also persisting within narrative as a material force, serves as a guide in the following chapters. These look at various forms of digital media, considering them as forms of narrative and therefore as socially symbolic. These narratives are explored not only in terms of what they say, or mean, but of what they do. Lyotard wanted to divide out affect from meaning, but contrarily both of these are involved in the production of narrative here. In a particular way interpretation can move us – and affect can certainly mean something. As Jameson said, 'history is what hurts' (Jameson, 1991: 81).

Notes

1 'Matilda shouted fire, fire / The only answer "little liar" ' (Belloc, 1907).
2 I want to avoid the implication that technology is the ultimately determining instance either of our present day social life or of our cultural production ... Rather I suggest that our faulty representations of some immense communicational and computer network are themselves but a distorted figuration of something deeper, namely the whole world system of present day multinational capitalism' (Jameson, 1984: 79).
3 Tzvetan Todorov coined the term 'narratology' in 1969 (Mander, 1999: 1).
4 Saussure never suggested diachronic studies of language should not be made, as Culler (1976) and Crowley (1996) both point out.
5 A second Italian/US branch of narratology grows out of Peircean semiotics and is developed by cultural theorists including Umberto Eco.
6 This unit is the sentence for Chomsky, but not for Saussure. Culler also points out that the boundaries of *langue/parole* were always disputed (Culler, 1976).
7 This banishment might add to the fascination with cyberpunk evident amongst a generation of film theorists.
8 Murray's account has its parallels with Walter Ong's discussion of television as a new form of orality. For Ong, what might be lost in book or chirographic culture could be compensated for in a return to an originary immediacy of the kind celebrated by Alfred B. Lord, Milman Parry and Havelock Ellis in their consideration of oral tales (Ong, 1998).
9 Relying on a basically structuralist definition of narrative to explore various CD-ROM based video games, Andy Cameron points to their branching structure, and the continuous activity or intervention in the tale demanded from the user. His suggestion is that both the structure of these tales and the activity demanded of the user to 'make' them break the line of the narrative (Cameron, 1995). Linearity and closure are required components of narrative. Neither is deliverable within interactive productions and for this reason interactive narrative is essentially an oxymoron. Cameron bases his argument in part on the relative lack of success of forms of interactive narrative offered as a new genre distinct from gaming. The best interactive productions can offer is the 'pleasure of gaming'. Implicit in this account is an evaluation of 'true' narrative as worth more than the narrative-style gaming the interactive platform is said to offer.
10 Borgmann's account of technology as diremption is based on the discourses of technology he finds present in contemporary society. One of these, the apodeictic discourse, is that of the natural sciences as they seek universal

explanations. The paradeictic apes the apodeictic discourse but is episte-mologically deficient and is 'most readily seen when the social sciences seek the certitude of the physical sciences' (Grange, 1994: 166).

11 A 'reification of the isolated linguistic element to the neglect of dynamics of speech' (1973: 77).

12 This tendency is embedded in the work of Vossler and Humbolt, both of whom are discussed in *Marxism and the Philosophy of Language*, for instance.

13 *Brave New World*'s newspeak is a fictional example of a non-heteroglossic language.

14 Metz noted the irony that 'the language we speak has become what American logicians call "natural" or "ordinary" language, whereas no language is needed to describe the language of their machines' (Metz, 1974: 35).

15 As Augustine expresses this directly: 'the soul distends itself *as it engages itself*' (cited in Ricoeur, 1984: 19).

16 He is also insistent that 'only history can claim a reference inscribed in empirical reality' (1984: 82).

17 In the final chapter of the *Political Unconscious*, Jameson references Ricoeur in a discussion of positive hermeneutics, pointing out that Ricoeur's sense of eschatology, which figures as the utopian moment in his understanding of narrative possibility, has its parallels in Marxist accounts. The utopian moment has always been a feature of Marxist writings – famously, for instance, in the Luxemburg formulation – socialism or barbarism (see Luxemburg, 1970: 269).

18 Jameson is unhappy with the word but offers no other.

19 Jameson discusses this in terms of the need for the text to 'draw the Real into its own texture'.

20 Here the contrast is with praxis – the mode through which such a resolution might be arrived at through action in the real world.

2

'Beautiful patterns of bits': cybernetics, interfaces, new media

[I]f plugging into the digital machine means plugging straight into the heart of the most advanced expression of contemporary capitalism, how is this relation to be conceived in terms other than those provided by industry? (Terranova, 2000: 117).

The automata . . . have come into their own. (Wiener, 1961: i)

Preface: an artificial paradise?

Technologies transform cultures and those who live in them. But they themselves are not simply formed by, but are integral elements of, cultures at particular moments in their history. To argue this is not to cheat, to suck the puissance out of the technological no sooner than it has been admitted and revert to culture and discourse. Nor is it to argue that the social stands *in advance* of the technological – this would amount to claiming technological transformation is at root *only* social transformation. Rather the two engines of transformation are inextricably linked. The world in which we live and struggle and play is irreducibly technological: struggles against cold, against ignorance, against hunger, but also against domination, against stupidity and struggles for freedom, for happiness, for justice – all are pursued *technologically*. So also are forms of play: cinema, television, sex, friendship, love, all have their technological (or bio-technological) aspects and are, in some respects at least, technological. The existence of connections between technologies, societies and cultures is not at issue. It is *the forms these connections take that compel investigation*. This is important not least because particular understandings of these connections, which may be viewed as either historically contingent (and therefore technologically specific) or in transhistorical terms (when a certain indifference to the specifics of technologies is inevitable), operate with a particular ideological force, implying what it is possible to change and what is destined to remain.

Digital technology is caught up in this web of connections and in the debate around the forms that these connections take, being variously understood as a technological or non-technological formation, as natural or unnatural, artificial or organic, purely cultural, absolutely technocratic, all new or rather old, for instance. The question of the particular cultural forms and practices that digital media technologies might enable or disallow, transform, reproduce or express, within different historical contexts, finds its context within this more general problematic; and one of those forms, of course, is narrative, which has become a touchstone within a series of accounts of this relationship.

My starting point here, in this consideration of a particular relationship between technology and culture, is not computer culture per se. I turn first to an account of mass culture. In *Signs Taken for Wonders*, Franco Moretti discerns the end of literary culture at the hands of mass culture, this new order being prefigured in tensions and strains within literary productions which cannot contain its logic. The move Moretti makes is from the *Waste Land*, taken as a boarder production where myth proliferates promiscuously (and impossibly), tending towards polysemy rather than closure, to mass consumption, viewed as an artificial paradise that operates according to a new law. The dynamic of this new order is not focused on the satiety of the consumer through the satisfaction of her or his perceived needs (as Adorno and Horkheimer thought it might be); rather it expresses itself in the form of an insatiable curiosity (insatiable because continuously refreshed; this is *why* it is a paradise of a kind). It is thus viewed not so much in terms of a demand for the discrete products of mass culture, but for experience itself (Moretti, 1983: 231).

In this new world significance comes second to experience, if it comes at all, and it is certainly rethought, since now the referent is routinely divided from the sign so that the principle of literary fiction (which is that it operates *beyond* a certain kind of truth and falsity) becomes a *general* principle: it is the society within which this principle becomes operational that is defined by Moretti *as* an artificial paradise. It understood as artificial *both* in the sense that truth is not at issue – judgement is based on the manufactured experience that is assessed on its own merits (essentially aesthetically) – and in the sense that this culture is based on the technologies of mass dissemination and mass production. Paradise is artificial because it is a world constructed and experienced through media technologies.

Moretti's 1980s consideration of a culture coming adrift from its referents (and in this sense becoming increasingly immaterial) while simultaneously becoming bound up in communications networks (and in this sense being *made* increasingly technological) is an intriguing starting place to begin to think about contemporary digital media networks and the cultural forms and practices they enable. The artificial paradise arguments stand well in advance of these developments so that Moretti's (elegant) groping towards a new understanding of the relationship between information technology/communications technology and culture prefigures a series of fresh takes on this connection, which is now being explored in relation to newer media forms.

Moretti's work has roots in the tradition of cultural Marxism. When he asks what happens to a particular form of culture when a particular kind of infrastructural shift takes place, one that is intrinsically techno-logical but that is also bound up with a social totality, one of the questions that he asks concerns not technology but society: to paraphrase, what *kind* of world is it that lets itself be pervaded by *this kind* of stuff? Fredric Jameson, writing at around the same time, spins another tale of new technology and new cultural form (and the two accounts are, naturally enough, related, by way of other theorists of postmodernity, including notably Baudrillard) in his account of the *Cultural Logic* (see Chapter 1). His account also focuses on the emerging cultural forms operating within a technologically inspired reconfiguration of capitalism. Jameson's essential argument, however, is that the forms of information present themselves as 'what there is', as a new logic, and that they thereby stand in for the logic of late capitalism itself, which underpins them and which moves through them and behind them. This is a *faulty* logic, as Jameson notes, but its force as a shared cultural analysis, as a way a culture understands itself, as a cultural field within which subjects are constituted, is anything but impaired. This raises a question: given the force of the technological, how are we to approach it as an object? Should we begin with technology? Should we do so even if it stands in for something else? And if so, how?

Moretti's work might provide a way in here, since it might be under-stood as a form of medium theory and it insists on the technological nature of cultural production, from now on, if not before. This insistence on the materiality of mass mediation finds its parallels in the work of theorists such as Friedrich Kittler and Katherine Hayles, both of whom have argued for the irreducibly technological nature of literature in the era of computa-tion (Hayles, 2002; Kittler, 1997). A difference, however, is that Moretti explores the *end* of a literary era and its *replacement* with the artificial paradise of mass consumption, which in his current work he seeks to map in different ways, while Kittler seeks to configure a different form of literary criticism through a stress on the importance of the medium.

Moretti, however, even in making this move, stays with signs. He spins a tale in which particular technological developments in the sphere of

cultural production (in terms of form, reproduction, distribution, dissemination) are desired and even preconfigured in particular ways, not only
because they are social needs (this is essentially Raymond Williams's
argument), but because culture itself can no longer be contained within
older forms such as the novel, here read as synonymous with print,
perhaps. This might be a form of literary theory that is sensitive to the
medium – but then again Moretti's account of 'artificial paradise' begins
and ends with a modernist poem and remains within the terrain of signs;
and even if these are taken to be wondrously real, this is largely as they
are understood in relation to each other. Confirming this trajectory,
Moretti's later work concerns itself with a cultural geography of literature,
a form of taxonomy as an engagement with a new form of literary material
(Moretti, 2003).

Somehow a question about technology, about the specific forms of
media and information technology that are in part, at least, the subject of
Moretti's analysis, about which it turns, slips away. In short, while much
ink has been used considering the cultural ramifications of these kinds of
analyses, much less has been spent wondering about the *specific* understandings of information that these models deploy (even Jameson buys his
informational analysis in, in his case from Mandel by way of a critique of
Marxist accounts of production). And yet these specifics matter – not only
in influential historical examples (which reverberate today), but now. It
is partly with this neglect in mind that I agree with Tiziana Terranova
when she says that media theory does not often begin with technology and
that more of it should (see below). Without a clear sense of what is meant
by technology, without beginning with technology *at some point in the
analysis*, we cannot explore the naturalized connections between
technology, cultural forms and the social world that are offered to us
as a firmament, an overarching sky variously called the information
revolution, postmodernity, or posthumanism, a particular understanding
of the technology-culture relation that becomes not the subject of inquiry,
but its horizon.

So in this chapter I begin with technology. The point, however, is not
to end there. The intention is to explore how the connections between
technology and culture have been drawn – and may be drawn – in relation
to new media technologies. To some extent this is a historical account. I
have adopted this approach partly because I believe it is possible to gauge
contemporary technoculture in new ways by exploring earlier formations
and asking how they have conditioned contemporary understandings. In
addition it seems important to inquire into the dynamics of ongoing
processes of technological innovation, to ask how innovation itself, the
question of the new, informs the ways in which the technology-culture

relationship is understood. One key issue here is how and why newly introduced information technologies are so often perceived to be powerful or transformative, able to create new cultural forms and practices, remediate others and render others still entirely irrelevant – and why they so often disappoint. The first sections of the chapter consider this issue, exploring the interplay between innovation and determination and showing how the circuit as whole has a certain ideological force. I conclude by suggesting that these circuits of reception and acculturation temper the critical and popular reception new media technologies receive.

In the middle sections of the chapter I go on to suggest that this dynamic also conditions ways in which developments in the history of information technology are understood within cultural theory. Constant attention to the 'all new' obscures the degree to which continuity pertains. It might therefore produce a particular view, not only of the status of an object as new but also of what this object can do. Here this is traced out through an exploration of interface computing and/in its relationship to earlier forms of computing, and through an exploration of significant moments in the early development of what only later came to be called techno-cultural theory. My point here is to suggest that each of these moments may be understood as in part a reaction to the earlier moment – and that this reaction may include within it a form of amnesia.

The final sections of the chapter bring these arguments about the relationship between technology and culture up to the present. Here I explore the contemporary techno-cultural climate, considering various ways in which information technology is understood within the contemporary constellation. I am at pains to make some sense of the fundamental divisions between posthumanist understandings of information drawing heavily on Deleuze and Guattari – and through them on various forms of vitalism – and a series of more or less historically materialist accounts operating with a different sense of agents and structures and the relations between them. However, I also want to ask where there are connections to be made. An encounter between a form of narrativity and a form of thinking about the technological that emerges in Actor Network Theory thus forms an exergue here and tempers what might otherwise be a simple return to Marxism. It may also operate to redirect attention to narrative.

Part 1: the thing itself – technology and determination

If media theory rarely begins with technology then this may be because media theorists, haunted by the spectre of technological determinism, are afraid of material technologies in their specificity and their particularity, preferring to deal with technology by 'dissolving it in culture and discourse' (Terranova, 2000: 111). Medium theorists and contemporary information theorists may also be haunted, in this case by a fear that the cultural specificity of particular technologies might contaminate the beautiful patterns of bits, the material geometries of information systems. Despite the threat of various forms of haunting in this chapter the focus is on technology itself; to think about the force of networked new media technology as a cultural form, and within that to inquire into its relationship with narrative formations, it is necessary to grasp its materiality.

The material technologies underpinning a new-media formation thus come under the spotlight here. However, I do not assume that these technologies are simply 'objective objects' standing outside of social processes. Consideration of these technologies within the social totality makes it possible to grasp their *specific* materiality without reducing them to this 'objective' form, and to do so without reducing the terrain on which they emerge to the networks formed by their simple and exclusive combination, the latter tending to constitute a techno-social domain (P. Graham, 2000: 132) rather than a social totality. Instead it is argued that networked new media can best be understood as a historically specific system that takes a particular material form, rather than being viewed through abstracted concepts such as *techne* through which (all) technology effectively and indiscriminately becomes discursive mediator or distant essence rather than material object. This approach is taken partly to avoid the more or less conscious ahistoricism of some forms of medium theory. Defining new media technology in non-essentialist terms, it is here understood as something *historically* developed, produced and used, something whose form is therefore not fixed. In other words, technologies are forged within the social relations pertaining at a particular time and are also, and as technologies, the *bearers* of those relations over time. As such, technologies may tend to influence particular *future* possibilities, and not only those that are narrowly technological (in the sense that existing standards influence future designs) but also those concerning what Marcuse called 'reason and freedom' (Marcuse, 1972: 14).

New media artefacts/systems are assembled out of bundles of silicon, plastics, metals and glass, as well as being constructed through and in code. They are in different measure more or less solid, more or less flexible. As a consequence of their coded aspect they are to some degree reprogrammable; they make take different forms; and they may change form or be relatively easily translated rather than copied across media.

New media systems engage with (remediate, perhaps, but not in simple ways) many existing symbolic systems and operate through and with multiple sensory inputs and outputs. They articulate language, image and music, for instance, rendering each as code, but also rendering worked-upon code as image, as a form of language or as a musical work. When language, music or images become digital media streams they are thus reconstituted as symbolic systems through this new material articulation; this is a digital photograph, and this is what it does, and this is how it can be remade.

Invoking the problematic distinction between form and content is useful for a moment here. It allows us to insist that computer code itself, a material form, is *also* a symbolic system, and also to insist that there is a meaningful distinction between this and other symbolic forms even if this distinction is precisely what is confounded through remediation, which blends and remixes these systems.

Use impacts on questions of materiality which is why bringing use into the definition of the system and into the consideration of its materiality at the outset is important. The point is to go beyond a simple form of social construction that says systems are shaped over time by the uses to which they are put – essentially through product-development cycles. A more thoroughgoing sense of how use intervenes in the system is required. New media networks only fully unfurl *as systems* in their use, and use is therefore to be regarded as an integral part of the whole, rather than as epiphenomenal. Use is itself a part of the material.

Finally, there is the question of imagination. The material/symbolic forms and practices that form new media systems of various kinds and at various scales also intersect with and to some extent produce a diffuse new media imaginary, a cultural logic that exists *beyond* and *before* media systems when they are regarded as instantiated objects, and that informs the everyday environment in which we live. Informational culture thus has at its heart material digital objects, systems and networks, the political economy that organizes this production *and* the cultural imaginary that arises from it. Having made this division we have immediately to blur it, since each of these term also contains the others. The cultural imaginary may be contested producing not only new cultural logics for information but new media systems and new forms of technological life. Seeking to begin with technology 'itself', I am not presuming a simple 'culture or technology' division.

With these considerations of the material in mind, I begin by exploring ways in which new media technologies are conceptualized as new both in the critical and popular registers. The new has a complex relationship to the question of determination and it is this that is explored here.

The new and the determined

It is a common conceit to imagine one's own times are of unprecedented historical importance. (Robins and Webster, 1999: 63)

> The digital revolution is whipping through our lives . . . causing social
> changes so profound their only parallel is probably the discovery of fire.
> (Rossetti, 1995: 14)[1]

Hyperbole is not unknown in the history of new media technologies;
Martin Luther once said the printing press was God's highest act of grace
(cited in Gospel Com, 2001). In its launch issue *Wired UK* declared a
'peaceful inevitable' revolution based on the Internet, which it declared to
be as important as the discovery of fire (Rossetti, 1995: 14).[2] This kind of
overestimation may be a general feature of popular understandings of
new technology. Robins and Webster claim that successive generations
have believed that their times are of unprecedented historical importance,
adding that this popular belief has been sustained by a sense of living
in *technologically* significant times (Robins and Webster, 1999: 63).
Certainly many generations have believed that the technologies emerging
in their own time would change the world (Marvin, 1988).

When technologies are understood as world changing they are also
understood as determining, having characteristics that make them at once
compelling but impossible to assimilate by the society into which they
emerge. As a consequence, it is felt that these societies will themselves be
changed by (assimilated by) technology. Popular histories, and songs such
as 'For the want of a nail', demonstrate the purchase of this trajectory
as a means of explaining historical processes. Working in a different
register, Lewis Mumford took this to a beautifully argued conclusion in
Technics and Civilization, where he defined every era by a prime mover
(Mumford, 1946).

The picture changes as new technologies become bedded down. They
then no longer seem autonomous from political or social processes, and
as a consequence are less likely to be regarded as 'world-changing' or
exceptional in themselves. In other words, the social shaping of new
technologies tends to become more visible in popular discourses as these
technologies become established and/or as the history of their
development comes to be revised. The moon landings are one example of
this trajectory (Bryld and Lykke, 2000)[3] and atomic bombs another (see
Sassower, 1997). A corollary of the increased visibility of the social
processes shaping technology is often that the technology *itself* tends to
become *less* visible. That is, it becomes an unremarkable feature of society,
a naturalised part of the landscape (Gibson, 2000: 20). Carolyn Marvin's
study of 'when old technologies were new' provides examples of this
trajectory, one of which is electric light, hailed at the moment of its
inception as a new form of spectacle that would paint the sky itself
(Marvin, 1988). Today electric lighting is not a wondrous technology but

is actually almost invisible *as a technology*[4] (hence the shock value of McLuhan's description of the light bulb as a medium).

In sum, in the popular sphere, new technologies tend to be regarded initially in ways that are highly technologically determinist. This changes as technologies become more established, when their social shaping within society becomes more obvious. This circuit is continuous so that 'new' new technologies displace 'old' new technologies which are redefined at the moment they recede from view. Within this cycle, technology is at its most visible when it is regarded as determining, and tends to become less visible in the popular mind as it comes to be regarded as socially shaped. As a consequence, a technology becoming 'old' is also often regarded as less *powerful* than it was previously thought to be.

Finally, these circuits extend to future technologies. The current preoccupation with the near future of technologies (bio-technology, AI or human cloning for instance) within popular science, the *Matrix* series in popular entertainment, and perhaps also *Minority Report*, are examples of this. They suggest that we are often more preoccupied with how near- or mid-future technologies (regarded as likely to be determinant) might come to control us than we are afraid of how *existing* technologies (RFID, existing biometrics, for instance) might be used by particular groups within a society as *embedded* forms of social control. Thinking about future technology is useful here in that it also points to how popularly based technological determinism of all kinds might find its roots in a Utopian desire for new forms of life (for a world *made* better). New technologies, both fictional and real, can come to hold for us the promise of a wished-for future (see Silverstone, 1994, 1999). The counter to this is what Adorno and Bloch described as the tendency of utopian wishes *delivered* through technology to disappoint (Bloch, 1992): like the ancient gods we can now speak across vast distances, but we know that this is (only) telephony.

Within academe too there is a marked tendency to stress the significance or transformative force of a particular new technology *qua* technology in its early days. This is followed by a period of reappraisal in which the significance of the technology and the claims made for its relative auton- omy tend to be reassessed. Finally, the moment comes when the claims made for a particular technology fade; as it becomes embedded it seems less exceptional, indeed less interesting. At this point attention shifts back towards the horizon as the next potential 'world changer' hoves into view.

This is inevitably a caricature of what is a complex, multi-layered process. There are always dissenting voices – indeed entire fields have been established to dissent from precisely the kinds of technologically determinist accounts that tend to dominate as new technologies emerge

(Raymond Williams's *Television, Technology and Cultural Form* punches for cultural studies/media studies against Marshall McLuhan's medium theory). On the other hand the pattern holds up, not only if the discrete history of many media technologies are considered (Marvin's 1988 account of electricity is again notable here, but see also Armstrong, 1996) but also if the historical dimension is considered;[5] as Stallabrass notes, many of the world-changing social and political promises now made for the Internet are familiar to those who read media histories because they are precisely the *same* promises that were made about earlier new media technologies at *their* moment of inception (Stallabrass, 1999: 114).

If the case for determination tends to be revived with *each* significant new technology, within both the popular and academic spheres, a difference between the two is that in the latter case this may also involve a shift in forms of thinking about technology *in general*. In other words, it is not simply the reading of a *specific* technology that tends to shift in critical writing in response to the cycles of innovation I've described. More fundamental conceptions of technology 'itself' are also vulnerable to Robins's and Webster's 'common conceit'. Over and over again we succumb to the sense that the new technology of our own time is exceptional. That is, the case for the autonomy of technology (for technologically produced transformation) is very often explicitly made or implicitly adopted in the analyses of new technologies, while the case for the social shaping of technology, which reorganizes this relationship, tends to re-emerge as technologies lose the patina of the new.

These theoretical shifts are complex and the circuitry overlaps. Perhaps it might be said to operate at many different scales at once, so that micro-level oscillations form part of larger, longer-term swings. More, innovation itself is continuous, and a feature of digital media, indeed, is the speed at which they can be remade – not least through recoding. Even taking all of that into account, however, the trend remains: *technologically and culturally deterministic accounts of technology alternately appear and disappear in relation to ongoing cycles of innovation and assimilation.*

Grasping this dynamic is crucial to thinking through the cultural/critical reception given to the development of information technology in the past sixty years or so. It has a bearing both on how various information technologies have been gauged at various times, and on the ideological force of claims made for information.

Computing *was* transformed at least three times in the twentieth century, not only in the popular imagination or even in critical writing, but also in material ways. First came the founding moment of computing, the first computers and the development of early forms of computer science and cybernetics, the science of control and communication. Second came the development of personal computing in the mid-1980s, and here the major innovation was focussed on interface computing and the development of new forms of interaction between user and machine. The final transformation was the rise of networked new media, which extended interface computing to include interaction between multiple users and multiple machines, which became a popular form with global reach in the 1990s. In the early twenty-first century, we live in a world permeated by global media networks in the 'network society' (Castells, 1996), the 'information age' (Appadurai, 1990) or the 'new media' age (Manovich, 2001), and mobility is increasing so that the networks of which Castells wrote are increasingly also locative – connecting a position in physical space with a position, or node, in virtual space.

Each of these three waves of transformation, despite the fact it relied on the previous one, has also been widely understood as a distinctively new technology. Each moment, indeed, has been proclaimed revolutionary *in its own right*, so that, in popular rhetoric, the original computer revolution was later superseded by the home computing/personal computing revolution and this was eclipsed in its turn by the rise of the network society or networked computing (the Internet). More, each of these moments, never entirely separate and indeed connected in fundamental ways, has inaugurated a popular impulse towards technological determinism, defined above as a characteristic response to the shock of the new. And each has produced a particular efflorescence of critical thinking: a series of reappraisals of the role of technology and/in culture which have, indeed, been made more often than the technology itself has been substantially refreshed. I refer here to the claims made for the cybernetic society in the 1950s (see Gere, 2002; Edwards, 1996), to the proclaiming of the information society in the late 1960s (Schiller, 1997), to claims made in relation to personal computing in the 1980s (Levy, 1995) and, most recently, to claims made for a new form of society based on networked computing ('the Internet') made in the late 1990s and continuing today in relation to Web 2.0.

Some of these moments are traced out below, but it is important to point to the implications of this repeated stress on rupture: networked new media *can* be viewed as another moment in the continuous history of the development of computing, a history which includes changing conceptions of the technical reality, cultural significance and power of automation. However the circuits described above have *tended* (and still tend perhaps) to deliver new media to us as a moment of discontinuity and this has conditioned how they are understood, conceptualized, explored, used and imagined.

Finally, it is through these circuits that the Internet 'revolution' has been presented to us as a revolution making computer technology new once again in critical theory and in the popular imagination. The Internet in this sense marks a *refreshing* of the promise of computerisation. Now, given the relationship between the shock of the new and understandings of technology discussed above, it will be evident that this categorisation will have certain consequences. It will affect how networked new media technologies are understood *as technologies* (how they are socially constructed as 'powerful', or exceptional), how they are thought about in relation to society, how visible they are and how they are conceptualized within various critical traditions. To the extent that defining this technology as new, or accepting it as new, *excuses* critical thinking from consideration of the question of technology and the social world, or suggests that technology supersedes this totality, this refreshment of the promise of computerisation is ideological. Here also we might return to Jameson and his sense that:

> Our faulty representations of some immense communicational and computer network are themselves but a distorted figuration of something deeper, namely the whole world system of present day multinational capitalism. (Jameson, 1984: 79)

Our representations, then, may be less faulty than infantile – in the sense that they are based on *early* impressions of what appears to be a distinctively new moment in the development of an information society. The legacy of earlier critical engagements with computer science, and indeed of the connections between new media and earlier forms of computing, both have to be reassessed if new media are explored as a development that may often *seem* 'all new', but is only partly so, being at least as much about continuity as transformation (see McKay and O'Sullivan, 1999).

The account of innovation, information technology and culture so far is highly schematic. Below some arguments are unpacked. First I consider the relationship between earlier understandings of computers as calculating machines and contemporary forms of computing that stress various aspects of the interface. Developments in the interface are understood as a defining feature of new media, and are central to the way in which the promise of computerization has been refreshed both in relation to personal computing and in relation to contemporary new media.

From giant brains to interface computing

In order to put a problem into this machine – just as with other machines – first a mathematician . . . lays out the scheme of calculation. Then, a girl goes to one of the hand perforators. *This sounds like it's going to hurt!* Sitting at the keyboard, she presses keys and punches out feet or yards of paper tape expressing the instructions and numbers for the calculation . . . [two copies are made independently, for error checking] . . . a girl takes them over to the processor and puts them both in . . . if the two input tapes disagree, the processor stops . . . Next, the girl takes the punched tape made by the processor over to a problem position that is idle . . .' (Edmund Berkeley, cited in Leonard, 2000)

The first computers were built in the US and the UK at the end of the Second World War. Alan Turing's paper 'Computable Numbers', laying the groundwork for programmable computing and the universal machine, was published in 1936 (Hodges, 1983). ENIAC, arguably the world's first computer, was built in the US in 1945 (Singhal and Rogers, 2000: 212), although another early computer was developed in England through the work of Alan Turing around the same time (Hodges, 1983). In their early iterations these were giant calculating machines, clumsily mechanical when viewed in relation to their modern successors, and they were non-digital, relying instead on a system of valves. They were also enormously power hungry. Running the ENIAC computer at Pennsylvania would drain the electricity grid, so that the lights of Philadelphia, on the far side of the river, dimmed.

Developed through a series of collaborations between the academy, industry and the UK and US governments, these computers were intended to automate large scale and complex calculations of the kind embarked upon by governments and perhaps the largest corporations. Their uses were envisaged as largely, but not entirely, military. Various accounts of these early years point to a growing awareness of the complexity of mass society, provoking a search for new means to control this complex social system amongst governments of the time. Thus Vannevar Bush, Director of the US-based Office of Scientific Research and Development, responded to the prospect of an information explosion with the tract 'As We May Think' in which he envisioned the Memex, a system for the organization and combination of information, not precisely a computer, but rather a blueprint for knowledge architecture. The Memex was something like Xanadu, Ted Nelson's hypertext system designed to address the same problem of information overload some decades later (Nelson, 1987), although Nelson's sense of computer liberation placed him far from Bush in political terms. The question of how to use and interact with information held by, organized by and worked upon by machines (a process through which more information might be generated) was thus posed early in the history of computing, although it was rarely posed *as* an interface problem. This came slightly later, as we'll see.

Talking to machines: interface computing

Basic input/output mechanisms are essential to all forms of computing. Alan Turing's universal machine, widely regarded as the progenitor of the modern computer, was, after all, programmable (Hodges, 1983), but its mechanisms did not constitute an interface, as we now understand the term. Indeed, writing a history of the transition from mainframe to personal computing, Paul Cerruzi notes that in the early to mid-1970s, before the invention of even the earliest personal computer, the very notion of using a computer interactively would have been quite simply scandalous, as would the suggestion that a computer could be used for anything other than the work of calculation (Ceruzzi, 1999: 65).

Today, the turn to the interface is evident in new media of all kinds: in new communications network protocols that operate at higher levels than previously, in the design of individual products and in applications software allowing an increasingly tight coupling between machine and user, for instance. All these developments are still relatively new to computing; it is a measure of our rapid habituation that they already seem normal (invisible) to us as we draw on them in everyday use. They reflect a real shift in the concerns of those designing and building computers, and in the ways in which the computer industry has developed and expanded.

Bush was a pioneer, but more systematic moves towards human-centred computing began as far back as the 1960s, associated with the work of Donald Licklider, an early computer scientist. Licklider's work signals a change in emphasis since he set out to develop a 'symbiotic' relationship between humans and computers, in which computers would do more than simply handle information (Preece, 1994: 18). This was the difference that grounded the work of the emerging field of Human Computer Interaction (HCI) based on computer science and human psychology and often crossing into industry. HCI was underpinned by a series of developments in the late 1960s/1970s, including user-friendly input/output devices – GUIs (graphical user interfaces) and the WIMP (Windows, Icons, Mouse, Pointer). A more-or-less standard history of these developments has emerged over the past decade. Briefly, Ivan Sutherland's Sketchpad included novel input possibilities (1960s), Xerox's Dynabook and Star (1970s) provided early stabs at graphical rather than command-line interfaces, and the Apple Lisa (early 1980s), brought these together[6] and marketed them (see Nielson, 1995; Levy, 1995; Preece, 1994). These developments led by increments to the elaborated graphical user interface of the Apple Macintosh (1984) and later to Microsoft Windows, and to the use metaphors that became the standard mode of interfacing with computers from the late 1980s/1990s onwards (Levy, 1995). These now influence interface designs for new forms of mobile and small screen interactions, some of which are also locative (McCullough, 2004). Developments such as augmented reality, voice input and intelligent assistants build on these beginnings, and virtual reality (VR) emerges out of many of the same traditions (Nielson, 1995; Laurel, 1991).

But this is looking ahead, and I want to briefly stay with HCI, which first coalesced as field in the mid-1980s (Preece, 1994: 7),[7] largely in response to the diffusion of new generations of smaller, faster, cooler and cheaper computers for business use. Around the same time, computers were becoming available to the general population for private use for the first time. If this trajectory seems natural, once again our memories are short; the idea of home or leisure computing seemed as scandalous and unlikely in its time as the idea of interaction had done initially (Haddon, 1995: 15).[8]

The central focus of HCI in its early years was developing human–machine interfaces and interface principles that redefined human-computer interaction. It may be tempting to regard interface developments as making modern computers easier to use, just as developments in hardware (the shift from valves and tubes to increasingly precise and miniaturized digital circuits inscribed on silicon) have made them faster, and to leave it at that. However, interface computing has been defined and understood within the discourses of the computer sciences and within the computer industry as a new form of computing. The key shifts here are three.

Firstly, with the advent of interface computing, interaction, once confined to the tedious processes of inputting data and obtaining (printed) read-outs, and therefore something all too easily understood as peripheral to 'computing' itself, becomes more tightly and more visibly tied into the whole. Secondly, interaction becomes more elaborate both spatially and temporally. The ubiquitous employment of spatial metaphors in interface design (desktops, cities, communities) makes clear the purchase of this kind of theorisation of interaction. Brenda Laurel's exposition of (personal) computers as theatre is an example of its development. Laurel conceptualized the computer screen as a stage on which actors (users) played and worked, one that solicited some actions and discouraged others. She also recognized, as did others, that richer forms of interaction require user investment (and therefore consent) rather than simple comprehension or competency to operate (Laurel, 1991; Kay, 1990). Thirdly, there is a recognition that authority (who or what tells who or what what to do) now passes between user(s) and machine(s) in more complex ways than it did in earlier forms of computing. Here HCI's reliance on affordance, a perceptual concept developed by J. J. Gibson,[9] is relevant since affordance concerns the use suggested by an object (Norman, 1998; J. J. Gibson, 1950: 129). Via affordance the interaction between user and machine is be viewed not as a turn-taking process but as a process in which each side configures the other in response to various solicitations, although always within the limits of programmatically defined and policed legality. It might thus be argued that the interface configures or solicits not only the user but also the machine of which it is a part (which is, after all, otherwise only a general-purpose calculator). Affordance is different from visibility since the point is not to *display* everything that might be possible but rather to *solicit* a particular response, and it provokes consideration of embodied/embedded forms of use.

Designs for networked virtual space (browsers in particular) relate closely to ideas of interface space originally developed by those designing stand-alone machines for personal computing (Mitchell, 1995). And while it is the case that HCI discourses increasingly seek to make interfaces transparent, designing systems to help users *feel* they can interact directly with content or reach 'through the information to underlying contexts and meanings', as Terry Winograd has put it (Winograd, 1994: 53–54), this is an extension of interface rather than its negation – which is also why increased transparency here does not imply increased control; on the contrary it tends to decrease it. This trajectory continues so that invisibility is now commonplace as a desired end in various manifestos for future directions in computing (Norman, 1998), particularly in relation to dispersed, mobile computing. The turn of the screw here is that these invisible interfaces obscure not automation but the fact of mediation itself (nobody in HCI talks about unmediated access, only about the *visibility* of the mediating process, we might note). Clearly these developments do not negate but extend Licklider's original agenda, and indeed remain pretty much faithful to it.

HCI functions as a bellwether for change. Consideration of the HCI agenda points to the degree to which the 'turn to interface' marked a real shift in approach, a reconceptualization of what computing itself entailed. More, these shifts in computer science and within the growing computer industries parallelled changes in popular fictional understandings of computing and computer use. The genealogy of fictional accounts of the technological reflects this: interface computing is far closer to the fleshy human–machine connections of the *Matrix* series, with its bio-tech version of the Internet, than it is to the disembodied 'giant brain' of *2001*'s HAL, that enigmatic figure for mainframe computing as control run out of control.[10] These popular understandings were promoted by the industry. Most obviously, the commercial, directed by Ridley Scott, launching the first Macintosh computers in 1984 explicitly set the new Macs up in opposition to the automated totalitarianism of monolithic forms of information technology.

If there are real distinctions between interface computing and older forms of computing there are also important continuities to be noted. The basic notion of interaction is not new but is *intrinsic* to the original conception of the computer as a programmable, or *universal*, machine (Hodges, 1983). Cybernetics is a system of circular causality that requires interactivity between different components of the system. Interface computing is not *synonymous* with interaction, rather it is a *form* of interaction that expands and extends the possibilities of computing in new ways. HCI is an interdisciplinary field but, in so far as it leans on computer science, it is, in the end, bound by the logic of computation and consequently by that of automation. If the practical activity with which HCI concerns itself is the development of interfaces, these are deployed in order to allow the automation of an extended range of tasks. The following is a textbook definition, in more ways than one:

> The discipline of computing is the systematic study of algorithmic processes that describe and transform information; their theory, analysis, design, efficiency, implementation and application. The fundamental question underlying all of computing is: 'what can be (efficiently) automated?' (Denning *et al.*, 1989: 15)

Exploring the discipline of HCI thus underscores what is new about interface computing while also insisting on the close relationship between interface computing and the core function of the computer as that which automates. New forms of computing essentially *combine* automation with more sophisticated forms of interactivity between humans and machines. Interface computing allows for real-time interactions between task and calculation, so that computation becomes not a single task, but an ongoing process, and computing becomes an operation that is feasibly carried out in vastly extended arenas, and in relation to problems previously not amenable to calculation.

There is a caveat here, since I do not want to underwrite a conception of the interface as a thin layer operating at the surface of things. On the contrary, the interface is central to contemporary computing precisely because it does not only operate *at* the surface, or *on* the screen. (Affordance, defined as a process of mutual configuration, implies this depth model for interaction.) The processes of the human computer interaction are extensive, reaching beyond the screen in spatial terms and beyond the proximate transaction in temporal ones. The interface can be defined as a relation that organizes automation which may operate at many different levels or scales. This approach can be contrasted with accounts focusing on simulation or 'life on the screen' (Turkle, 1995), more or less exclusively.[11] It is also markedly at odds with modernist accounts of computing which, like a certain generation of hackers, seek the truth 'near the metal' (see Taylor, 1999). And finally, it is different again from Brian Massumi's sense that the human-machinic fusions he discerns in various artworks go beyond any notion of a distinct human–machine interface, with its implication of exchange, however fuzzy, and are to be preferred to it (Massumi, 1995).

HCI thus provides useful descriptors. However it does not consider the social or cultural implications of interface computing. Indeed, in so far as HCI leans first towards computer science and an abstract imperative to automate and secondly towards cognitive psychology to explain the user, rather than seeking social explanations for the force of new media, it is unable to grapple with questions of control that relate less to flexibility and ease of use as formal possibilities than to power. Indeed, the two are often rolled up into one through the use of that specious term 'empower-ment', so that it becomes impossible to ask the question: who decides?

A fresh perspective on the relationship between automation and interface that lies at the heart of contemporary computing can be derived from a return to various traditions of critical thinking around technology. Below I look at the relationship between the cybernetic moment (beginning in the late 1940s) and contemporary new media (beginning in the mid-1990s), focusing on various breaks and reconnections with cybernetics, and asking what replaced it as a system. This opens up a view of the horizon within which various strands of contemporary critical writing around networked new media have emerged. These may accept, reject, rewrite or forget cybernetics, and do so partly as a consequence of their reading of contemporary media technology *as new*.

'Beautiful patterns of bits':[12] from cybernetics to new media
The function of a bit of information is to 'reduce uncertainty, reduce possibilities, reduce choice'. (Wiener, 1967, cited in Strate, 2000: 280)

Cybernetics grew up alongside the early development of computers themselves. Turing's paper on computable numbers (1936), laid the groundwork for programmable computing and the universal machine and a decade later cybernetics was beginning establish itself in the US. Cybernetics (from the Greek for 'steersman') is defined by Norbert Wiener as 'the science of control and communication in animal and machine' (Wiener, 1961). Cybernetics understands common processes or functions – notably feedback loops producing steady states or self-regulating systems – to be at work in teleological mechanisms, the latter being defined as mechanisms which behave with a purpose. Cybernetic systems therefore exhibit a circular causality – Wiener's example is a ship's steering system in which the actions of the steersman continuously feed information back into the ongoing movement of the ship (Wiener, 1961: ix). The example is useful since it is made obvious that the actions involved here are interactions. And indeed, cybernetics understands information or intelligence as an attribute of an *interaction*, rather than as a commodity or a form of content which might be stored in a computer or elsewhere (Pangaro, 1994): Code works upon (coded) data.

Computers are reprogrammable machines and Wiener formulated cybernetics as a 'general concept' model (Heims, 1991: 12). Indeed, the field of cybernetics came into being when the concepts of information, feedback and control were generalized from specific applications to systems in general (Pangaro, 1991); the promise of cybernetics is thus that *all* systems displaying cybernetic dynamics can be precisely mapped. Cybernetic systems can therefore include social structures and biological organisms (Jarry and Jarry, 1991: 104; Levinson, 1997: 1).[13] Viewed through the lens of cybernetics, the individual human and her or his community thus both became understandable as mechanical systems. As Heims puts it, 'life is described as an entropy reducing device and humans characterised as servo-mechanisms, their minds as computers and social conflicts as mathematical game theory' (1991: 27).

Cybernetics was quickly taken up in communications theory, where its promise was to offer a verifiable and scientific account of mass communications processes. It became the founding principle of Shannon's 'general system of information' or Information Theory (Heims, 1991). A key notion of Information Theory, as it draws on cybernetics, is the priority of the logic of the process. The message itself, or its hermeneutic possibilities, is of no import to information theorists. The world is reduced to the unambiguous certainty of the bit. The demand for isomorphism arises from this, along with a concomitant belief that anything that disrupts the perfect mapping between sender and receiver amounts to noise in the system and is to be rooted out as undesirable (Mattelart and Mattelart, 1998: 44).

Proselytising for the extensive application of cybernetic principles from the hard sciences to the soft began very early. A series of meetings hosted by the Macy Foundation ran from 1946 onwards, bringing together hard and soft science researchers, and playing an important part in this process (Wiener, 1961).[14] However, as Steve Heims points out in his excellent account of the Macy events, this forum was dominated by psychology and psychiatry at the expense of social science or political economy. The symmetry already discernable between behaviourist models of the mind and cybernetic accounts of electric circuits might have produced this imbalance, and the Cold War was also a factor (Heims, 1991: 12). Coverage of cybernetics at the time in the US press often set out to frame developments in this area in the context of rivalries with the Soviet Union as my own research has shown.

Wiener himself was dubious about the possible 'social efficacy' of cybernetics, believing problems of scale would emerge. As he put it, 'we are too small to influence the stars . . . too large to care about anything but the mass effects of molecules' (Wiener, 1961: 163). Wiener also recognized, if some of his followers did not, the crucial factor of ongoing and unplanned human interventions into theoretically discrete social systems (1961: 163).

If the Macy meetings marked a series of formal engagements between disciplinary camps, the more general influence of cybernetics within the human sciences has been profound. Its touch is evident in systems theory and in the systems-theory influenced work of Habermas. It influences the structuralism of Levi-Strauss's social anthropology (Callinicos, 1999: 266) and the structural psychoanalysis of Jacques Lacan. The latter, who memorably claimed that the unconscious was 'structured like a machine'[15] (Kittler, 1997: 79, cited in Bennett, 2000: 116), delivered a treatise on cybernetics in his *Seminars* (Lacan, 1991). Cybernetic influences are also clear in apparatus theory, both as it is indebted to Althusser (see Copjec, 1989) and in so far as it draws on structuralist accounts of narrative systems to explore cinema (Metz, 1974: 35).[16] Frederick Kittler, the literary theorist, has declared that structuralism quite simply *is* cybernetics (1997).

Finally, the diffusion of the cybernetic metaphor, with its stress on process rather than content as a popular mode of explanation for *everyday* processes, should be noted. Here I refer again to Heims's history of the Macy meetings:

> The language of cybernetics gained popularity as the new communication and computer technologies became everyday objects in people's lives . . . presumably a commonplace system of metaphors is indicative of the structure of people's experience, and in particular of the focus of their interest and attention. When learning and teaching came to be discussed in terms of transmitting information, or even 'bits of information', in analogy to certain processes in digital computers, it shifted attention away from understanding. (Heims, 1991: 191)

Heims's account is supported by media representations popular at the time. The metaphor of the computer as 'giant brain' and its inverted image which depicts the brain as 'giant computer', for instance, were influenced by the cybernetic vision of the organism as system, partly owing to the cult success of *Giant Brains, or, Machines That Think,* a primer in computing written by Edmund C. Berkeley in 1949 (Berkeley, 1949), which was also a manifesto.

Transmission interrupted – breaks with cybernetics

Cybernetics was thus for a time a key motif in critical thinking in the human sciences and in cultural analysis. By the mid-1970s, however, the *general* influence of cybernetics within the humanities was already much diminished, and new writing re-exploring the relationships between technology, technological innovation and cultural forms and practices had emerged. The eclipse of cybernetics within the human sciences and within cultural analysis is related to a revolt against scientism in general (Jarry and Jarry, 1991: 104). Elements of this revolt include the break with scientific Marxism and the turn back to Marx's early humanist works (see Callinicos, 1999: 271), the rise of ethnomethodology and symbolic interactionism (Mattelart and Mattelart, 1998) and the break with structuralism made by Derrida and others. These developments are connected, although they occurred at different times and operated in partial ways. The strands of critical thinking explored below each marked specific breakpoints and transitional moments in the shift away from cybernetically influenced thinking, and each takes us to a new place, a new way of understanding how media technologies might be understood after the demise of first wave cybernetics[17] as a tool for cultural analysis.

The invisible village

In the late 1940s a gathering of communications scholars, including Irving Goffman, held a meeting in what was to become part of Silicon Valley. This gathering, later known as the Invisible Village, argued against the use of cybernetic approaches to study society and social intercourse. Participants demanded a reinstatement of conceptions of the principle of meaning – defined as something produced intersubjectively through the actions of individuals in contexts (Mattelart and Mattelart, 1998). Their case was that cybernetic models could not be applied to what Goffman called the 'irreducible variables' of complex social systems (Mattelart and Mattelart, 1998). The claims made for cybernetics as a total system, able to comprehend the social totality, were thus undermined. The call was for a focus on the particular instance rather than on the systemic model, for the study of meaning and significance rather than message. It was taken up by others: British cultural studies arose in part as a direct response to dissatisfaction with conceptions of communication based on information theory, as Stuart Hall acknowledged in *Encoding/Decoding* (Hall, 1992).

Other cultural studies scholars have gone further. James Carey, in particular, critiqued Hall's retention of any form of communication model, with its emphasis on transmission, for the study of social processes, and stressed instead the ritual aspect of culture in the places and spaces of everyday life (see Carey, 2002: 129).

The development of anthropologically inflected approaches to media technology, innovation and everyday life in European media studies arose in part out of this tradition (Silverstone, 1994; Berg, 1996: 2; Feenberg 1999; Bakardjieva and Smith, 2001), although thay also drew on French everyday-life theorists including Lefebvre and De Certeau.

Conceptualizing technology, these theorists have tended to draw on various forms of social construction diverging sharply from the cybernetic tradition. Their accounts vary, but Social Construction of Technology (SCOT), as defined by Pinch and Bijker, is a theory within which the malleability of technologies and the provisional nature of scientific knowledge are emphasised (Pinch and Bijker 1984, Kline and Pinch, 1999, MacKenzie and Wajcman, 1999) which has been influential over some years. For SCOT, scientific truths and technological innovations emerge within broadly defined development contexts (at home, at work, in the lab) within which various actors operate. These contexts are more important in conforming technologies and truths than empirical knowledge of an objectively existing and knowable world, or of objectively existing and fully knowable technologies. Indeed, for SCOT, no such world and no such technologies exist (Gram Hanssen, 1996: 94). Against technological determinism what is stressed is the complexity of social processes through which technologies come to be made and understood. The production of currently realisable and contingently stable objects is understood as an ongoing process involving imagination, fantasy and social manoeuvring so that technologies are shaped by 'relevant social groups', and those who play a role in the development of the artefact are then defined as sharing 'a meaning of the artefact' (Kline and Pinch, 1999: 113). These 'meanings', which are in fact interpretations based on user or developer perceptions, are flexible and may be understood differently by different groups, giving the objects themselves a certain interpretative flexibility (Pinch and Bijker, 1984). A consequence of the attention paid to the power of the user to shape technology may be that these approaches can neglect what Bruno Latour has described as the 'obduracy' of the technological object (see Latour, 2000a), its capacity to resist reconformation, even after the social realities it crystallizes have changed.

Silverstone and Hirsch's work on technology and the household systematizes the kind of processes implicitly accounted for in many similar accounts (see Bergman, 1996: 2; Frisson, 1996: 3; Feenberg 1999;

Bakardjieva and Smith 2001). This work considers the process of the integration of technology into the 'moral economy of the household' (Silverstone and Hirsch, 1992: 220). For Silverstone and his co-researcher the passage into the home marks the entrance of 'objects and meanings, technologies and media' into a private sphere where they are appropriated into a personal economy of meaning (Silverstone and Hirsch, 1992: 22). The process is formalized by way of a four-part programme[18] in which acculturation and domestication are key steps. Within the Silverstone/ Hirsch account, households who find a place in their homes (lifestyles) for a particular technology are portrayed as having been successful at bringing in technologies 'from the outside'. The crossover of a technology into everyday life is thus figured as a victory for the forces of the lifeworld against the system. Technological artefacts are stripped out of their production contexts as they are 'appropriated' by users and taken into these spheres.

At issue here is whether these artefacts can be understood *as* technological artefacts once they move across the line from the public to private space? Is this understanding of the process of appropriation one in which technology is dissolved into discourse, as those medium theorists who believe media studies cannot grapple with the real aver? Does a successful negotiation of the public/private boundary both bring the technological object into the lifeworld and produce its invisibility or even its dissolution – as a properly and specifically technological object? In this case the newly arrived household object would become, not a technology precisely, but (i) a consumer object to which households have attached identifications to a greater or less degree; (ii) a portal to the outside which has been successfully brought under 'domestic' control; and (iii) something that now articulates the moral economy of the household and perhaps reveals its tensions. What might now be understood as the *apparent* technicity of the object could then perhaps be understood as something that might be dictated by culturally capitalized style choices (Brunsden, 1991), which rate or demote technology in particular fields.

It is tempting to suggest that the passage of a technology from the system into the lifeworld is understood as an instance of appropriation rather than being feared as an instance of encroachment or coloniza- tion precisely *because* this process of dissolution occurs. At any rate, the willingness of Silverstone and Hirsch to recategorize technology as a part of the lifeworld, evident in the theory of acculturation and domestication discussed above, is interesting. Perhaps it simply extends to technology the optimism, or even the Romanticism (Bowie, 1995), that often underpins discussion within the tradition of the study of everyday life. It may also be, however, that a certain reluctance to tangle with the object emerges as part of the legacy of the break with cybernetics represented by the Invisible Village. The everyday-life tradition is highly productive. However, replacing technology with its placeholder, to the extent that it does occur here, makes it more difficult to approach key questions concerning technology and use practices, and difficult in particular to approach questions of cultural *innovation*. For theorists of everyday life, these might cohere around how social groups might reshape, repattern or transform old practices around new technologies. My point is that what goes under the same name may be a practice that has become materially different, and that this has consequences. Discourse, in other words, may smooth over material difference that *makes* a difference.

Cybernetics to the structure of delay

I call this view essentialist because it interprets a historically specific phenomenon in terms of a transhistorical conceptual construction. (Feenberg, 1999: 15)

A very different break with early cybernetics comes with Derrida's early work on deconstruction. This is to be read as *at once* an indictment of first wave cybernetics *and* as a response to ongoing computerization. It is remarkable in that it at once displaces the cybernetic principle as a regulatory model whilst simultaneously instantiating a (different) sense of the technological (*techne*) as central to thinking all systems of speech and language. In this early writing Derrida explicitly set out to undermine the general authority of structuralism, 'the [Saussurean] regulatory model [critical theorists] find themselves acknowledging everywhere' (Derrida, 1972: 62). In doing so he also undermined forms of thinking about technology or technics influenced by cybernetics, exposing and undermining the rigid demarcations between content and form this kind of system entailed.

A crucial term connecting language and technology in Derrida's work is *writing*, understood as a form of constitutive inscription, and therefore as technological. For Derrida a 'certain sort of question about the meaning and origin of writing precedes, or at least merges with a certain type of question about the meaning and origin of technics' (1976: 8). Tracing the connection (or merger) discerned here leads Derrida to explore the distinction between speech and writing and consequently to consider the *priority* generally accorded to speech over writing. This priority tends to be given because writing, taken here as a form of inscription, makes clear the existence of delay and of a break between the sign and what it might have been intended to signify. As such, it has been regarded as secondary to speech as the primary act of communication, something merely 'technical and representative' of a reality beyond itself (1976: 11). It is the *distinction* between speech and writing Derrida sets out to deconstruct. His argument is that all speech is in a sense already writing, already a form of inscription, in that it too is always deferred, since there is always a distance – the distance of a breath, or the universe of language – between thought and self.

Derrida's claim is that computers, as new forms of inscription technology, may raise writing from its subordinate status since they reveal what was 'already always a machine' (because speech was always writing and both were always inscription) *as* a machine (Johnston, 1997: 23). New computer technology is thus viewed here as the beginning of a new form of writing and, given the links already made between writing and technology, the inauguration of a new kind of writing can also be understood to inaugurate a new (or rediscovered) sense of technology as *techne*, or constitutive inscription.

Previously, the links between writing and technology and the priority accorded to speech over writing, to immediacy over delay, and to absolute self-presence over absence, have produced a conception of *technology* itself as secondary. Like writing, technology in general has only been allowed to be instrumental – again secondary – rather than being in any way regarded as constitutive. In Derrida's thought the understanding of technology as instrumental is addressed by opposing the concept of *techne* to the straightforwardly technological. Derrida's claim is that the intrinsically technological moment of speech/writing produces a structure of delay, by which means a perfect, and perfectly instantaneous, mapping between 'sender' and 'receiver' (or self and self-presence) is *always* confounded. As he argues:

> [D]ifférance would not only be the play of difference with language but also the relations of speech to language, the detour through which I must pass in order to speak, the silent promise I must make; and this is equally valid for semiology in general, governing all the relations of usage to schemata, of message to code, etc. (Derrida, 1972: 67)

In instantiating the structure of delay through an insistence on the intrinsically technological, Derrida thus points to the impossibly of the perfect – and perfectly transparent – mapping between sender and receiver which cybernetics takes as its ideal. The groundbreaking insight here is that this kind of cybernetic perfection is made impossible precisely *because* of the presence of the technological – this time as detour – in all systems of communication. For Derrida, the 'irreducible variable' that confounds the cybernetic model is thus not found in the complexity of human-to-human interactions when these are contrasted with closed 'mechanical' systems. It is found in the intrinsically *technological* nature of *all* of these transactions.

It follows from this that if Derrida's sense of *techne* is accepted, then the basic opposition between the human as primary and the merely technological as secondary also falls (Coyne, 1999: 235–237). Here the anti-humanist current in Derrida's writing becomes very evidently directly linked to his conception of technology and to what might then be understood as both a *détournement* and a rewiring of a certain kind of cybernetics.

Derrida's sense of technics might thus be understood to stand in opposition to early forms of cybernetics (as well as in opposition to structuralism). At the heart of the structure of delay is a sense of technological detour. This operates to deconstruct the hopes of cybernetics that social systems including humans and machines might be mapped as teleological mechanisms. The system Derrida envisages, in contradistinction to the cybernetic systems envisaged by Weiner, is thus one that is always open to noise. Indeed, it is one in which noise, *read here as interference by the medium in the message and vice versa*, becomes part of a now constantly deferring system.

Here I note that in his early writing Derrida considered 'cybernetics' in general (see for instance the discussion in *Grammatology*, 1975: 10). More recently he has written on e-mail and 'tele-presence' (Derrida, 1995; Derrida, 1996). While these later explorations refer to actually existing technologies, they also always reach beyond them – or rather around them. There is little space within Derrida's sense of *techne* as an intrinsically constitutive moment operating within all forms of inscription to differentiate *between* particular technologies, and/or the circumstances of their production and use. Derrida's work, while crucial as a defining moment in the relations between critical theory and cybernetics, and crucial also in forcing a rethink of presumed divisions between form and content as they are policed by technology, is thus always non-specific about computer technology 'itself'.

Transitional writings: reports from the databanks

A different post-structuralist critique of cybernetics, one that discusses computerisation and society more directly, commenting in particular on the growth of databases, is Jean François Lyotard's *The Postmodern Condition: A Report on Knowledge* (1984). This was published in the year the first Apple Macintosh computers were launched (see above), inaugurating the era of mass personal computing. Lyotard's immediate target in the *Report* is Jürgen Habermas's systems-influenced theory of communicative action, but the *Report* is also a broad critique of cybernetic approaches to communications theory and an attack on information theory in particular. Jameson, indeed, sums it up as an attack on the concept of 'of a "noise free", transparent, fully communicational society' (Jameson, 1984: vii). For Lyotard, computerisation, read in terms of the instantiation of cybernetic systems and the rise of the cybernetic principle, has produced a crisis of legitimation in which all forms of knowledge become suspect (1984). This postmodern condition is one in which 'the rise of operational criteria . . . make it impossible to decide what is true or just' (Mattelart and Mattelart, 1998: 148).

This crisis is not only recognized but in some sense *resolved* by Lyotard since, firstly, the continued existence of the (now relativized) truth claims of science are allowed through their rearticulation in terms of the performative as a new principle of knowledge. Secondly, 'the people' are invited to take solace in the consolations of small narratives and localized truths. It is striking that both of these resolutions route around computer technology. Lyotard's relativism, his declaration of the abolition of narratives of progress and of a correspondence theory of truth, does not apply to computer technology itself. In the *Report*, the rise of computerisation is thus introduced as an objective reality in a world where few other such realities are left. As a consequence, the *Report* presents the reader with a paradox. On the one hand, it stands as a polemic against those conceptions of the political and/or those defences of modernity that seek to go *with* the grain of information theory/cybernetics. On the other hand, this is an attack that fails to engage with what might be presumed to be its most obvious target – since what is left standing in this account is precisely a grand narrative about cybernetics. Lyotard's pessimistic analysis of the postmodern condition, therefore, is one that entails the perfection of a cybernetic circuitry and the production of a (database) space from which all noise, all humanity, is increasingly purged. Humans are simply left to play – meaninglessly – on the margins, a development which itself cultivates a new focus for critical attention, which switches from signification to affect, from meaning to sensation. In this context, Lyotard's pronouncement that an appropriate political demand for this age would be to 'open the databanks to the people', can only be understood as a fatalistic gesture since, following Lyotard's own logic, the databanks lie beyond the reach of any possibility of meaningful interference (Lyotard, 1984).

The manner in which Lyotard dispenses with the grand narratives of history, progress and Enlightenment while leaving another grand narrative – that of technological supremacy – in place, puts the *Report* in a transitional space within critical writing on computerisation. As an account that fuses end-of-history predictions with 'silicon gee-whizzery' (Witheford, 1994: 88), it has come to be emblematic of a moment in which information seemed to become more important than history as a determinant of the future. On this basis commentators such as Braman (2000: 308), have assumed that Lyotard's analysis is of a piece with new formulations of information society, including those emerging in response to the rise of networked new media systems. Arguably, however, Lyotard's approach to information technology in the *Report* places it as a dissenting piece of writing located at the *end* of the era of first wave cybernetics, and at the end of the era of mainframe computing, rather than as an account looking ahead to new developments in information, particularly those that prioritize interaction in space (first virtual and now increasingly physical) through the development of more flexible and extensive interfaces. These developments began to be theorized by writers such as Donna Haraway, and it is to the latter that I now briefly turn, since in Haraway's early work we find another transitional writing.

Transitional writings: the cyborg

[Cyborg politics] is the struggle for language and the struggle against perfect communication, against the one code that translates all meaning perfectly, the central dogma of phallogocentrism. (Haraway, 1991: 176)

Like Lyotard's *Report*, Donna Haraway's *Cyborg Manifesto*, also written in 1984, stands between two worlds. Haraway is starting from an era still dominated by a form of thinking about computers that is essentially cybernetic – where the notion of the system whose loops may be modelled as a closed abstraction rather than the notion of interaction in contexts is dominant. However, the direction of her gaze is into the future. The *Manifesto* looks towards an age of personal or intimate computing, recognising the imminent expansion of computers and information systems (here defined as 'informatics') into areas previously unmediated by information technology. The expansion of information technologies into the body itself is regarded as particularly significant since it forces a reappraisal of 'what counts as nature' (the human) and 'what counts as culture' (the artificial). Haraway's argument is that new and untidy forms of connection, a different kind of interface between humans and machines, might confound cybernetic certainties.

Haraway's argument is configured in feminist terms, and centres on the question of gender and technology. She suggests that there may be complex relationships between humans and information technology, so that progress in technology is defined in terms of the culmination of masculine strategies of domination over nature – but is also seen as the perfection of the cybernetic principle. For Haraway these are two faces of the same coin. That is, the contrast between the embodied, leaky cyborg (both as it is coming to be and as it might become) and the pure, closed, logic of code, can be expressed in terms of a contest for a polyvalent language: a contest for *noise*. Haraway can then define cyborg politics as:

[T]he struggle for language and the struggle against perfect communication, against the one code that translates all meaning perfectly, the central dogma of phallogocentrism. (1991: 176)[19]

It is clear that for Haraway the *Manifesto* itself, and in particular the figure of the cyborg that she creates, constitutes a form of performative politics, a political fiction rather than a theoretical system, or a way to 'think the future differently' (Braidotti, 1996: 10). What is being 'thought differently' here (or produced differently if we accept the efficacy of the cyborg as performative) however, is not only gender 'itself' *but also technology*. Just as gender is cut free from its essentialist associations with nature/culture binaries, so information technology, cut free from cybernetic essentialism, also becomes something rather more indeterminate. The extension of the post-structural/post-cybernetic principle of relativism to technology 'itself', which does not occur in the *Report*, is thus clearly a key distinction between Haraway's reading of technology and Lyotard's.

There are tight connections between the trajectories identified in Haraway's work and developments within computing itself. Understanding new forms of informatics in terms of fusions and leakages, Haraway envisages new forms of increasingly intimate connection between embodied users and the information systems in which they are embedded. Thus if the *Manifesto* sums up a particular historical moment, this is partly because it followed computers 'themselves' out of the laboratory and into everyday lives and everyday spaces. In tracing out more intimate and active connections between users and machines, which are characterized by indeterminacy and partiality, Haraway starts a process of writing and thinking about computers within the humanities and social sciences which is based on thinking through questions of interface and interaction in a hybrid world and within indeterminate systems, rather than working on the premise that cultural logics can be tied up in the closed loops and feedbacks of first wave cybernetics. Secondly, Haraway's cyborg, reflecting the prioritising of the human–machine relation that occurs with the growth of user-friendly interactive systems, was a figure that fitted the times.

Haraway then becomes an exemplar of new forms of critical thinking about computing emerging alongside developments in computing in the 1980s which, in their focus on the intrinsically hybrid nature of communications between bodies and machines, challenge the assumptions and priorities of first wave cybernetics, and convincingly disrupt ideas about its applicability to the social sciences/humanities. More, if the

Manifesto relies on post-structuralist semiotics in making its feminist claims (see Stabile, 1994 here), and in that sense remains within that 'turn to language' that characterized a particular moment of feminist thought (Coward and Ellis, 1978), it does so in an attempt to consider new forms of material transformation/hybridity, prefiguring a concern with the material that became important to later forms of cyber-feminism, and indeed to techno-cultural thinkers of many kinds.

Finally, I note that Lyotard and Haraway offer accounts of information technology in which particular forms of cybernetics are vilified but are also understood to produce grounds for play. In the case of Haraway, new forms of the technological are lionized. In the case of Lyotard, play is appropriate because, placed in the increasingly perfected cybernetic environment, in that space where there is noise, affect, emotion, sensation, but increasingly little possibility of signification *outside* the databanks although *inside* a computerized society, there is little *else* for humans to do.

Part 2: contemporary technocultures

One day the day will come when the day will not come. (Virilio, 1997)

[A]bstract machines are not Turing machines; they work in different ways and have other relations with our bodies and our brains ... An abstract machine is rather a 'diagram of an assemblage' in which computers or computations can of course figure together with us. (Rajchman, 2001: 70)

In the mid-1990s *Wired* declared that by means of networked information technology we could start the world again. Once again this is hyperbole, yet it caught a moment. For a significant critical body of theorists networked new media combine with other components of a digital shift to pose foundational issues about ontology and metaphysics. For these theorists a digital revolution is transforming life in ways that largely render everyday issues of technology and/in the political irrelevant, at least as they might previously have been conceived of (see Stone, 1995; Pearson, 1997; Plant 1996, 1997). Even for more reserved critics, the break is again declared (see, for instance, Castells, 1997).

This critical response to what was widely perceived as a new computer revolution, this time a revolution in everyday life (although very different from the one originally envisaged by the French situationists and counter-culturalists of the US West Coast), led to a re-evaluation of forms of theory and forms of critical practice that continues into the 2000s.

Around the time of *Wired*'s launch a series of abrupt breaks from the discourse theory of the 1990s, with its centre in language, and from the social-shaping discourses dominating within media studies/cultural studies, can be discerned, and there is also a distinctive shift from the 'transitional' forms of thinking about information technology and culture identified above. If *Wired* wrote the manifesto in the business/popular sphere, publications such as *Mondo 2000* did the same within geek subcultures, while Nick Land, Sadie Plant and others at Warwick, Manual De Landa in the art scene, and those around Haraway in California, operated within the universities. Coming from different traditions, theorists including Constance Penley (for cultural studies) and Andrew Ross in New York (for a form of cultural Marxism) switched on the humanities and social sciences.

At the same time, however, there are many continuities, and a series of returns, acknowledged or not, to earlier theories, frameworks and structures. New writing on technology at this period continuously refers back to previous eras of technological change. The triumphant return of Marshall McLuhan, widely discredited in the 1980s, on the back of *Wired*, which at one point declared him their patron saint, is a case in point here – and an interesting point of connection between the popular and the critical (Taylor, 2000; Ferguson, 1991). One indication of this sensibility is found in the flourishing of media histories at around this time, including the telegraph as the 'Victorian Internet' (Standage, 1998) and a series of histories of early radio (revealed as a prefiguration of the net) and telephony (always a collective medium *in potentia*). McLuhan said that new media contain old media as their content, and critical thinking might here evidence this kind of dynamic.

The peculiar mix of high theory and medium theory that is now known as techno-cultural theory also makes a series of returns, and I discuss those below. This field is defined by the initiators from the late 1990s, some of who are mentioned above. It also includes, for instance, Terranova (in the sphere of communication), Parisi (on feminism) and Lovinck and Fuller (within medium theory). To one side stands Hardt and Negri's *Empire*, which is essentially an account of the advent of the biotechnological continuum as the instantiation of the social factory. These theorists form an influential cross-section of the population of a fluid and shifting (but none the less real) field of techno-cultural theory, which often also takes in a return to cybernetics, approached in its early and also in later forms. Once again then, the question of innovation tempers popular and critical appraisal.

There are other inhabitants of this field, although they may not go by the name of techno-cultural theorists, and they have been less dominant. The engagement between various adherents of determination and various forms of social shaping continues in new forms. One of these forms appears as a dispute between adherents of the abstract vitalism of techno-theory, as it has been influenced by Deleuze and Guattari, which has often produced writing characterized by a peculiar form of mystical cybernetics founded on the 'improbable chance' (Rajchman, 2001: 7) as statistical probability and life affirmation, and those who explore the question of materiality somewhat differently, operating within horizons where chance is what is taken where possible by actors within a history they do not entirely control (see Marcuse, 1972).

Vitalist critiques of the contemporary situation thus confront (but also temper) a more recalcitrant Marxism, a form of historical materialism that (also) insists on the irreducibly material nature of cultural forms and practices (even those that are increasingly light) while at the same time insisting on the socially shaped aspects of immaterial technologies, the two essentially being in a dialectic relation. I note here that this division operates not only in relation to material technologies but also in relation to social subjects – individually and collectively. That is to say, it operates in relation to the who we are, as we are made by technology and culture.

Debates around these forms of thinking about information crystallize in various ways, around the technological itself, around the constitution of forms of being and forms of collective being (debates around cyber-feminism are key here), around definitions of informational culture. These nodal points around which debate coheres are – of course – connected. Thus, for instance, questions of intellectual property and forms of immaterial production begin with the question of value and resolve into questions of ontology, as the Free Libre/Open Source Software (FLOSS) movements, show (see Lessig, 2002).

Here these engagements are explored in relation to the circuits of innovation/determination already identified as new wave techno-cultural theorists, rejecting both social construction theories of media studies/ cultural studies and cultural Marxism, revive an essentialist approach to technology.

Within this world-view an expanding 'virtual' world, which is located both-on and off-screen, incorporates 'machinic' bodies into new machines and into new rhizomatically organized networks. The concept of the machinic is derived from Deleuze and Guatarri's *Thousand Plateaus*, where it is argued that human and machine can be understood to come together as a universal (machinic) mechanism, operating between different levels of materiality (Armitage, 1999; Deleuze and Guattari, 1987: 256). The sense of increasing lack of differentiation between humans and machines, encapsulated by the notion of information networks as 'machinic assemblages' (Deleuze and Guattari, 1987; Pearson, 1997: 183), that characterizes this form of thinking is accompanied by the sense that there are few *connections* between the old world and its people and this brand new one – in fact by a *deprioritization* of the old. Indeed, the divorce between the existing worlds of the everyday, as this latter might have been thought before this technology came along, and the world *begun again* through technology, as *Wired* suggested it can be, is fairly absolute.

The twin senses of rupture and connection, the sense that information technology might restart the world, and that in doing so it might place humans and machines into a new relation, thus takes some of its force from Deleuze and Guattari. However, this is also an approach influenced by Heidegger's conception of technology (1993) since it is also marked by the sense of a return to a more authentic relationship with technology. This influence may seem unlikely; given that gloomy predictions of techno-cultural disaster (Feenberg, 1999: 17) are a characteristic of Heidegger's approach to technology, one could be forgiven for wondering how his work has figured in contemporary techno-cultural thinking, much of which has been markedly optimistic. However, Heidegger's 'Question Concerning Technology', an account which functions as a polemic against modern technology, has been directly influential within techno-cultural writing, and 'outing' the influence of Heidegger within techno-cultural thought is useful. It forces a reappraisal of the forms of anti-humanism habitually employed by techno-cultural theory to describe the human–machine relationship, undermining the radical edge this takes on through its articulation by way of the language of Deleuze and Guattari and revealing its essential conservatism.

Peter Osborne's discussion of reactionary modernism can help tease out ways in which Heidegger and techno-cultural thought connect. Osborne characterizes reactionary modernism as the temporal structure brought about when backward-looking politics is combined with the affirmation of technology. His argument is that this temporal structure is a novel but integral part of modernism in its own right, one of a number of revolutionary temporalities that might be discerned operating in modernity (Osborne, 1995: 160–168).[20] Heidegger's hostility to technology might seem to rule him out as a reactionary modernist, however, the links between Heidegger and such ideas are clear. Osborne himself takes this up, noting that Heidegger, despite this hostility, does share much with this counter-revolutionary current. In particular, reactionary modernism's,

> . . . image of the future may derive from the mythology of some lost origin . . . but its temporal dynamic is rigorously futural . . . Conservative revolution is a form of revolutionary reaction [because] it understands that what it would 'conserve' is already lost (if indeed it ever existed which is doubtful), and hence it must be created *anew*. It recognizes that under such

circumstances the chance presents itself to fully realize this 'past' for the first time. The fact that the past is in question is primarily imaginary is no impediment to its political force, but rather its very condition (myth). (Osborne, 1995: 164)

I would suggest that such reactionary modernism is also an integral part of some influential strands in techno-cultural thought – and would connect Osborne's sense of this temporality as 'revolutionary' to the energy with which the techno-cultural theorists affirm the technological.

Heidegger's account of modern technology is conceived within a framework that is neither instrumental nor anthropological. Rather, it is concerned with ontology and with essence. 'The Question Concerning Technology' is a critique of modern technology that finds its target by way of a meditation on the distinctions to be drawn between *techne* as the essence of technology and the instrumental understandings and deployment of technology prevalent in the modern world. The relationship between *techne* and technology is complex, since while the essence of technology will not be found in actually existing technology, the latter can point towards this essence.

For Heidegger, indeed, *techne* is not an object at all, but inheres in a process. *Techne* is a revealing (a coming to presence) in which man plays a part, but of which he is never the master. Heidegger's definition of *techne* as a form of working upon that reveals a truth (*alatheia*) derives from this sense. For Heidegger (as it was for Aristotle, in fact) *techne* is exemplified in skilled craftsmanship, so that as well as being a revealing, *techne* is a making – a *poesis*. Heidegger's critique of modern technology is that it is no longer a process setting out to be a revealing of truth, as *techne* should be. Instead, modern technology 'throws its frame around experience forcing us to see the world as sets of object opportunities for exploitation' (Grange, 1994: 162). Modern technology thus turns all that it touches into a 'standing reserve'. It is an ordering process that disembeds, thereby turning to inauthentic uses, all that it touches. As Heidegger understands it, all of nature in the industrialised modern world is 'spread before us, like so much supply' (Grange, 1994: 162).

Heidegger's conception of authentic *techne* as a process of revealing and modern technology as a process of ordering, when set in opposition to each other, thus also have things in common. Both are forms of what Heidegger calls bringing into presence – and are therefore not the work of man alone (1993: 324).[21] For this reason the control modern technology seems to offer is illusory. Even as man (sic) sets out on the process of enframing (industrialisation) that seems to offer him ultimate control over nature, he is in fact the most enchained by it. As Heidegger puts it, believing himself 'lord of the earth' he is actually 'everywhere secured'

(1993: 322). In fact, he too becomes part of the standing reserve: a creature disembedded by his own actions, now 'standing' in relation to technology rather than in relation to being.

Thus for Heidegger the process of industrialization articulated through technology is that process by which nature is finally enframed by technology (Grange, 1994: 161). However it also represents humans' ultimate loss of control over their environment. Given this, Heidegger can argue that the correct response to modern technology cannot be found in the realm of the political, since this form of control is based, at root, on the same illusion. Heidegger, indeed, argues that modern technology cannot be resisted at all. All that can be done, he says, is to open oneself to the essence of technology, in which one finds what he calls a 'freeing claim',[22] something which is discussed more generally in his thought as a meditative openness to the world (see Cheney, 1995: 25).[23]

Even to glance at Heidegger's sense of technology is to become aware of how widespread – in popular and critical writings on new media technology – is the double sense that founds his writing. The first sense is that modern technology, which is not neutral but whose meaning is found outside of society, increasingly controls and defines us. Even as we use it to control the world, the world slips from our hands. The second sense is that control might not be the issue; for Heidegger an authentic relation to technology does not involve mastery. A loss of control is precisely what is celebrated in many optimistic accounts of the Internet as self-organizing system.

In addition, I note that for Heidegger modern technology is unique. That is, the new forms of technology of which he writes represent a break with previous forms of technology (for Heidegger, from craft-based technology) and from the kinds of interfaces they offered with the world. In other words, they represent rupture rather than being part of a continuous history. 'The Question Concerning Technology' addresses that rupture by raising the very different prospect that through a form of attention to *techne* we might find the real. The powerfully articulated and dangerous nostalgia for the world as it was evident in Heidegger's thought does find an echo in popular representations and in technocultural thought – albeit in ways that are less alarming.

Uncritical identification?
We shall not make history. Let's go outside. (Pearson, 1997: 181)

Sadie Plant, the British cyber-feminist, is useful here in offering a representative, if also idiosyncratic, example of an account of cyberspace[24] articulated through gender that evidences the form of reactionary modernism outline above. Plant's basic take on technology stands rather neatly in apposition to Heidegger's. For Plant, as for Heidegger, modernity and modern technology are problematic. For Plant, however, information technology is not the apotheosis of inauthentic technology, but a technology that turns out 'never to have been modern' in the first place. Digital technology, therefore, holds the key to what is essentially a return to a newly configured but authentic form of life.

For Plant, cyber-feminism begins at the point when humanism is abandoned. Her analysis starts from Luce Irigaray's contention that for women a sense of identity is impossible to achieve since women cannot escape the 'specular economy' of the male (1985b: 75). This is an economy in which, through the controlling phallus and eye (the member and the gaze), woman is always understood as 'deficient'. For Irigaray, feminisms that demand for woman her place as the subject of history, her share of human domination over nature, have got the wrong goals. Pursuing the 'masculine dream' of 'self-control, self-identification, self-knowledge, and self-determination', as Plant puts it, will always be futile, since ' "any theory of the subject will always have been appropriated by the masculine" ' (Irigaray, 1985a: 133, cited in Plant, 1996: 173). For Irigaray, the only possible politics for the sex that is not one is a politics that takes as its starting point the destruction of the subject. For Irigaray, this is a work in language. Plant, however, explicitly turns to technology, and in doing so turns away from representation and indeed from the kind of cyborg narrative Haraway produced. She focuses in particular on the Internet, understanding it as an emergent system twisting out of the control of its makers. For Plant, self-organizing technology can be used to perform the work of destruction Irigaray prescribes.

Plant argues that the 'matrix', configured in her writing both as the actually existing Internet and as an emerging system, amounts to 'a dispersed and distributed emergence composed of links between women and computers'. The 'matrix' produces a space 'apart', a space beyond the specular economy. Here women are 'turned on with the machines' while man is also enmeshed in cybernetic space, becoming a component of a self-organizing process beyond his perception or control (Plant, 1996: 182). In other words, man, 'believing himself lord and master of all he surveys', to return to Heidegger momentarily, is caught in the technological nets (the cybernetic architectures) that he spread (or so Plant sees it) precisely to consolidate his own position.

The point here is that Plant's account depends not only on a particular analysis of women and phallogocentrism but also on a particular understanding of technology 'itself'. A first question arising here is how information technology, generally coded as masculine (Wajcman, 1994), becomes feminized in Plant's account. A second question concerns what

feminization might imply about Plant's sense of the essential characteristics of networked new media. Plant offers two explanations for this
gender switch. First, emergent technology is understood to have slipped
from the control of its makers by virtue of its actually existing technical
properties. Reading across from the new science, Plant claims the Internet
is an emergent system. An (unreliable) recourse to the authority of science
thus underpins her claim. Second, however, and this is where correlations
between Plant's sense of technology and Heidegger's are very evident,
Plant contends that there have always been interconnections between
females and technology, since she suggests that technology is feminine
in essence. Her point is that the 'nature' of women and the 'nature' of
new/old (but not modern) machines can now reconverge under the banner
of an authentic technology, now read as feminine. For Plant, indeed, there
is now no division between women and machines. Her sense of the
human-computer interface is thus one in which the trope of absolute
identification is adopted; women become technology/become nature/
become part of the process. Plant is discussing the subsumption of the
human into the machine, a newly configured continuum that now contains
women and (protesting but disarmed) men. In this subsumption, all
possibility of meaning or interpretation is given up, and any sense of
interfacing as an active process of exchange, through which humans make
meaningful what is solicited to them by machines – is also lost.

This newly rediscovered originary technology is about not only *techne*
but also *poesis*. Multimedia technology, says Plant 'reconnects all the arts
with the tactility of woven fabrications' (1997: 185). Information technology thus redelivers (or promises to redeliver) an authentic technology
and, as it does in Heidegger's formulations, this authentic technology
involves new kinds of fusions between technology and art. What we have
then is a revealing of truth, this time configured as a reascension of the
feminine principle in technology, cast out of the human–machine interface
throughout history and now re-emerging at its end, *even as its end*. Plant's
sense of information futures is powered by a radical nostalgia for a past
that is retroactively created, partly through an appeal to the new science
and partly through an appeal to actually existing technologies – in
particular to the promise of connection made by the Internet.

In so far as it avoids an engagement with real world technologies, Plant's
analysis is one based on a mythical future technology – a future technology
which is always deferred, and which is therefore both essentialized and
idealized. This orientation towards the future begins to explain the
distance between the analysis of the same object provided by the ecstatic
accounts of cyberspace promulgated by Plant and others working in this
tradition, and by accounts based on ethnography, other empirical work

or political economy. This distance is – apparently at least – vast and pretty much unbridgeable.

The purchase of ontological explanations of cyberspace technologies such as Plant's is that they can relate to the scale of change that new technologies such as the Internet are popularly understood to presage. Their revolutionary modernism is, in other words, fuelled by the promise of the new that is made by emerging forms of new media. For Plant, and for many others (see Kelly, 1994; Virilio, 1995), the Internet is taken as the guarantor of the Matrix to come (or of a biotech, infotech or nanotech revolution to come). Given this guarantee, it is easy to read the contemporary Internet as world-changing in and of itself – perhaps as something inevitably reaching beyond its own social context so that it can never be contained by this context. Finally, the priority accorded by Plant and others to ontological categories meshes with the popular sense that technology is changing our being in the world in ways we can *feel*. The burst of energy represented by Plant's early writing might be understood as a classic moment in the kinds of cycles of innovation outlined above.

The irony of the kind of essentialist determinism and the reactionary modernism evident here is that they fail to connect at all with real technologies. Following Feenberg, I would suggest that this form of essentialism targets the transhistorical abstraction of the concept of the digital, rather than the digital itself (1999: 15). My understanding of this form of thinking about technology is that, despite the fact that it is many ways marked by a preoccupation with materiality, being a response to the linguistic turn that followed cybernetics, it cannot touch the real. Despite the sense of the overpowering force of technology always evident in these accounts, they are not only future-orientated but also tend to be future-*analytical*. To approximate Virilio – the day will come when, because of technology, the day will not come (Virilio, 1997). Meanwhile, since we've gone outside, we can always cultivate our gardens.

As Megan Stern points out, there are accounts of cyber-feminism that are more flexible and nuanced than Plant's (see Stern, 2004: 47), including a European strand of queer cyber-feminism which wears its Deleuze/Guattari with a (political) difference, and various approaches based on political economy and social construction. Plant's account still stands, however, as the apogee of a particular historical moment in debates around techno-culture, and shares much with Parisi's later work on 'abstract sex' which appeared in the early 2000s, not least the deployment of myth.

Both writers draw on Dawkins and Margolis, and evolutionary biology and endosymbiosis respectively, as indicators of new forms and modes of (post-human) subjectivity. Plant's recourse to the bacterial continuum and her discovery of the instantiation of the feminine principle (mitochondrial Eve) essentially produces a myth of origins. Parisi's account of abstract sex, also influenced by Margolis, does not work through the myth of woman; rather, what is constructed is a myth of information technology and cybernetics (Parisi, 2004; Sandford, 2004: 35). In Parisi's work recourse is made to early cybernetics but also to second wave cybernetics and auto-*poesis*, as it was developed by Varela and Maturana (see Braman, 2000: 314–319), and alongside them to the new physics of chaos and evolutionary biology.

Parisi reruns and extends many of Plant's central arguments through a slightly different technoscience filter, and by way of a more highly elaborated philosophical approach. If Parisi does not have Plant's playfulness, as Sandford ruefully notes (2004: 36), she retains the twin recourse firstly to 'science' itself and to the authority of particular forms of informated science, so that in her hands the new biology, on the one hand, and second wave cybernetics/auto-*poesis*, on the other, become the very material of culture (and also that of abstract sex), and secondly to a sense of monism inspired by Deleuze and Guattari.

From the latter, Parisi takes on not only a particular critical tradition but also a particular form of thinking about the possibility of making connections and correlations, something which might be said to amount to a methodology, although this last term would perhaps be disputed by Parisi and others working in this current.

To me, at least, the coalescence of digital theory around Deleuze and Guattari has become an orthodoxy and has become rather problematic, partly through overuse. This is not because of the slippages and con-nections it allows between multiple theoretical approaches and various instantiated technologies. These are evident in Parisi's work on sex and also emerge in Terranova's account of informational culture, in which discourse continually slips between probability and the probable, between the realm of chance in history and the realm of chance in determining probability within information theory, between the virtual as that 'real' space that is to be found in networks behind the screen and the virtual as it is understood in Bergson, as the unexpected (see Terranova, 2004). Such slippages are often productive and certainly these works make intriguing connections.

My discomfort concerns the lockdown effect that occurs as the slippages-between that join these categories, which might once have been productive, no longer operate in *slippery* ways (as a form of opening), but are, on the contrary, locked into each other and begin to be deployed with extraordinary rigidity. Rajchman sums up Deleuze's philosophy as 'an art of multiple things held together by "disjunctive synthesis", by logical

conjunctions prior and irreducible to predication or identification'
(Rajchman, 2001: 4), but this synthesis has, in the context of writing
grappling with the materiality of new media, become expected and
predictable and the terminology into which it fits has been emptied out.

In this new orthodoxy the certain uncertainties of cybernetics (as a game
of probability), of virtuality (as a game of the unexpected), of chaos, of
post-human theory (as a site for hybridity) and of the Deleuze/Guattari
theory machine (as the grand narrative or central integrator) do not
produce lines of flight, in the sense of the genuinely new, nor do they
produce the unexpected in the Bergsonian sense of the word. On the
contrary, no longer slipping but attaching, they operate rigidly to rein one
another in, somewhat in the way that the mythic operates to pin down
meaning (here, oddly enough, we are back with Moretti as well as
Osborne). In this immanent plane that holds theories, information
technologies, bodies, knowledges and social structures as undifferentiated
material abstractions (through Deleuze and Guattari), it would always be
difficult to explore the instantiations of technology, but here, where desire
is conjoined with the fact of information, this becomes almost impossible.
This is not the unlimited plane that is desired (Rajchman, 2001, 4) but a
limiting plane, and one that is, *contra* Deleuze himself, extraordinarily
judgemental (Rajchman, 2001: 5).

In this new formation, somewhat reminiscent of the Borg in Star Trek,
it is to be hoped that resistance is possible, but it is not always clear where
it might be found or what forms it might take. We may remember that
Scott Lash, who doesn't quite go there in the *Critique of Information*,
thinks that mourning, at least, is available (Lash, 2002). New forms of
medium theory, working with Deleuze and Guattari but avoiding cybernetic certainties, do better in this respect – and might be regarded as arising
in response to these abstractions and/or to the difficulty in engaging
politically that they produce.

In its modernist aspect, medium theory has its connections with Kittler's
structuralist sense of literature as a diagram. However, in the place of the
turn to language that defers meaning and that takes politics into the realm
of discourse, in this case code becomes material possibility. Mathew
Fuller's (art) work on Microsoft Word (Fuller, 2003), defined as an
example of speculative software by the author, is a marker here.

Medium theory of this type is profoundly at odds with linguistic
theories (in this it cleaves to Deleuze and Guattari), but maintains a sense
of material technology that is grounded not in abstract cybernetic
conceptions of information but in information as a material social form,
instantiated within contexts of power and dominance. Information can
become both the grounds for, and an instrument of, struggle, but it also

needs to be exposed in its 'usual' iterations. This understanding of software as political practice demands an understanding of information which both stresses its material effects over its discursive construction, its form over its content, and seeks to confound the distinctions between them.

Here we see instantiated, perhaps, a particular form of post-Marxism. And if it begins with technology, it certainly ends in the real world, this being a return to a form of conceptualization of the technological that is material (rather than discursive/semiotic) and that defines itself within a social totality at least as much as within technical horizons. This form of speculative software, or critical medium theory, owes something to the autonomist inspired *Empire* (and vice versa). In *Empire*, the priority of the labour process in constituting the (sometimes resisting) subject is reversed: all innovation on the side of Empire is understood as a reaction to the capacity of the multitude to create, and this in a terrain of struggle that is massively expanded to take over all aspects of everyday life. Both for the speculative software theorists/activists and those taking the *Empire* approach, politics is founded in the conviction that creative production is located in the multitudinous tactics of the dominated in that sphere of action defined as the social factory; it is this rather than the strategic responses of those who dominate that produces *ontological* innovation.

There is a clear division between those who understand information to have inaugurated or made visible (variously) the revealed dynamics of a particular form of possibility – which is the possibility of action by the multitude, defined as a collective which springs to life after the end of conventional politics, from which all that is vital comes (see Terranova, 2004) – and those who retain a purchase on a dialectical view of the relationship between structural limitations and forms of resistance. On the other hand, there are also connections, and these are seen in the restitution of an avant garde gesture (a very different form of modernism) in the work of the critical medium theorists, at least in those who espouse critical medium *practice* as well as theory. Their unashamedly interventionist attitude is also what marks them out from relentless constructivist approaches in which whatever is shaped, whether within technological or social horizons, appears to be shaped *right*.

Exergue: Actor Network Theory and the technical social (versus social construction?)

The adjective social now codes, not a substance, nor a domain of reality (by opposition for instance to the natural, or the technical, or the economic) but a way of tying together heterogeneous bundles, of translating some types of entities into another. 'Translation being the opposite of substitution.' (Latour, 2000a: 5)

In contrast both to abstract essentialism and to the discursive emphasis of social construction, Actor Network Theory (ANT) offers a systemic view of the exchange between the social and the technical. ANT offers a theory of innovation in which networks of humans and non-human actors (artefacts, objects, documents, standards), organized by a model based on narrative semiotics, produce a new social-technical constitution (Latour, 2000a). This might be contrasted with the Marxist argument that social relations as a whole, rather than technical networks in and of themselves, constitute the context and logic of technological change.

Actor Network Theory, developed by Michael Callon, John Law and Bruno Latour, is a 'ruthlessly' semiotic (Law, 1999: 3) and to a large extent a Foucauldian approach, which understands the constitution of technologies and knowledges as truth effects derived from networks containing humans and non-humans as actors or actants (Wilbert, 1996: 3). ANT attempts to think through the question of how different kinds of objects (bodies, texts, hardware or viruses, for instance) combine together in various forms within networks in order to produce 'finished' technologies and accepted scientific truths.

ANT has been widely adopted as a research methodology for exploring the constitution of particular technologies. More broadly, it is concerned with exploring the mediated constitution of all kinds of knowledge, particularly the mediation of accepted technical and scientific 'truths' (Latour and Woolgar, 1979: Latour, 2000b). These knowledges and truths are taken by ANT to emerge through a process of technological mediation or *translation*, during which objects may take many forms. An example here is to be found in Latour's work on Aramis, a Rapid Transport System (RTS) planned for Paris. Aramis was a paper plan, a model, a series of physics problems, a political project, all of those things, and potentially a successful actor network. Finally, dropped as a viable project, it was rust (Latour, 1996).

The different material forms technologies/knowledges take in the process of translation make these potential technologies anew to some extent since, as Latour puts it, translations are not *substitutes* for the object, and nor is translation itself a processes of substitution (see above). Latour, however, is also interested in isolating the factors ('immutable mobiles') that ensure the developing object or developing knowledge continues to be recognizably the same object/knowledge as it translates across different modes and is transformed through the mediating processes that make it – or unmake it. (Latour, 2000b: 426). The mediating processes through which technologies and truths are produced, as ANT sees it, thus do not move between 'truth' and its 'representation'. On the contrary, they are understood as productive and constitutive (Latour, 2000b: 422–424).

ANT *couches* the process of mediation essential to the discursive construction of knowledges/technologies within a theory of actors and networks. ANT claims that the production of scientific knowledge and technical objects can be understood as a process by which 'actors' – the humans and non-humans that come to be involved in a particular project – are enrolled into networks. Networks, then, essentially both organize the process of mediation and contain it. It is in this way that ANT reads the successful production of a technology, or indeed the shape a technology comes to take,[25] as more or less a 'network effect' (Wilbert, 1996: 4). This is also why Latour can define a technology as quite simply the *intersection* of all the sets of acts carried out in its name (Latour, 2000b).

ANT has an obvious relevance to techno-cultural thinking for two reasons. First, doubts and uncertainties about human–machine boundaries, discussed above with reference to Haraway and also evident in popular discourses around computing, find a resonance with ANT. In particular, they resonate with its insistence that techno-scientific knowledges are constituted by hybrid networks that include human and non-human operators on equal terms (Law, 1999: 3). More fundamentally, ANT offers a means by which to think about the malleability of technologies and knowledges (their non-essentialism) on the one hand, while simultaneously holding on to their materiality and the material processes of their production, on the other.

At this point ANT also looks like a theory that balances the social world and the complexity of the materiality of technology. However, when we come to consider the logic of ANT's networks more closely, the distinction between ANT and pro-social theories of technology become evident. Actor Network Theory draws on a form of narratology to conceptualize its networks and the actors enrolled within them. Of particular relevance here is Greimas's work on narrative structure, explored through a theory of actants, actors enrolled within a narrative to perform a limited series of actions (or *translations*, perhaps) and thereby to take the story forwards to a successful conclusion (Greimas, 1987: 116–121). For Greimas these translations are often organized by way of the semiotic square as he develops it, and there are fairly evidently homologies to be found between Latour's sense of translation across networks and Greimas's sense of movement around the square.

Greimas's model, as noted, works not with actors but with actants, and ANT – despite its name – generally does the same (Law, 1999).[26] Actants are not actors playing roles, but rather embodiments of key elements of narrative with a predefined series of functional themes and a limited array of possible roles (Lenoir, 1987: 124); they gain their attributes from their – prescribed – *relations* with other entities in the network (Law, 1999: 3). Actants are a key to understanding Actor Network Theory since they enable the actions of non-humans as well as humans within networks to be taken account of. Indeed, these two groups can be considered in a symmetrical way (Lenoir, 1987: 142),[27] so that, so far as any actant has agency in this account, humans and non-humans have it equally.

Critics have pointed out that the symmetry between different kinds of actants in a network is bought at the cost of a calculated indifference to the specificity of the actor. The blindness to gender, race or class positions in ANT, as it has been deployed to consider industrial/laboratory processes, has left it open to justified charges of managerialism (see Cockburn, 1992: 42(44). Underpinning this charge is another concerning the exclusion of wider social forces, social power, social inequality – and indeed *the social itself* – from actor networks. Pickering and others have argued persuasively that to posit this kind of symmetry between humans and other objects is to banish society and/or social relations from the ring (Pickering, 1992; Collins and Yearley, 1992).

Behind the engagingly 'hybrid' cast of actors, humans, machines, inscription devices and other animals, is thus a highly rigid structure. The essential point here is that the structure offered by narrative within this account *stands in* for the orderings that might otherwise be imposed by the social totality. Indeed it *bounds* the world of the connected networks that Latour and others envisage. For ANT there is little beyond these narratologically derived networks, which essentially organize what Latour calls the 'techno-social' on their own. In this sense ANT's actor networks and ANT as a mode of thinking about socio-technical relations refuse social contexts in favour of an internal coherence. This is summed up in Latour's claim that technologies 'do not occur in context but give themselves a context' (1996: 133(134).

As Latour puts it, the social, as coded by the network, collapses assumed distinctions between 'natural', 'technical' and 'economic' (Latour, 2000b: 5). Latour and others in this tradition thus declare they are seeking a new constitution of the social, which is found in networks, which are also to be understood as narratologically constituted. *Technologies write their own stories.* At this point, we can see in Actor Network Theory the logical extension of Lyotard's position. Here, however, the idea of narrative knowledge is extended deep into technology, no longer the universal exception around which local and partial narratives dance. For Latour and others involved in Actor Networks technology itself becomes a narrative construction, albeit a fiercely formal one. We are suddenly back dancing at the foot of Lyotard's databases – but now we find that they too, are constituted as a material truth effect.

Here, with the problematic of human agency in relation to the agency of machines raised by ANT, I turn to Marx. Actor Network Theory, indeed, has its parallels with Marxist understandings of technology since ANT, like Marxism, understands what technology is by locating it within a system. In the case of Marxism, however, the system in question is not an abstract structural model, but the totality of social relations.

Marxism, technology and social relations

Whatever has no will may provide a service, but does not thereby make its owner into a master. (Marx, cited in Caffentzis, 1997: 29)

All our invention and progress seem to result in endowing material forces with intellectual life, and in stultifying human life into a material force. (Marx, 1980: 655)

A Marxist approach provides a different framework within which the connections between cybernetics and the principle of automation, on the one hand, and interface computing as an extension of interactivity, on the other, can be explored – in this case within a historical context and one that stresses the development of technology as a techno-social process.

Marxism stands in stark contrast to information society theory, which insists that information produces a breakpoint, bringing us into a new form of life. Schiller, drawing on Bell, defines information theory as entailing a 'massive discontinuity . . . not a projection or an extrapolation of existing trends in Western Society . . . a new principle of social-technical organization and ways of life' (Schiller, 1997: 116). For information theorists it is thus the ascension of technology itself to the role of prime mover that marks the rupture with previous theories of society. In this new world previous forms and relations of production are overwhelmed, communication reorganized and old forms of social life and social organisation superseded (Schiller, 1997). The information society analysis thus fragments the Marxist understanding of the social totality. It is in this sense – and others – that Robins and Webster could long ago declare Bell's formulations to amount to 'informed anti-Marxism' (1986: 33), while Witheford points out that the work of Bell, and other early information theorists such Drucker and Brzezinski, was 'explicitly framed as a refutation of the Marxist thesis' (1994: 87).

This break is not total, and nor is the division between information theorists and Marxists absolute. From the Marxist side, Jameson's account of the cultural logic of postmodernism was explicitly tied to Mandel's theory of late capitalism and never posited a total break with Marxism. On the other hand it does, as Sean Homer notes, posit a form of restructuring as a consequence of which postmodernism and late capitalism 'both come to signify the same object and to be equated with totality itself' (Homer, 2006). More recently, Manuel Castells has argued that information networks operate *semi-autonomously* from social forces, producing a break with older forms of organization, but also maintaining forms of continuity (1996). Appadurai goes further towards a break, exploring different aspects of a networked global world through the concept of the 'disjuncture' between relatively discrete spheres (media, finance, information) (Appadurai: 1990). Finally, there is *Empire*, an account that gathers up into its skirts whole tribes of fellow travellers. *Empire* is an account drawing heavily on Italian autonomist Marxism, but one that certainly operates on the basis of technologically produced rupture since biotechnology is the operational principle of a new world order. This final section considers distinctions between Marxist and information society approaches, while remaining aware of these hybrid accounts.

Few would dispute that information technology transforms capitalism; the debate is around the limits and quality of this transformation, the degree to which it remains a part of those trajectories in capitalism already. discerned by Marx or breaks with them. The question of the relationship between technology, labour and the social individual is at the crux of these debates, and to begin to explore this we might turn to Marx's own writing on technology. Information society theory loudly proclaims its reliance on a technology as prime mover, something that might be thought to tie it to Marx, who famously suggested in *The Poverty of Philosophy* that the hand-mill gives you society with the feudal lord, the steam-mill society with the industrial capitalist. To make this connection would be to misread Marx as simply a theorist of the industrial revolution. More can be found that is useful in thinking about technology and cultural form in Marx's work than this. Indeed, there is something ironic about dismissing Marx in this way given the force and intent of his lifelong project – an exploration of how men and women can make history given their situated positions within a particular historical constellation. Technology is radically decentred when Marx's political ambitions are placed centre stage.

If Marx is supposed to have been a crude technological determinist, then, aphorisms aside, the charges relate to place of the technological in what has been characterized as the reductive economism of his earlier writings (see, for instance, Lie and Sorensen, 1996, and Witheford).[28] Emphasis on these writings has meant that Marx's wider views on technology and the cultural implications of technology are largely disregarded and are rarely taken up into debates around technology 'itself'. Even in broadly sympathetic collections on technology and social construction, such as Mackenzie's and Wajcman's, Marx is explicitly disbarred from consideration in discussions of production *in relation to* broader social or cultural issues (1999). To read Marx as a determinist in this way is at best a selective reading. Its widespread adoption might be influenced by the dominance of structural or scientific Marxism in the 1970s and by the later eclipse of this form. Today it is recognized that there is a 'humanist' Marx (see Soper, 1986), but humanism is rarely looked for in Marx's discussions of technology, rather it has resulted in stress being placed on different areas of his work.

Accounts stressing technological determinism tend to neglect the fact that Marx's account of the development of productive forces is contained within a more general theory, that of the relations of production. The *relations* of production include the forces of living labour (humans) as well as the forces of dead labour, including what Marx called automation (see MacKenzie, 1984; Marx, 1977: 370–382).[29] As MacKenzie points out, the Marxist understanding of surplus value (valorisation) can be used to make the founding distinction between productive forces and relations of production clear. For Marx, the production of surplus value is derived from living labour, which is to say, from humans. The basic distinction found here, that humans not machines create value (see Marx, 1973: 767–769, cited in Caffentzis, 1997: 39), shows that Marx was arguing for a theory of societal causes of organisational and technical changes in the labour process. Thus, for Marx, the development of technologies, or of what MacKenzie describes as the apparatuses of technology, is not a determining factor in history, and nor indeed is technology a prime mover of history. On the contrary, as Langdon Winner noted, Marx's remarks on technology add up to a means by which to think through technologies as the outcome of a particular set of social relations (Winner, 1999: 38).[30] The 'question concerning technology' posed by Heidegger in the realm of ontology was framed by Marx far earlier as a question of machinery.

In his writings on technology Marx set out to consider the place of new industrial technology ('machinery') as an element in social relations as a whole, and as an element in the production of the social individual (Caffentzis, 1997: 42). This individual being is conceived of, not as an abstraction, but as an individual wrought through 'sensuous activity', existing within a world defined as 'the total living sensuous activity of the individuals composing it' (Marx, 1977: 175). Marx's assessment of the technology of industrial capitalism emerges from this understanding of the activity of labour. In particular, Marx stressed the importance of what he termed the working machine (the tool – or it is tempting to suggest the interface arrangement) over the automating force behind it (coal, steam) when what is at issue are 'social relations of man' and material modes of production. He points out that it is the tool that concerns the *direct* action of the human on the object to be worked upon (Marx, 1977: 526 my italics).

In an article celebrating the *People's Paper*, also operating here as a reminder that the concept of alienation from labour is central to his account, Marx compared the effect of 'progress' on workers and on machines. As he put it: 'all our invention and progress seem to result in endowing material forces with intellectual life, and in stultifying human life into a material force' (Marx, 1980: 655). This inversion prefigures the supposedly contemporary paradox of increasingly sophisticated (information) machines and increasingly dumbed-down workforces.[31] In the *People's Paper* discussion Marx thus extends the question of human and machine labour from the sphere of production, taking it into the sphere of ontology. Life itself, as it is lived by those operating industrial machinery, is characterised by a process of exchange that eviscerates the human. The body gives up its intelligence, its fluidity of movement, or its *liveliness* to the machine, and is left only as a material force. The form of work and its technical character is thus linked to the process of the constitution of the human as a social being. It is thus the whole human, rather than the human operative (the actant in a closed system), who is reduced to a 'material force' being acted upon by the system. In sum, following Marx, we can see that this unequal exchange between human and machine increasingly tends to conform the human in particular ways, and in so far as this process is not resisted, subsumes her or him to the logic of the industrial system.

The *People's Paper* article explores a progression. The relationship between humans and machines is continuously reforged with the introduction of new tools, as the nature of work changes, and this has a bearing on the formation of the individual, who is increasingly made mute. As Marx notes this is 'progress' under capitalism. Robins and Webster are also exploring a progression when they argue that features commonly used to define the information society are better understood as representing an *intensification* of the system of capitalism already in existence than as representing a break from it (see also Witheford, 1994: 95). They point to three related features of a highly computerized society often flagged as evidence of the information society, each of which they suggest points at least as strongly to the intensification of the existing system as to something new. Certainly all of the features they mention are prefigured in the *People's Paper* consideration of life under early industrial production. These three features are: (1) the tendency for mental and manual labour to be increasingly separated;[32] (2) the extension of consumption;

and (3) the tendency for capital to increasingly dominate social life (Robins and Webster, 1987: 48). The important point here is that, like Marx, Robins and Webster are arguing that the alignment of everyday life and of social subjects operated through technology is an alignment with capital, rather than with technology per se.

Marx considered intensification through the concept of subsumption, understood by Witheford to refer to the degree to which labour is increasingly integrated into capital's process of value production (1994: 93). The worker of the *People's Paper*, subsumed, not into the machine precisely but rather into the system, might embody this process, and it is clear that questions of mental and manual labour are bound up with subsumption as a form of integration. As Witheford notes, drawing on Negri, formal subsumption is a property relation. Real subsumption results in a wholesale reorganization of work aimed at reaping economies of scale, a reorganization that might also relocate the workplace and reorganize the body. In other words, a component of real subsumption is that everyday life (as cultural form, as cultural practice, as a practice of the self) is increasingly directly practised according to the aesthetics and logics of a particular mode of production. An integral part of this reorganization is also an extension of consumption typified by the 'cultivation of new needs . . . in an orgy of "production for production's sake"' (Marx, cited in Witheford, 1994: 94).

If interface computing, a new form of automation, is regarded as a key element in the intensification of the existing system of social relations, then this is because it stages just such a series of realignments: the reorganization of work, the more thoroughgoing penetration of the commodity relation which extends more deeply into areas previously only lightly ordered by this relation. These include the private but often collective realm of the home, the intimate life of the individual, and the collective emotional life of a nation or other group as it might be articulated through rituals, ceremonies, customs, monuments and memorials. These realignments produce uniformity and there is an increasingly tightly drawn relationship between these zones.

This is produced partly through a *material* isomorphism between (computerized) work and (computerized) leisure. The same kinds of equipment, similar forms of software, are found at work and home and demand to be used in similar ways. Keyboarding/using a mouse, operating a system (Mac or Windows), word-processing and image-processing, searching and browsing, *interacting*, are all tasks performed at work and at home – and both sites are gathered under the same networks.

Ubiquitous interaction with new media networks produces other commonalities: surveillance is an integral part of both work and leisure, not as it has been computerized per se, but as computerization has increasingly come to involve interface computing. If the work of being an active media user at home (see Andrejevic, 2005) parallels a life being watched at work, then a third space, homologous to these two, comes into being with the advent of pervasive CCTV. The cultural form expressing that relationship is clearly reality TV, where content precipitates out of a formal arrangement of a non-reciprocal gaze that itself mirrors what we now tend to do every day, all day.

In the sphere of emotions and affect another series of parallels emerges as these areas become increasingly vulnerable to computation – and therefore to systematization and exploitation – through the development of more sophisticated interfaces. Here the increasingly skilful manipulation of 'emotion engines' in forms of entertainment including, most obviously, gaming are mirrored by the exploitation of emotional labour in automated workplaces such as call centres.

Manovich too finds contiguities between 'perceptual experiences in the workplace and outside it' when he suggests that humans feature as part of 'human machine system' both at work and at home (Manovich, 1996: 184). Manovich reads the consanguinity between (computerized) cultural forms and cultural practices and (computerized) work in terms of the production of new rhythms. These are shared across the old work-leisure divides and are characterized by abrupt moments of alternation between periods of shock (and intense work) and periods of waiting (or downtime). These rhythms pattern leisure activities such as arcade, PC-based or console games (Manovich, 1996: 185). Manovich thus offers an insight into the relationship between immersion and disjuncture, intensity and boredom, that many be characterized as part of the new media experience.

This account might be extended here in two ways. Firstly, the abrupt swings between action and inaction that Manovich identifies let us in and out of worlds (spaces, sites) operating at different speeds and operating according to different ground-rules (we cycle between windows, including the one marked 'real life', as Turkle put it in *Life on the Screen*, 1995: 13). Amongst the changes to be negotiated might be those dividing the pace of contemporary work and the pace of contemporary leisure. Secondly, I want to insist that the discrete moments of action and inaction are more connected than they may seem to be in Manovich's account (where they resolve into an insistence on abrupt *changes* in rhythm). This is the case in part because these rhythm changes might be understood to constitute *shifts* in attention rather than absolute breaks (Crary, 2000; Bassett, 2003), and in part because these moments may be continuously renarrativized so that they become components in a broader circuit (and once again attention is useful in understanding how this might occur). In other words, we mind the gaps for ourselves. This mindfulness, part of our activity, part of use itself, has to be written into this model, since it is precisely what interface computing provides for and indeed *demands*. It is partly in this way that we come to understand our culture's insistent demands for the tale.

Thirdly, I would extend Manovich's account in one more direction. It is clear that the kind of contiguity between work and leisure of which Manovich writes operates beyond those activities involving *direct* use of computer technology within everyday life. The increasingly widespread use of information machines and the increasing degree to which virtual operations *thread* in and out of non-virtual operations, produce a more general transformation. These kinds of transformations thus extend beyond the moment of computer use itself, being reflected in all our activities, desires and pleasures. It might be argued that everyday activity, taken as a whole, is constituted in part through the kinds of jarring rhythms Manovich identifies, and the kinds of narrativizing responses to these shifts I have described. I note here that Manovich's argument was made with Walter Benjamin's discussion of film as a 'complex form of [industrial] training' in mind. This points us to the final component here, which is that these experiences shape our desires and pleasures; perhaps, to return to Marx, they cultivate new *needs*.

Whether Manovich's argument for discrete bursts of interaction or the case for narrative continuity is followed here, the general case for intensification is made. The difference, perhaps, is that for Manovich the argument is made through a rather more formal reference to the static logic of a particular system that is – essentially – on or off. The case for narrative is made through a stress on process: interface computing is read as a form computerization that can only be understood *in process*. Both accounts produce a trajectory in which the felt experience of everyday life taken as a whole becomes *more closely aligned* to the logic of capital. Here, then, are the second and third forms of intensification to which Robins and Webster refer (Robins and Webster, 1987: 51).

Finally, I want to stress that the material isomorphism between information systems operating in the spheres of production and of consumption and everyday life does not break down or render meaningless real distinctions between the arena of production and that of consumption (nor actually does it change the location of value production). The place of information technologies in the consumer sphere is non-identical to their instantiation in the sphere of production (whether this is in a new or old sector), and so are the places of their users in these two different sites. Computer-sector advertising notwithstanding, work taken home, or even work taken to the beach, remains work. The ways in which this difference is understood (and the ways in which it is revealed or concealed in discourses around computing) matter. Material isomorphism often performs a work of concealment here. Which is why we need to be clear about its limits. As Spivak once put it, contrasting Marx with Foucault, Deleuze and Guattari, exploring only the concrete or concrete actions (here taking the immaterial form of a transferable code) can mask the ideological aspects of particular operations (Spivak, 1988). This is one essential difference between accounts of technology and society as seen from the Marxist perspective and accounts proffered by post-Marxist information theorists seeking to develop new forms of radical politics in response to a post-ideological era.

The intention here has been to defend the proposition that Marxism (still) has something useful to say about technology itself in its relation to the social world – that it can help us conceptualize the human–machine interface as well as the cultural formations that might arise through it. The question of narrative and its transformations, and indeed the question not only of what is done with narrative but of how this is conceptualized, become part of an exploration of the material, symbolic and ideological forms that this intensification might take.

For Marx, technologies emerge, reflect and are involved in the repro-duction of social relations in their totality. The cultural formations that emerge in a techno-culture, which may cross boundaries between work and leisure, sites of production and sites of consumption, in new ways, and in doing so may seem to dissolve or reshape them, are not purely the artic-ulations of a particular logic of production nor purely the articulations of a 'machine logic'.

Marxists, unlike information society theorists, can presume a con-nection between technology and social and cultural life on the one hand, and understand that it is not *predetermined* by technology on the other, either in its concrete form or as a form of discourse. For Marx, indeed, it is in only in this way, when technology is understood as socially embedded and socially shaped by production, that the force of technology in society – its role in the production of the social individual – can really begin to be grasped.

Exergue: Marx and Latour

The intention in the second half of this chapter has been to consider forms of thinking about technology which are able to admit the force of technology as a technical object while also considering its relations within the social world. This aim might be encapsulated as a search for an approach to networked new media that would allow the reinsertion of the hermeneutic possibility (the possibility of interpretation and construction) on the one hand, and the reinsertion of particular forms of structural constraint on the other. I have briefly considered this through exploration of Latour's call for a new techno-social constitution and I have discussed how Marxism might be used to locate technology as an element within the totality of social relations so that the progress of technology might be read within this context. Here it may be helpful to characterize the differences between these two ways of thinking as follows.

1. For Latour, the human becomes an object among other objects. The principle of symmetry amongst actants in a network obliterates difference. For Marx, the human is subjugated through technology, which articulates existing social relations, but the human remains a subject of history, at least potentially, since technology is regarded as part of the social totality. For this reason the human is a body capable of refusal. This is something that Latour explicitly allows machines but virtually refuses to humans. For Marx, the human is also capable of judgement.

2. For Latour, the social is never given except by the context of the network that constitutes it. For Marx, on the contrary, the totality within which technologies and humans are forged is the totality of social relations. The specific force of the technological object is understood within this totality.

3. For Latour, symmetry between humans and nonhumans forms the basis of his techno-social constitution. For Marx, the lack of symmetry – the *difference* between humans and machines – is fundamental to his economic theory and to Marxism as a theory of emancipation.

4. For Latour, the technological object emerges into the social *as* a technological object – his sense is that social construction theories have replaced the technical object with a placeholder, the social object. For Marx, the technological object is always also a social object: it is commodified through the processes of its insertion into everyday life and through its insertion as an element in the forces of production it is part of a social system.

5. Finally, then, one might conclude by suggesting that for both Latour and Marx the interface between humans and machines is one in which both humans and objects can speak, but not as fully human. This is what they have in common when they write about technology. For Latour, however, this is a consequence of attempting to think through a Parliament of Things, a techno-social constitution which respects objects

(2000a). For Marx, the silencing of humans as fully human is a consequence of particular sets of social relations which ought, he thinks, to be overturned. If machines become more intelligent and humans more inert then this attenuation of the human is not intrinsically a consequence of the relationship between technologies and humans, it is as a consequence of the forging of a particular interface in conditions not of our choosing.[33] Facing these different possibilities (and misquoting Haraway), I'd rather be a human if a Marxist analysis pertains than a human object in a Latourean network.

In conclusion

This chapter set out to consider the terms of our contemporary engagement with networked new media: to ask how we plug in, and to what. I have worked with a sense that this engagement between humans and machines within the social totality constitutes the human–machine interface, understood in its broadest terms. This interface has been considered at a number of levels or scales, and from a number of different critical locations. Starting with the object, it has been demonstrated that what constitutes the interface can never be reduced to purely technical questions, since 'plugging in' is always a historically located social process as well as a technical reality.

I began by pointing out that networked new media are forms of computing which are both new (in so far as they concern interface and the extensions of interface), and old (in so far as they remain centred on automation and calculation). The task then was to find a means to critically assess this form of computing, not to define a 'sociology of the interface' (Kirkpatrick, 2000: 1), but rather to explore its relationship to a particular constellation or historical moment.

I set about this task firstly by locating critical writing around networked new media within broader cycles of critical writing and within popular senses of technology and innovation. Working within this framework it was possible to reach behind recursive cycles of social and technical determinism, within which new technologies are framed, to find a different view of processes of computerization. Taking key moments as landmarks, I considered developments around cybernetics/interface computing in social and critical theory. These movements map the oscillations characteristic of technological innovation which were identified at the outset, and evidence the kinds of critical *lacunae* described in that account. In other words, shifts in critical theories of technology relate to cycles of innovation, and to a sense of the new. This has led to the widespread conception that networked interface computing is something new and to writings that have responded to this sense of rupture.

My response to this misrecognition has been to return to the cybernetic moment and trace a series of writings marking various breaks and returns to cybernetics as a cultural theory. These shifts and turn are complex, but might be understood in terms of a move from cybernetic determinism to various forms of post-structural relativism – within which technology 'itself' is configured in different ways. Two such configurations, implicitly read in contrast to each other, are Derrida's sense of technology as a constitutive, even determining, force, but one that is always an abstraction, and the social constitution of technology as an approach used by everyday life theorists. Here the technological object remains, but is essentially detechnologized.

The current constellation has been marked by a return of another kind – this time to transcendental conceptions of information that draw on new forms of science and on old and new ideas of cybernetics. Here accounts based on the newly revived essentialism of cyber-cultural theorists are considered. I have described these accounts as displaying a form of reactionary modernism – reading their intent as being to recreate a (mythical) past, albeit in a coming future. There are parallels between the considerations of technology and ontology evident in the metaphorically inflected writing of the early cyberculture years (see Thrift, 1996), and in more directly politicized biotechnological accounts such as *Empire*, which is in the end underpinned by some of the same theoretical formations. Each produces a new attitude towards an engagement with the political.

This was taken up in the final sections of the chapter, which explored new media computing an intensification of existing social relations, making the case for a form of Marxism that is not technologically determinist through an emphasis on the key role that struggle – and the possibility of freedom – plays in his writings.

I conclude the chapter with some remarks on the characteristics of networked new media as they have emerged through this discussion. In the course of the chapter I have considered various ways in which networked new media have been approached within contemporary critical contexts tempered both by cybernetics and by the earlier turn away from cybernetics as a critical theory within the humanities. My suggestion here is that this has produced an environment in which it has been easy for critical theorists considering networked new media to 'start the world over again' – to consider this new media technology as entirely new.

Refusing the connections between networked new media and earlier forms of computing is a mistake. We need to think about networked new media as an example of interface computing, as both distinct from but connected to earlier forms of computing of which it is only the latest development. Marxism, which reads the dynamic of technology within the logic of the social totality, then suggests that we can read this development in social as well as technical terms. Bringing these two propositions together leads to me to consideration of networked new media/interface computing as a form of what could be termed 'fuzzy cybernetics'.[34]

I have argued that the reach of information technology increasingly extends from work to culture and everyday life. Interface computing can solicit responses from the user in increasingly elaborated and extensive ways, ways that might be tolerant of imprecision, to use the technical definition of the fuzzy. New interfaces are therefore instrumental in that general process of the extension of the reach of technology defined above as a form of intensification of capital. Given that we have argued that networked new media are a development of computing itself, which has at its heart a principle of automation, this extension might be taken to represent an extension of the principle of *automation*.

But this leaves open the question of the *kinds* of extensions that might be at stake here. What gets automated, and how? First we can consider interface computing and networked new media to provide for an absolute extension of automation. Network computing, for instance, which invites interactions between distant users to take place within the grounds of the machine, begins to automate relations over longer distances, and between larger groups, than previously possible. Networked or populated computing is a logical extension of the fuzzy computing principle that began with the development of stand-alone interfaces.

Second, networked new media extend the reach of computing to places hitherto closed to it because they seemed too imprecise or to difficult to define as calculable tasks. This is where it becomes evident that interface computing does not operate at the surface of machines with hidden depths. Fuzzy cybernetics of the kind offered by interface computing does not function only as an ameliorative cosmetic. The point of interface computing is not to produce a 'homey' interface to make us feel better about 'using' at home, perhaps, or a 'comic' interface designed to make us work more efficiently – although interfaces might well be designed to do those things. Interface computing is fuzzy at a more fundamental level. It is fuzzy because it is designed to be more robust – to produce automated circuits in less 'scientific' environments than hitherto. In other words, it is designed to work within mechanisms that are increasingly complex and far less easy to map than those first wave cybernetics sought to organize.

Pre-eminent amongst these mechanisms are those of everyday life and everyday consumption, but we have noted that these mirror production processes and draw on them: while those running call centres are seeking to write 'emotional labour' (Golzen, 2000) into the systems they design through interface computing, Sony engineers building the Playstation claim to be developing 'emotion engines'. There are connections here.

Because interface computing takes automation into places previously closed to it, and because it engages subjects (in labour and leisure) in new ways, interface computing and interactivity can be viewed as an extension and intensification of the logic of capital – an intensification working through the logic of the machine. This both recognizes the scale of the changes wrought by computerization and grasps their broader (historical) significance. In other words, the changes that HCI understands as (only) technical developments, that Haraway can analyse within the grounds of science studies/cultural studies, that Latour can build new worlds with, can be considered also within the logic of the social totality.

Finally, it seems important to stress here that to recognize and reassess the link between the cybernetic principle of automation and feedback, and the networked new media is not to assume that it is necessary to adopt a cybernetic *approach* to the analysis of new media. Deploying a cybernetic analysis, which would be to understand the social totality as determined by a purposive mechanism (the logic of the machine), would not help explain the force of technology within the social totality. I do not believe that there are only emergent networks left – and the arguments made above suggest that claims that emergent networks are 'beyond' society or determine the logic of society are disputable to say the least. In addition, unlike Latour, I do not believe that the socio-technical is a truth effect of connected but always discrete networks.

In contrast, in this chapter I have turned to Marxist approaches. A Marxist view of technology allows us to reverse the technologically deterministic approach without losing sight of the material, and to think about interface computing as a social relation. As I have shown, this does not condemn us to a consideration of new technology located only in the narrow sense of its use in production. Nor does it have to imply a direct correlation between feedback circuits and interfaces in work and leisure situations – for instance call centres on the one hand and circuits involved in gaming, or learning, or artworks on the other. I would suggest indeed that a Marxist approach opens up a broad field of inquiry concerning the extended relations between users and machines in culture.

The material culture and the cultural processes that industrial capital is seeking to 'automate' using networked new media are complex and non-discrete. The networks of interaction are open and ongoing. In addition, the sophistication of interface computing means that what the machine solicits from the user can be *interpreted* by this same user in different ways, depending in part on the user's structural position, but not only on that.

Beyond the arcane and formal command-line is a process of thick interaction, the interface as a developing form of mediation which may or may not offer true communicative options to the user but which is – and actually precisely because of this ambiguity – deeply ideological. In this book the question of mediation is considered in terms of narrative when narrative itself is considered not as a geometric model, in the fashion of Latour, but as an interpretative practice through which humans make sense of their world. Indeed, we might talk about the *narrativizing* of the interface.

Notes

1 *Wired UK*'s proclamations have a certain irony given that the magazine, which regarded itself as the torchbearer of the good news from Silicon Valley, closed after less than a year.

2 The fire analogy is part of Internet lore. See John Perry Barlow's 'railroad' speech of 1994 (Barlow, 2000).

3 See also Constance Penley's study of NASA as a cultural formation (Penley, 1997).

4 Visibility changes with scarcity. The California 'brown-outs' were an example of this.

5 As individual studies have shown, most notably Raymond Williams's work on television and cultural form (1990).

6 Apple's Steve Jobs appropriated mapped video, GUIs and mice in the 'daylight raid' on Xerox PARC, which had developed the technologies but was not marketing them (Cringely, 1992: 189).

7 Light's definition is useful. Human Computer Interaction (HCI), the name given to the tradition of studying the role assigned by developers to 'the user' in product design, dealing with interface design and product usability; a study which locates itself within computer science, but which sometimes seems not entirely welcome there (1999: 268).

8 Haddon cites a UK journalist on the prospect of home computers then being widely promoted in the US: 'These crazy Americans . . . they seem to think people are going to buy computers for their own entertainment! . . . What's really strange is that Americans being crazy . . . some of them are! (Haddon, 1995: 15).

9 For Gibson an affordance was equally a fact of the environment and of behaviour. Gibson's theory of direct perception has much in common with Merleau Ponty's sense of the 'active solicitations' of the sensory world (Abram, 1995: 99). Gibson understood that the solicitations of environment would change depending on who was being solicited – as he put it of surface tension and water, 'support for water bugs is different' (Gibson, 1950: 127). Norman's early use of affordance is actually far more limited. The indirect relationship of HCI to Merleau Ponty is also of interest given that Paul Virilio's highly critical account of virtual space, read as producing the loss of sensory connection with the lived environment, draws heavily on Merleau Ponty (Virilio, 1995: 28).

10 HI, AB, LM = IBM. Some websites claim Clarke has declared that the acronymic transposition was accidental. This seems unlikely. A press officer for IBM once told he was not at liberty to discuss the connection.

11 Kittler goes further, suggesting that not the screen but the software itself is a simulation – the reality of computers is hardware, as the Gulf war shows (1997: 156).

12 The phrase is borrowed from Kittler (1997: 116). It was pointed out to me by Matt Bennett.

13 'Biological and technical systems both run on patterns of information dispersal, including feedback' (Levinson, 1997: 1).

14 Apart from Wiener himself, a key figure was Jon Von Neumann, the mathematician who played a key role in translating Turing's theoretical machine into a 'general purpose computer'. Leading figures from the human sciences involved in the conferences were Gregory Bateson, Margaret Mead and Paul Lazersfield (Heims, 1991: 12).

15 Bennett also notes, via Kittler, that for Lacan the world of the symbolic is already called 'the world of the machine' (Kittler, 1997: 45).

16 Metz, considering cinema as a narrative machine, declared that 'cybernetics and the theory of information . . . has outdone even the most structural linguistics' (1974: 35).

17 First order or first wave cybernetics was followed by second wave cybernetics and by the theories of auto-*poesis* and self-organising systems. Notable here are the biologists Maturana and Varela (Braman, 2000: 314–319).

18 Appropriation, objectification, incorporation, conversion (Silverstone and Hirsch, 1992: 21).

19 For Haraway, *pace* Lacan above, the unconscious is no longer a *cybernetic* machine.

20 Two others are revolutionary modernism and hegemonic capitalism.

21 'Modern technology, as a revealing that orders, is no mere human doing' (1993: 324).

22 This is consistent with a Heideggerian view of language, one which results from a meditative openness to the world and which lets go of the metaphysical voice (Cheney, 1995: 25). In his development of bio-regional narrative and ecological subjectivity Cheney understands this as a form of listening in which things can come to presence in terms of a 'storied residence' (see Wilbert, 1996).

23 Heidegger's own complicity with a regime that automated genocide precisely through the calculated use of information technology might suggest why this kind of fatalism is pernicious.

24 Plant's work was widely taken up by Internet activists and artists such as VNS Matrix in the late 1990s, and is much cited in critical theory (see Squires, 1996; Robins, 1996; and mainstream and specialist media).

25 Olga Amsterdamski has rightly critiqued ANT for this conflation. She argues that ANT reads the success of a technology as synonymous with the form that technology assumes (Amsterdamski, 1977: 501). This is a lethal form of self-justification which amounts to arguing that whatever is, is right.

26 Latour says that 'since in English "actor" is often limited to humans, the word actant, borrowed from semiotics, is sometimes used to include non-humans in the definition' (Latour, 1999: 303).

27 Underpinning Actor Network Theory, therefore, is an extension of the sociology of science's demand for symmetry in explanations of successful and non-successful science (the failures of one cannot be explained in social terms if the success of the other isn't). Actor networks include an extra symmetry, claiming symmetry between the entities which become known in these theories as actors and which operate within the networks that allow technologies to gain their 'reality' (Lenoir, 1994: 124).

28 Lie and Sorensen state: 'the orthodox Marxist account of technical change held that technology, understood as a force of production in the long run would undermine capitalism' (1996: 5).

29 In this section of the *Grundrisse*, Marx considers living and machine labour in a discussion specifically concerned with how or if 'automation' might change this relation.

30 Langdon Winner used nuclear technology as a limit case, concluding it was 'an inherently political artifact' (Winner, 1999: 34).

31 Macdonalds' cash tills, which are said not to not require literacy, offer a well-known example of this. The popular fear is that as machines learn to speak, we forget how to read.

32 The increasing *division* between mental and manual labour should not be *simply* equated with the rise of immaterial labour, although it is clearly linked to *perceptions* of the latter's ascendancy – for instance amongst those (first world) subjects who tend to presume that production has become immaterial because the material component production has moved 'off-shore' to an invisible factory which is not part of a brand identity.

33 One way to think through this possibility is to address the question of skills transference. In *Abstracting Craft*, Malcolm McCullough explores the 'craft' of the digital artisan, suggesting that there are compensations for the loss of hapticity. In exchange for the responsive engagement with material involved in crafting wood or stone, the digital craftsperson may find new ways to engage with material (McCullough, 1996).

34 Microsoft's dictionary definition of 'fuzzy logic' is as follows: 'Fuzzy logic [is] a form of logic used in some expert systems and other AI applications in which variables can have degrees of truthfulness represented by a range of values between 1= true and 0 = false. With fuzzy logic the outcome of a problem can be expressed as a probability rather than a certainty' (Microsoft, 1994: 180). I use this metaphorically.

3

Those with whom the archive dwells[1]

ROM stands for read only memory; [the PC] can read the contents of a ROM chip but it can't change them. A ROM chip's software is there for good . . . the only real threat to ROM is an electrical mishap such as a power surge . . . (Heid, 1991: 266)

The body turns in its sleep and says 'I'm dreaming of you, user'. (Harwood, 1997c)

Chapter 2 of this book set out to consider the terms of a culture's contemporary engagement with networked new media; to ask how we plug in, and to what. I argued that the engagement between humans and machines within the social totality constitutes the human–machine interface, understood in its broadest terms. Interacting with machines, at whatever scale, is therefore, and *inescapably*, a historically located social process as well as a technical reality. This position has implications for how contemporary interfaces are understood and investigated, not least because, viewed in this way, interactions across the human–machine interface can never be reduced to purely technical operations but are not to be regarded as purely discursive either.

Here I consider the role digital technologies might play in the constitution of contemporary identity, when this is understood in narrative terms as a life story and its narration. The life stories at the centre of this inquiry are those of a group of inmates of Ashworth Hospital, a secure institution for the criminally insane. This group participated in the making of *Rehearsal of Memory*, a piece of speculative software produced in collaboration with the artist Harwood with input from the art collective Mongrel, and others. *Rehearsal* takes the form of a navigable composite body made up of skin scans taken from the inmates, from Harwood, and from Ashworth staff. This body holds fragments of memory, experiences of life at Ashworth and other places, held as images, texts and audio spots. Users of the artwork are invited to explore the body and its associated objects, but are only able to do so in ways allowed by the project architecture. This functions to organize the interactions between the body and its users in ways that tend to undermine the conventional relationships operating between the inmates of such institutions and the general public. A certain sense of distance is lost. More than that, in *Rehearsal*, the body looks back out at the user, and in this way effects an *escape*.

Rehearsal began in 1995, when Harwood, a digital artist and activist, entered Ashworth High Security Hospital, near Liverpool, and began a series of twice-weekly visits that continued for three months. The result of Harwood's time inside was *Rehearsal of Memory*, first shown at as an installation in 1995 at the exhibition Video Positive and shown in this form at digital art festivals and art galleries around the world. Later, funding from the Arts Council of England enabled the creation of a CD-ROM version of the project, developed by Harwood with assistance from former students of Artec, a London-based digital arts training centre, some of whom later went on to become members of Mongrel, the digital art collective. The CD-ROM was published and distributed in 1997 by Artec itself, in collaboration with BookWorks, an art publisher. Given this history, *Rehearsal* is hard to pin down as a single artefact. The CD-ROM version might be regarded as an archive of the installation (an *aide memoire*) perhaps, but it is also a work in its own right and certainly involved extensive recoding, the rerecording of voices, and the reorganizing of the project interface. Traces of *Rehearsal* are still to be found on the web today, documented on the Mongrel site; discussed in various web mailing-lists; found by search engines in the context of madness, ISEA, Montreal, Serious Games, Nettime, sanity, and (oddly enough) jellied eels and English beach resorts.

This discussion is based on *Rehearsal* as it operated, both in CD-ROM form and as an installation at *Serious Games* at the Laing Gallery in Newcastle (1996) and the Barbican in London (1997). I also draw on formal interviews and a number of informal discussions with Graham Harwood, and formal and informal conversations with those involved with supporting the project at Artec. Although Harwood here speaks for the work, I note that, partly *because* it has taken multiple forms and has an unusual production history, the authorship of the work is by no means clear. There is Harwood himself, there is Mongrel, which was involved in later versions of the artworks, and there are, of course, the inmates who participated in the project. There is also the question, not of the work, but of the body, the anonymous computer personality that appears on screen. Perhaps all of those who contributed their skin or their views 'own' the body. If so, the *terms* of this ownership need to be considered.

Rehearsal is biography or autobiography, database and narrative; it incorporates elements of all of these things. It is 'about' memory and 'about' identity, and if it documents a particular form of memory loss, it simultaneously operates as a form of retrieval system. Finally, it is about narration as a process whereby an individual's life story comes to be told by machines and by other selves, in different spaces and different social contexts. It is about narrative identity understood as something collectively produced. While *Rehearsal* explores these themes in relation to a series of very particular circumstances (incarceration, madness, criminality) they also arise in relation to the vast tide of personal homepages, personal blogs and personal Wikis that swells through the web; the flotsam and jetsam of everyday life, endless assertions of the self, extending outwards into an ever-expanding virtual domain. *Rehearsal* might be regarded *as* a particular kind of home site critically engaging with these forms of identity production. Certainly many of the ambiguities and collisions this piece plays on are intrinsic to negotiating forms of identity involving everyday digital spaces, where identity emerges between producers, users and machines, within specific local economies but also within vastly complex webs and networks.

These negotiations are not always successful or easy. Identity is both secured and made more fragile by its partial translation onto a machine. It is secured because code does not degrade through successive translations (it is not 'lossy', to use an old technical term). To become digital is in this sense to be immortalized, and if there are virtual graveyards[2] offering permanent memorials on the web, there are also cryogenic storage facilities that promise more substantial versions of this kind of upload at some undesignated future time. In both cases immortality operates in theory only. Actually existing digital media systems are not secure as repositories and neither are they efficient as engines for narration. On the Internet, memories are held on servers that may be owned or controlled by different concerns. Addresses are lost, servers die, links are broken, software is updated so that files become obsolete. More commonly, life stories held on the web are simply forgotten. The production of a personal homepage or a blog and its uploading have never guaranteed that it will be read, or viewed, or used. The Internet is infinitely more reliable as a *repository* of life stories than it is as a system offering any kind of assurance that these tales will be *rehearsed* or narrated. Many homepages are never accessed at all and neither are most of those digital photographs that document our lives.[3] In the UK, at least, it seems likely that *official* records of our identity, which may or may not render a good account of who we are, are accessed far more often than these personal ones. Translated into a digital form in which it might seem to be inviolable or at least more resilient, identity, understood as something that requires meaningful *rehearsal* or narration and rehearsal in good faith, is thus a precarious affair.

That so many take up the slim chance of narration in various digital fora indicates the depth of what Adriana Cavarero would describe as our desire to be narrated (Cavarero, 1997). It also underscores the degree to which digital forms ('the media') are bound up with a collective understanding of what constitutes meaningful publicity, or publicity in good faith. Forms of intimate web presence shade into talk shows and reality TV, but also connect with mass forms of collective narration, including funerals, concerts and protests, all of which promise liveness but do so through a guarantee of its mediation. At any rate, *Rehearsal* engages with both the uncertainty of digital identity and, within that, with the desire for narration that forms a part of the contemporary narrative economy. It does so in ways that set out to question the implications of being made digital, of *being partly archived*, on the one hand, and the issue of who controls this process, on the other. It says something about the fragility or disposability of such forms of digital identity in other ways too: as an artwork *Rehearsal* is widely disseminated and documented, but I can't play the original CD-ROM version on my upgraded laptop.

Rehearsal is also an artwork that is part of 'a redefinition of a . . . field of aesthetic awareness' (Druckery, 1999: 18) provoked by digital technologies, and it is *as* an artwork that *Rehearsal* explores emerging conventions of computer use and plays on emerging expectations of interactivity. However it also intervenes in debates beyond 'digital art' as it might be more narrowly conceived, performing a commentary on the use of computers when it is regarded as a mainstream work/leisure practice, an everyday means by which groups and individuals connect with each other, a means through which identity is negotiated. In so far as *Rehearsal* sets out to use digital technology to reveal what society prefers to forget (*whom* society prefers to forget), it can be understood as a form of 'hactivism' (see Taylor, 2001). Its highly aestheticized approach resonates with online art activism sparked off by the likes of RTMark and with the activists who famously aroused the ire of the UK tabloids by modifying Churchill's statue during the World Trade Organization protests in Seattle (see Naomi Klein, cited in Street, 2001: 210).[4] However, its principles are not strictly hactivist since it is not concerned with coding virtuosity per se. Rather, *Rehearsal* operates critically to expose particular aesthetic *norms* for new media through their production and disturbance. It might be regarded as an early (1990s) form of speculative software, connecting with Matt Fuller's later definition of this as a politically aware art practice that 'plays with the form not the content [of new media] or rather refuses the distinction while staying on the right side of it' (Fuller, 2003: 14). The distinction between (1990s) hacker and (2000s) speculative software tactics here coheres around goals centred on 'truth' (the truth in code, or getting as near the metal as possible) and 'exposure' (where the intention is to expose ways in which code is used and deployed as a control mechanism) that understand the potential of software itself rather differently. Harwood himself once described *Rehearsal* to me as 'an art piece about the social uses of new technology' (Harwood, 1997a). It is an attempt to *exploit* the communicative possibilities of new media that simultaneously *exposes* how new media technologies are used in ideological ways, and that reveals also how these uses are being naturalized.

Rehearsal, a reflexive exploration of the various political/social potentials of a new medium, itself operates on many levels simultaneously, but I want to suggest that narrative is at the heart of this attempt – at the core of *Rehearsal* itself. This is so in a common-sense way, since the work gives voice to some life stories that are generally not heard, but also because questions about narrative identity and technology, about life stories and their automation, are integral to the processes of naturalizing of digital technology with which the work deals.

In this way *Rehearsal* might work to reframe some debates around narrative 'itself' and, in particular, it may shed new light on that aversion to narrative, that keenness to consign it to oblivion both as a mode of inquiry and as a cultural form, that circulates in techno-cultural debate. My own insistence that narrative is a productive mode of analysis is based on what I recognize as the persistence of narrative, even its extension, within new media forms. But it also arises for another reason. The case to be made is that an insistence on the continued *theoretical* centrality of narrative as a mode of analysis of cultural form is also important, having implications for a cultural politics centring around new media. Exploring Jameson's defence of narrative in the *Political Unconscious,* Dominick LaCapra insists that his sense of narrative's central importance operates 'in relation to the *ideological* operations on the subject, or lived experience'. LaCapra adds that the political that is repressed (rendered unconscious) when this horizon is not recognized is what *theory* represses about itself, so that the term 'political unconscious' designates 'that which has been repressed in contemporary thought, *notably academic thought*' (LaCapra, 1983: 236). This argument bears reframing, being put into operation, not in relation to the particular conflict of interpretations with which Jameson was concerned in the early 1980s (where it centred partly on a clash between different *modes* of analysis of narrative as a cultural form) but in relation to contemporary disputes around narrative's

centrality and importance per se. My contention is that narrative *itself* is
what is now repressed. Given that, my intention here is to re-excavate the
importance of narrative and of a narrative *analysis* within a world where
the argument that 'we are beyond such things as stories' is in tension with
ever more strident demands that we *account* for ourselves, that we get
our stories *straight.*

Digital technology, as it is deployed today, increasingly codifies the
life stories of individuals by way of identification cards or database
records, but behind this operation stands the individual existent, whose
reduction to a coded interpellation institutionalizes a form of automated
indifference and judgement, passed *at* the flick of switch and *as* the
flick of a switch: refugee, crank, non-payer, security threat, identity card
non-holder, terrorist. Without a story we are nobody. In these conditions
a theory that tends to suggest that narrative has declined into the
indifferent honesty of the database is pernicious, at least in so far as it
obscures the degree to which narrative remains both central and powerful
in 'real life'.

This argument is not about making a case for the persistence of
traditional forms of story, or indeed about traditional forms of identity.
On the contrary, the point is to develop a narrative analysis through
which demands and claims for the reconsideration of human possibilities
within cultural formations and cultural bodies that combine with or take
up technology in *new* ways can be assessed. This may amount to
an account of the generation of new forms of narrative – as it is lived and
as it is written and told.

Memory, of course, is crucial to all this, because it is intrinsic to a
conception of a narrative form of identity in so far as this hinges on the
persistence over time of the sense of the self *as a self* (see Ricoeur, 1992),
and because it is at the heart of digital technologies. All digital media
systems are archiving systems or memory banks of one kind or another.
For greater or lesser periods of time they *store* information, and in that
process they organize and control access to various kinds of data,
including data that concern individual and social memories: the kind of
data that helps to constitute the self as a self, over time and across space.
In *Archive Fever*, an exploration of new technologies of inscription and
storage, Jacques Derrida declares that those 'with whom the archive
dwells' are given 'hermeneutic right and competence' over its contents
(Derrida, 1995: 2). The question of who (or what) controls the archive,
and how it is interpreted, is at the heart of what is explored here in relation
to the production of identity in digital spaces.

This process of storage is active as well as passive; what is stored is
organized. However, given that this technology is also *interactive*, and

thereby places the end-user in a particular position in relation to the production of content, archival control in these spaces is less obviously in the hands of the archon, or archivist. This raises questions about the *limits* of the archive and/or the limits on the degree to which this archive is *constitutive* of identity. Derrida refers to this question of limits as the question of what is outside the archive. A rather different issue concerns the relationship *between* identity as it is electronically mediated and produced (archived) and identity as it exists before and after such mediation (such archiving) – in the life stories of existents and in the narration of end-users. What happens if we come to rely on *artificial* memories, stored outside ourselves, to maintain our sense of our self as a self? What happens when personal memories are stored as collective memories in new ways, when archives of the self and public archives become integral, or rather when they connect in new ways? If the *rehearsal* of such memories, their *narration*, produces *new* forms of identity, what *political* questions might arise, when this narration is enabled or refused in particular ways? And are there limits to this form of identity? In all of these ways memory is central to the kinds of transformations of the economy of narrative identity under examination. In this chapter these threads are brought together and some questions concerning the digital archive and artificial memory are explored through a consideration of narrative identity, defined here, following Adriana Cavarero, as the story of a life, and the possibility of its faithful retelling by another (Cavarero, 2000).

Those with whom the archive dwells:
narrative, memory, identity

In the popular register, identity is often discussed in narrative terms. Life stories define who we are, and condition what we may become. Obituaries are obvious examples of this way of thinking about a life but so are ongoing soap-opera stories of celebrity purveyed in popular magazines, or the biographies of public figures, groups, or whole populations, whether these last are produced to account, to explain, to condemn, to forgive, or perhaps in restitution for an injustice done. Identity theft, as it is adumbrated in the press, by definition relating to *personality* as well as to plastic (a part of oneself is stolen as well as a credit card), is also viewed as the theft of a life story.

These formulations have theoretical resonances, of course. Later in this chapter I consider accounts of narrative identity developed by Hannah Arendt, Adriana Cavarero and Paul Ricoeur. All three have elaborated accounts of the connections and relations between various actors, spaces and texts that might constitute an extended *narrational economy*. All share a conviction that 'the life' *exceeds* 'the text', although in different ways in each account. In fact it is the *relationship* between the life story and the life, and the degree to which both are included in a broader narrative arc, that constitutes the problematic of narrative identity in each of their accounts. For various reasons cyber-cultural theorists have not generally explored narrative identities but have tended to consider digital subjects as textually or cyber-textually produced, and/or as discursively *performed* (see Stone, 1995; Turkle, 1995; Farquhar, 2000, for instance). This theorization of the subject within cyber-theory, stressing 'life on the screen' (Turkle, 1995), led to a focus on immersion to the neglect of interactivity, with its focus on *processes* of connection between different places, spaces and forms of embodied use.

I have already argued that interaction can be usefully be explored through narrative. Bringing identity into the mix develops these possibilities. If narrative identity is *automated* in particular ways within digital systems, then how might life stories be archived, edited and reassembled in forms influenced and constrained by the architecture of the system, by users who may in the end narrate or refuse the tale? My hope is that addressing identity from this perspective might open the way to different forms of thinking about how digital identity can be understood. In particular, it might offer new ways in which the surveillant subject, on the one hand, and the theoretically weightless and 'free' cyber-subject, who is now so often regarded as entirely 'enchained', on the other, can be reconceptualized beyond these dichotomies. It is feasible and productive to explore the role of technological mediations in the production of an identity (or a life story), beginning with an account of social existence that is, as Kottman put it, not predicated on interpellation (Kottman, 2000) but that might be said rather to subsume and exceed it. Thus a turn to narrative might begin to suggest new forms of political response to forms of identity emerging within informational culture.

Narrative relations

Narrativity, as a construction or deconstruction of paradigms of story telling [is] a perpetual search for new ways of expressing human time, a production or creation of meaning. (Paul Ricoeur, interviewed in Valdes, 1991: 17)

Ricoeur's account of narrative identity, focusing on the persistence of identity over time, is an extension of the narrative hermeneutics developed around fiction and history in *Time and Narrative* (see Chapter 2). Explored in various texts, notably *Oneself as Another* (1991), this account retains an insistence on narrative as an arc of operations that exceeds the moment of the text, so that prefiguration and reconfiguration are not the 'before' and 'after' of the act of narrative, but are an intrinsic part of it.

Consonantly with this, when identity is considered in terms of narrative, the latter is understood as intrinsic to the whole process of identity formation and maintenance. In other words, there is no fall into narrative at the end of a life, no sense in which narrative identity is (only) a recapitulation after the act. Nor is there a way in which a life is predestined by narrative. Rather, the extended relationships operating between the human actor who acts and lives, the life story of this actor, and the narration of this tale are the subject of the inquiry. Ricoeur, indeed, is asking not only what identity consists of, taking the question of how it persists over time as the key, but also what narrative is and what it may become. For Ricoeur the limits of narrative identity are also the limits of narrative itself – and vice versa.

As in the earlier work, the writing on identity explores the problematic of time and experience but the focus switches from literary or historical forms of narrative, with Ricoeur arguing that narrative can be used to explore tensions between two aspects of identity when the latter is understood to inhere at once in selfhood (*ipse*) and in sameness (*idem*) (Ricoeur, 1992: 116). This very old tension/distinction might be redrawn as bodies and selves are drawn into increasingly intimate relationships with technology and as they operate in increasingly technologized spheres. In particular, it relates in suggestive ways to the widespread notion of identity confusion and to the lack of 'warranting' of bodies as they move between virtual and real-world spaces (Stone, 1995). Stone's argument, still influential, was that identity online is a performance and/in technology of a subject that is fundamentally multiple. The individual puts on cyberspace 'like a garment' and in doing so can put on an identity more or less at will. The (non)relationship between the online self and the (more continuous) self offline can be understood through the embrace of the principle of a schizophrenic self and/or the multiple personality, now depathologized (Stone, 1995: 90).

Ricoeur's argument is that sameness, found in physical continuity (the grounding of the body) as well as in identicality, tends to warrant selfhood. Exploring aspects of identity as selfhood without this warranty in place, by finding conditions where the self/same relation varies or where sameness does not pertain, exposes a question inherent in *all* consider- ations of identity (in sameness too), which is how its persistence over time, its persistence as a temporal form within time horizons, can be understood. Selfhood and sameness are 'two poles of permanence in time' (Ricoeur, 1992: 148). Ricoeur addresses this problem by reading identity as a mode of narrative emplotment.

Identity is resolved in narrative through a process of grasping the actions of a life, 'a story yet to be told' (Ricoeur, 1991: 434), configuring it as text, and reopening it on to new horizons through narration. Because narrative itself continually operates within new horizons (continual reconfiguration is part of its structure), this resolution is always ongoing and is never complete; we are *narratable* rather than narrated selves (the distinction is Cavarero's rather than Ricoeur's, but pertains to his work). For Ricoeur, the significance of the life story is fully realized only as it is opened on to the horizon of another through its narration. This moment configures the tale at its fullest extent since it is the moment in which a lived life is *transfigured* and well as *described*. As a consequence narrative identity, the significance of a life story, reconciling these two poles of temporal permanence, has to be regarded as something that finally 'wells up from the *intersection* of the world of the text [the life story] and the world of the reader' (Ricoeur, 1991: 430, my italics). Ricoeur characterizes this intersection as a *hinge* operating between the internal and external configurations of the work and the life (1991: 432). It can function because there is already a degree of symmetry between the organization of a life (its prefiguration as *meaningful* action or what Valdes calls the 'area of cultural participation through language' (Valdes, 1991: 28) and the formal organization of tale of the life as it is narrated (Ricoeur, 1991: 432).

This is not to argue that narrative determines the shape of a life, since here the flow between text (what is narrated) and world (the lives of the protagonist and the narrator) is bi-directional, moving both from and towards life and text. As Ricoeur himself observes, this is rather different from assuming that a formal narratological logic is to be found in the world (1991: 432), or from assuming that an entirely textual logic could determine or even destine (narrative) identity. Here the existent is not made a subject through an act in language, and nor are they destined by an act in narrative. In this sense, for Ricoeur (as for Cavarero), the individual is someone who *already* lives.

Finally there is the question of identity and ideology. If the solicitation between text and life is understood as reciprocal (although never identical), then the narrative text that 'tells' the individual can be understood to take its form from human *actions* in the world, actions which are themselves always already articulated in signs, rules and norms. The narrative form that reflects a form of life can now be considered both as contingent and as intersubjectively produced. Ricoeur's sense is thus that the *relation* with life *conditions* the form narrative takes, and that this form may be ideological. Ideology itself then comes to be socially constructed 'on the basis of countless layers of narrativity' (Ricoeur, 1991: 34).

The link between narrative and identity is thus to be found through consideration of the problem of emplotment, when this is regarded as a dynamic and *innovative* process, one that moves between text and world.

Ricoeur thus defines narrativity, as 'a construction or deconstruction of paradigms of story telling ... a perpetual search for new ways of expressing human time, a production or creation of meaning' (Ricoeur, interviewed in Valdes, 1991: 17). Narrativity itself, as a textual form, is *forged* and *transformed* by a search for human meaning which is also *generative* of identity, and is a process that is historically inflected, as Ricoeur himself recognizes. The limits of this transformation are where the limits of the human (of human *life*) are reached; indeed, he explores this explicitly in a series of thought experiments in 'the realm of conceivable technology' through a consideration of cloning in the 'Sixth Study' of *Oneself of Another* (Ricoeur, 1992: 48–50). For Ricoeur, where the maintenance of identity across change is no longer possible, where the dialectic of selfhood and sameness *gives*, narrative itself is no longer possible.

'*Real stories have no authors*'[5]

The problematic of identity and narrative is explored in a rather different way by Cavarero, who is in dialogue with Hannah Arendt's considerations of identity. Both theorists understand narrative identity as formed from three components: the protagonist, the life story and the narrator of the tale. The narrational economy of the self found here focuses on narration as the act of another, and as a public act. Interaction is thus once again central to identity production but in this case the focus is on narration and narratability rather than emplotment.

For Arendt it is the narration of a life story that produces the life as *memorable*, since an individual may act, but her or his life story can only be truly grasped by another. Narrative identity is thus biographical rather than autobiographical and is also *retrospective*, a means by which a life is made memorable, or a means by which restitution for injustice is made, after a life has ended (Arendt, 1989).

In *Relating Narratives*, Cavarero draws on Arendt's account to argue that narrative identity exceeds the actions and events that make up a life and require narration. Cavarero, however, breaks with Arendt when she argues that narrative belongs to lived human existence not to post-mortem fame (1997: 33). Narratability is not only how history interpreted a life, it is an *ongoing relation* of the self to the world. Through the concept of the narratable self, Cavarero sets out to consider narrative identity not as the end-product of a life story but as continuous with the production of the life, if also distinct from it in important ways. This account of narrative identity thus produces a reciprocal economy of narrative relations which includes a discursive moment but which also exceeds it.[6] *What* or *who* is narratable is somebody who is always *before* and *after* the text. Once again this suggests a very different route into thinking about digital identity than that offered by the performative: Cavarero argues that it is the knowledge that one has a continuing life story that confirms the individual in her or his everyday, and ongoing, sense of self. In contrast, Judith Butler has said of her performative conception of the subject that 'in the performative, there is no subject who precedes the reiteration of norms, rather it is the latter which precede, constrain and exceed the former' (Butler, cited in McNay, 2000: 16).

For Cavarero, all humans are potentially narratable since through our actions and choices we produce life stories. Narration, however, depends on another because while we may be responsible for making choices and pursuing particular actions, and therefore build life stories, the narrative patterns these actions and decisions might produce, as they are brought together, are not entirely transparent to us as we stand within them. For this reason, for Cavarero (as for Arendt), the individual is rarely the teller of her or his own tale. Bringing the contention that we desire narration together with our inability to narrate ourselves, Cavarero produces the paradox of the narratable self. This is the self who is always seeking the unity narration might provide, but who cannot fully satisfy her or his own desire to be narrated – to know herself or himself. In sum, Cavarero's narratable self could be defined as an individual whose narration (by another) reveals to the self *who* rather than *what* he or she is.

Recognition is a key element of the narrational economy Cavarero produces, since the individual who cannot tell the tale in its entirety must *recognize* the tale told as her or his own. It is recognition, rather than correspondence (for example, between two pre-existing narrative structures), that binds the life with the narration. This is not guaranteed, since the tale offered by another can be misrecognized, and the story told in good or bad faith. A narration in bad faith is one in which *narration* misrecognizes the protagonist of the story it narrates and so fails to deliver to the protagonist the narrative they desire.

Finally, Cavarero argues that the place and space of narration is important. Here she is clearly influenced by Arendt, and indeed draws directly on Arendt's discussions of the *polis* as public space in the *Human Condition* when she argues that for narration to be meaningful it must be performed in a 'plural and interactive space of exhibition' (Cavarero, 2000: 22). Narration is in this way opened up and becomes comprehensible as part of a more general, and indeed *reciprocal*, process, since while a narration cannot often be given by the self, it can be solicited. As Cavarero puts it, 'actively revealing oneself to others, with words and deeds, grants a plural space and therefore a political space to identity – confirming its exhibitive, relational and contextual nature' (Cavarero, 2000: 22).

Cavarero describes the kind of interactive public space where not only the gaze but also narration itself is reciprocal as 'the only space that deserves the name of politics' (Cavarero, 2000: 57). Within such a space existents might be opened to the real other within an 'interactive theatre where each is, at the same time, actor and spectator' (Cavarero, 2000: 22). The uncertain *processes* of ongoing identity formation and maintenance, understood in terms of the narratable self, are thus not only, by definition, intersubjective but also, at least in the sense that they are public, *collective*.

The conception of narrative identity outlined here does not depend on narrative content, nor in essentials on the internal form a narrative might take. Arendt, indeed, neglects almost entirely the internal arrangement of the tale and instead accords priority to narrative relations. Her interest is in 'the complex relation between every human being, their life story, and the narrator of this story' (Cavarero, 2000: 40). Cavarero follows Arendt in neglecting the tale and emphasizing the relations that produce its telling and the contexts that provide the necessary publicity for narration to be successful. For Cavarero, too, it is narrative *relations*, here operating between different actors at play in the interactive theatre discussed above, which are crucial. To set aside the internal organization of the tale is not to say that tellability is all. It might be more accurate to suggest that the *possibility* of narration conditions what a narrative identity is, and what *form* it takes.

Digital narration

The irruption of digital technology into the narrational economy of the self outlined above raises new questions. What does it mean if the 'interactive theatre' at the heart of Cavarero's conception of the narratable self reaches across virtual and real spaces? If the tale told by the narrator already exists 'independently' of the protagonist, as a digital archive? If the tale of the protagonist is *recited* by a narrator, but in a fashion largely *organized* by another, and organized using digital technology, then whose intentions are being respected: those of protagonist, intermediate producer, or narrator? Returning here to the image body of *Rehearsal*, already introduced, the problematic of narrative identity can be brought to bear on digital identity. Particular forms of narration can be enabled or disabled within these spaces when the interactive qualities of this medium are deployed in particular ways. This brings about a return to Ricoeur's question about the possibilities and limits for the reconfiguration of narrative, when these limits are understood, not in relationship to formal narrative models (whether a particular pattern of experience fits a particular model of story), but in relation to life, or rather to forms of life experience that can be made meaningful through particular forms of temporalization.

The narration machine

A presence was getting out which had a value for them. It told a different story about their lives. (Harwood, 1997)

Rehearsal tells a story not generally heard. Ashworth inmates are portrayed by the UK tabloids in a baroque fashion either as 'evil monsters' or as 'nutters', while the judicial system and the medical establishment categorizes them according to the provisions of 1983 Mental Health Act (at the time the work was made) and other relevant legislation. The individual life histories of these inmates are almost completely invisible (to the public) and relevant only in so far as they are part of the system of classification by which an inmate is known (in the eyes of the institution).

Rehearsal aimed to use computer technology to restore to a group of inmates some sense that their wider life experiences as well as the stories of their extraordinarily serious crimes might be heard beyond the walls of Ashworth. If the artwork could enable a rehearsal of these life memories and experiences in a meaningful way and in a meaningful context – in this case beyond the classifying institution – then those involved might feel that they were in some sense at least still people with identities, narratable selves perhaps.

For Harwood, a Foucauldian by instinct if not in fact, this restitution always had a wider intent. Setting out to give these life stories a public voice he also set out to critique categorizations that define the mad against the sane in contemporary society, arguing that these categorizations are perpetuated – and in part produced – by the media, the medical establishment and the legal system, and result in widespread ignorance both of those on the other side of the divide and of mental illness itself. On the one hand, those categorized as criminally insane are defined against 'us' so that we do not inquire into how they might be like 'us'. On the other hand, the cleaned-up discourse of clinical intervention (a form of technology) smoothes over the disquieting reality of mental disturbance. This redoubled form of censorship means that the rehearsed cycles of *familial* violence that are ubiquitous in the life histories of people in institutions such as Ashworth – and that have their echoes in many more lives – are not recognized. If the Ashworth authorities hoped that *Rehearsal* would have a therapeutic effect, Harwood's intent was always more ambiguous. *Rehearsal* set out to disturb in the *outside* world, rather than to soothe *within* the walls of the hospital. If it was effective, this was because it approached this from an unexpected direction, using computers to expose dangerous and dangerously disturbed people as *also* very ordinary, rather more like 'us' than 'we' might be comfortable with.

Computers are complicit in the production of the kind of classificatory discourses at issue here since they are used to place decision makers at a 'safe distance' from decisions or actions (who is imprisoned, who is dismissed, whose tissue was scanned to make the body in *Rehearsal*, whose real body and which real deaths sit behind the digital human specimens in projects like the *Visible Human*). Computers can thus make us 'ritually' free (Harwood, 1997b: 3) providing 'neutral decision making spaces' (Harwood, 1997b: 38) within which we do not have to fully accept the consequences of what we do. *Rehearsal* sets out to expose the distancing or neutralizing effect *as an effect* by organizing forms of *intimate association* between patient and user, art space and incarceration space, doing so with the technology that is supposed to offer a protective sheath against such interactions.

Rehearsal also explores the subversive potential of new information technologies and the possibilities for various forms of appropriation they might offer. Harwood's intention was to use computer technology as an alternative communication channel, one that could sidestep the usual 'routes of hygiene and distinction and of experts' through which inmates' and prisoners' stories are generally told (Harwood, 1997; Fuller, 1996). This sidestepping might be possible, he felt, because the Ashworth authorities misrecognized the potential of computers, widely understood at the time as 'clean machines' rather than as potential vehicles for cultural criticism.[7] The idea was that *Rehearsal* could 'get past the censorship' (Harwood, 1997; Fuller, 1996), in the sense that it would formally comply with the restraints imposed on the project by the hospital authorities (see below) but would exceed their intent. The wider reference here is to the kinds normative understandings of madness and criminality that might produce particular sets of responses to the artwork amongst users. This is a form of 'censorship in our heads' (Harwood, 1997a), which might block a faithful narration.

The strategy adopted to get around this censorship in *Rehearsal* echoed many prison scams, but also operated in the manner of packet switching: the inmates' tale was sent out into the world *in pieces* for later reassembly. This strategy informs the design of *Rehearsal*, which sets in motion a complex of relays between the life stories, the image body and the end-user. Here is a bid to use interactivity to *direct* or shape the user experience so that the narration of the stories, through the body and under the hands of the user, might be *faithful*, at least in the sense that it reaches around the official interpellations.

The final sections of this chapter explore this relay system in more detail, referencing the moment of making, the coded image-body that was made, and the moment of reception. The hinge here, between the internal economy of the work and the lives at each end of it, is the body itself, the anonymous *personality* at the heart of the artwork. This personality, planned on paper and then built in code, leaves Ashworth in pieces and is then reassembled by users through their interaction with the artwork, in their imaginations. Tracing this personality through each of its iterations suggests ways in which narrative identity might *persist* across networked environments, and through various transformations. The dialectic of *ipse* and *idem*, selfness and sameness, the *who* and the *what*, raised by both Ricoeur and Cavarero, and in both cases deployed to underscore transformation and its limits in relation to narrative forms of identity, is useful here. Perhaps this body is a *mutable* mobile.

The paper body

Narrative is part of life before being exiled from life in writing; it returns to life along ... multiple paths of appropriation and at the price of ... unavoidable tensions. (Ricoeur, 1992: 163)

The anonymous computer personality began life as a full-size paper model, the body of a man. It was composed of print-outs from body scans of inmates, staff and project workers, an office-party Xerox game in a peculiar space, and it functioned as a storyboard. Inmates also contributed various life experiences to the project in the form of texts, or spoken recollections. The paper body was then assembled in code, finding its final shape through a series of negotiations between those involved which were always delicate and sometimes difficult (Harwood, 1997a; Graham, 1997: 8). The form the body took was also conditioned by the restrictions placed on the project by Ashworth. *Rehearsal* was produced with the collaboration of Ashworth Arts, a group set up to provide art therapy for inmates, but it needed the approval of the authorities at Ashworth, and of the Home Office, which has ultimate responsibility for the regime at UK prisons and secure hospitals, before it could go ahead. Both sanctioned the work but also imposed a series of conditions. These included press restrictions – Ashworth was justifiably nervous about bad publicity.[8] In addition, the authorities[9] required a right of veto on the content, and a right to preview the work and to demand changes. Another constraint, the one which most obviously influenced the way the project took shape, was the requirement for absolute anonymity. Neither images, voices, nor specific stories, were to be recognizably those of individual inmates (Harwood, 1997). Finally, the work was influenced by the day-to-day rules governing life in a secure institution where surveillance of inmates is routine and is (at least in intent) seamless. Guards were present at the sessions alongside inmates, some taking part in the scanning.

Harwood's role at the production stage was partly to act as a coordinator organizing the scanning processes and assembling the jointly produced material. Harwood himself describes the production process as one in which he 'listened and imagined a space'. He denies authorship of *Rehearsal*, preferring to describe his role as one in which he facilitated the production of the tale the inmates wanted to tell. More convincingly, perhaps, he claims that, at any rate, 'it isn't my body' (Harwood, 1997a). This distinction underscores Harwood's ambiguous role in the narrational economy he sets out to enable. He might be understood as the archivist of the inmates' memories, as the narrator of their tale, as middleman or, quite simply, as a thief: a man who stole a body. This last reading essentially amounts to a charge of appropriation, and was laid against Harwood by some contemporary reviewers (notably Simon Worthington in *Mute* [1996]).

What is clear is that the body, produced with Harwood's skin scans amongst others, is partly an account of his own experience of the project itself and the conditions of its production. In this sense it is his narration. The themes with which *Rehearsal* deals, and the arrangement of the work, reflect the factors that directly intervened in its production. *Rehearsal* is as much a record of a dialogue and exchange between Harwood and the inmates, in very particular conditions, as it is an archive of the inmates own memories and feelings. The sense of uneasy complicity, of being engaged with a body in ways that are not entirely under control, that is produced in the artwork, resonates with Harwood's own experiences of its making. It is *as* a work that sets out to produce complicity that *Rehearsal* stands in contrast to – exposes – the far more general use of interactivity to produce that sense of ritual distance or *disengagement* from the object or the task, identified above.

The body in code

The paper body built in the institution became the coded image body, now an anonymous computer personality, visible on screen and possible to interact with in particular ways. Like Frankenstein's monster, to which it refers, this body is made from bits and pieces, but here no join marks are visible. The head is shot from three angles, head on and in left and right profile. The two profile shots lock their gaze on the full frontal counterpart, which stares outwards towards or beyond the user forming a rather decorative triptych. The torso, seen from the front, is unclothed and tattooed[10] and cut in various ways. Some of the tattoos and marks on the skin are clickable and open up to reveal images, texts, video and spoken words, the last sometimes little more than murmurs. Around the body are objects typical of life in a secure institution: pills, keys, clothes, prescriptions.

The body conforms to standard aesthetic norms through which criminals have been identified and classified *as* offenders. The headshots are reminiscent of Bertillon's early mug shots of prisoners, intended to be 'neutral', but quickly coming to signify criminality (Galton and Bertillon, cited in Sekula, 1986: 25; and Lury, 1999: 52–54). However the keys and pills, icons of imprisonment and of mental disorder, also have a quotidian feel. In this sense the body is found in its 'private' life, or perhaps the user is given a private view, hence the unease felt by commentators like Worthington.

The interface and the organization of interactive possibilities around this body reveal a different aesthetic: in use *Rehearsal* has the feel of a game. To use the artwork is also to use the body, to engage with it in that casual but also intense way that is characteristic of this new media form – and to switch it on and off. The disjuncture here between the form of a game and the gravity of the content raises the question of *who* or *what* is being used here, of the status of the body under the hand.

Rehearsal may be played with, but it does not cede control to the user. The image body clearly exists as complete body 'within the machine' (and not only as a coded possibility but as a image brought up on-screen) but it can only be *viewed* in pieces. No distanced perspective is provided; instead a peephole is placed hard against the screen, so that details – an arm, a leg, a face – fill it entirely, giving the impression that the body is on a giant scale. The dislocation that the close-up view produces is increased by the way navigation is organized, since no compensatory haptic control is offered in the place of visual mastery. The discrete stories the inmates tell, activated through hotspots on the body, operate with a similar dynamic; intimate fragments of life inside, old memories of moments in childhood, of cutting, drugs, hospitalization, are often 'let out' before the user who runs across them has time to take a decision about whether to linger over them or move on.

Rehearsal ensures that the luxury, or the hygiene, of the scopic view is not accorded to the user, who is left to stumble blind across this body. In addition, the close-up interface collapses the distance between the user and the body image to the extent that the barrier between them – the controlling interface – is easily overlooked. The illusion of dis-intermediation brings the user nose-up against the image body, forced to rub (digital) flesh with this body, as a condition of any kind of use. A tightly disciplined and highly organized encounter between the user and the body image, which plays on the tension between the felt transparency of the interface and its ability to move the *user* around, produces a form of intimacy. Playing with *Rehearsal*, you are 'up against a body, up against a machine' (Fuller, 1996).

These arrangements have implications for the ways in which this space might be understood as interactive. Certainly the body may be used, but it also reveals itself on its own terms. Indeed it might be justifiable to claim that the gaze is two-way, even if fictional on one side and deferred on the other, since the arrangement of the body, which is what organizes the gaze, reflects a choice on the part of the inmates whose body this is. The coded body always refers back to the original negotiations between Harwood and the inmates. It is in this sense that it takes their story *on*, and in this sense, too, that the narrational economy of *Rehearsal* over-codes the disciplining economy of the institution.

The tension between these two economies is found in the internal economy of the work, where two axes are brought into opposition with each other. The first centres on the visual environment of *Rehearsal* and concerns the disciplining of the body in the prison economy described above. The hospital/prison regime that tends to *reduce* the individual to an effect of its own economy is very evident in this aspect of *Rehearsal*. Cross-cutting this axis is the way in which interaction has been coded in the artwork to produce a particular kind of encounter for the user, since here *Rehearsal* does not only mirror the disciplining process of the institution but *counters* it. *Rehearsal* thus challenges the apparent interpellation of the body as *only* an effect of its categorization, a personality without a story.

Here then we can begin to reconceptualize the computer apparatus, which can now be viewed not in Foucauldian terms as a self-contained disciplining apparatus, producing a discourse of which the subject is an effect, but as a key element within an extensive narrational economy, one that reaches behind and before it. We might say that these life stories are *articulated* through the artwork, which is complicit in narration through its archival role, taking the force of the archive here to extend to what is rendered back as well as what is stored.

In that element of the *narrational* economy found in the internal economy of the artwork, here understood in its widest scope, the terms and *relations* of vision and communication are rearranged so that the discipline they impose is refracted away from the inmate – and some of it finds its object in the *user* of the work. Here interactive technology is deployed to mirror the prison economy and invert it – and if the inmates 'escape' to tell their tale in more propitious conditions, perhaps it is the user who is trapped.

Conditions of narration

Continuously producing new forms of surveillance through the extension of the apparatus of the database, as well as through the development of new forms of visual imaging, computers are extending the reach and efficacy of surveillance, as a series of commentators have pointed out (see Poster, 1995: 68; Andrejevic, 2005: 230).

Information technology is embedded in control and surveillance apparatuses of all kinds, including the ones at Ashworth, at once a prison *and* a madhouse. However, the museum and the gallery, other spaces of exhibition, could join Foucault's disciplinary institutions: the asylum, the clinic and the prison. Viewed in this light, the inmates' temporary transfer from the closed economy of the prison into the digital archive might not appear propitious; it may be just another transfer from one disciplining apparatus to another. Should *Rehearsal* be considered as simply a piece of exhibitionary technology? If Harwood facilitates the Ashworth inmates' fleeting (and partial) escape from their confinement within the institution, is this only to place them in a space of exhibition, to subject them to a different form of surveillance? Do those involved in the project become his exhibited objects, this time disciplined by being on public display? Reviewing *Rehearsal*, Simon Worthington argued that the project risked becoming exploitative. As he put it 'lives are treated in a voyeuristic way' (Worthington, 1996: xvii).

Tony Bennett argues that this conception of the space of exhibition is flawed. Given that museums are institutions 'not of confinement but exhibition', then they are not to be aligned with but *juxtaposed* to Foucault's carcereal archipelago, although they share with it an economy of affect (1988: 99).

For Harwood, reinscribing the inmates (or the body) within what Bennett might call a 'public dramaturgy of power', placing their life stories within a public space, is worth the risk. It subjects the inmates to the gaze of the public, it is true, but in doing so it brings them to the *notice* of the public. Computer technology itself, expected to be the machine that can *perfect* an apparatus of surveillance, thus fails to work as expected. Organized with intent, the interactive interface can function to deflect or scatter the gaze of the viewer/user, even turning it back upon itself.

The economy produced here exceeds Foucauldian conceptions of technology as disciplining apparatus – even while flirting with the suggestion that this is precisely what it is. In sum, the image body comes to stand neither in the accustomed place of the prisoner in the prison apparatus, divided from the world outside and from ordinary people, nor in the usual place of the exhibit, as something there to be looked at from any angle, since it seems at least to be able to look back but it is certainly situated within a controlled environment that restricts viewing. The result may be the production of something close to what Cavarero called 'a plural network of gazes' (2000: 23), even if these gazes are deferred, mediated, and in some ways also imaginary.

The player of games
Whoever is engaged in putting into play is also played upon . . . for the rules of the game impose themselves on the player. (Valdes, 1991: 26)

The final moment in the narrative arc occurs if the body in the machine encountered by the user in the gallery is narrated. This is an act of assembly to the extent that there is a capitulation to the terms of the work, but it is also a recomposition that produces something new; the coded body, as it is traced out through play, becomes a presence, at least, in the imagination of the user. Handing assembly over to the user demands that they take on board the *emotional* impact of the tale. It is in this aspect that *Rehearsal defers* narration, passing on responsibility for narrating the life story to the end-user.

This isn't to say that narration is entirely in the user's hands. It is the interface design, undermining the effect of ritual distance, that produces the peculiarly intimate terms of engagement for the user; and if Harwood isn't the author of the body he certainly *is* the producer of this narrative machine and promotes its deferrals and relays. The call to order issued by the interface means that narration is also Harwood's.

In fact, within this system of relays and deferrals, the question of archival control, of who controls the inmates' memories, becomes harder to call. Drawing on its etymological roots, Derrida called archiving a form of 'house arrest' (1995: 19). In this case the archive allowing the rehearsal of memories is 'released', but is 'released' in a form pre-agreed with the inmates, who are the subjects of the archive. To this extent Harwood, here viewed as the *archon*, at once does his best to disperse his own authority ('it's not my body'), however he also does so in a way that is consciously authoritarian, not in relation to the group in inmates he worked with, but in terms of you, the user. If the image body presses up against your skin, then this was *planned*. Harwood made this so by designing the interface to produce this effect. In this sense his 'hermeneutical competence' is articulated as an inscription in the design of the interface, and is reinvoked with each assembly. Cavarero's demand that the self requires narration within an 'interactive theatre *where each is, at the same time, actor and spectator*' (Cavarero, 2000: 22, my italics), thus begins to be renegotiated in new kinds of interactive spaces.

A postscript and three conclusions

A critical hermeneutic of imagination ... is one which demystifies the dissimulating property of phantoms in order to release the symbolizing power of images. *Idols must be unmasked so that symbols may speak.* (Kearney, 1984: 13, my italics)

Just as there is no innocent eye, there is no pure computer. (Manovich, 2001: 117)

The postscript is this: *Rehearsal* itself was completed more or less on time and enjoyed a great deal of success on the international art scene as an installation. It was later published as a CD-ROM by BookWorks, an art publisher, after a careful report on how to place it in a sensitive way (see Haskel, 1996) and was covered in art journals and computer titles as opposed to gaining tabloid notoriety of the sort feared. At the time of the original interviews with Harwood, planned screenings at Ashworth had been cancelled three times by the hospital authorities. All this might be an indication of who controls the body image, now considered an artwork, or of how the digital artwork finds its place within a broader exhibitionary economy. On the other hand, a viewing *inside* Ashworth was never the main point. Harwood states that the inmates themselves wanted their story to be told '*outside*'. As he put it, 'a presence was getting out which had a value for them. It told a different story about their lives' (Harwood, 1997).

Today *Rehearsal* stands as a relatively early example of tactical media, but one that remains incisive. It has influenced software artworks that followed it, and not only those from Mongrel. It was, however, *National Heritage*, a later work from Mongrel exploring race, identity and nation, that took on the unease around the question of ownership raised by *Rehearsal, demanding* of end-users formal and material complicity: your skin, your sample.

After the postscript the conclusion: despite the constraints that meant the body image of *Rehearsal* was of necessity an anonymous composite figure, Harwood produced an artwork that facilitates the narration of individual lives and individual people, a tale that can be faithful to a life story, to use Cavarero's terminology. The inmates who stand behind the body image 'envisioned' in one kind of technology, rather than imprisoned in another, can be discerned as narratable selves, and are narrated through and by the artwork and its users.

If the inmates valued their narration through *Rehearsal* and recognized it as their own, this might be because the manner of their narration disrupted their normal categorization: *Rehearsal* insistently looks beneath the 'monstrous' mask that mediates how we 'know' the criminally insane, to ask *who* this subject-in-process is. In doing so it argues against the kind of moral panics that define those in Ashworth and elsewhere, simply, reductively and unhelpfully, as monsters.

Digital identity is not finally *produced* here through a disciplining technological matrix, rather a life story is given *meaning* as it is reconfigured within a narrational economy constituted in part through the apparatus of interactive media. It is when a particular form of interactivity is deployed to allow a narrational economy to overtake normative interpellation or, in other words, when these two forms of interpretation are placed in tension, that it becomes clear how a narrative analysis can reach beyond the question of the individual narration of those involved in the project.

It is *through* the production of a narrative economy involving recognition (of the story as in some way one's own as well as that of another) and innovation (in that it is told in a way that is new) that *Rehearsal* operates to address social questions arising around normative discourses of madness and criminality. Here information technology is deployed in the service of the restitution of a form of narrative identity, but the resulting work also operates as a critique of those tendencies towards categorization, accelerated by informatization, that operate to warrant particular kinds of identities at the cost of declaring others illegitimate.

Finally, it is through the grounds of narrative that *Rehearsal* reconfigures the problematic of technology and society, the problematic of the information society. Here I return briefly to Fredric Jameson's sense of the expanding hermeneutic horizons within which the work can be understood, and ask how the kinds of forms of narrative identity produced here can be read at their widest extent. How is this rearrangement of narrative form *historical*? It is historical because, as I have already argued, the morphology of networks is socially determined. If narrative relations here operate through deploying and redeploying an identity *made* technological, then it is clear that the rehearsal of the life story; at the heart of Harwood's project is a profoundly *technologized* rehearsal. But it is also clear that the body of *Rehearsal* is finally not produced as a *purely* technological body.

The plays on proximity and distance, immediacy and deferral, which are evidenced in this digital production of identity, that might be said to constitute its formal economy, traverse the database 'moment' and weave between event, text and reception. In doing so, they also weave between different material bodies, different institutions and different economies. Increasingly, we understand this form to include artificial elements. When narrative relations are mapped across interactive spaces they become more complex. This is a process in which technologically organized time and space allow stories (about identity but not only about identity) to be *cached* differently, and released differently. In the process, identity 'itself' might be interpreted in different ways, and come to mean something new.

Rehearsal might suggest some of the ways in which these tendencies play out. The production of self, through the production of the tale, might be regarded as a process both potentially more extensible and dispersed, but also potentially more controlled, when it occurs across digital networks and interfaces. In the case of *Rehearsal*, this is inflected with a Utopian vision since Harwood sees technology as a plane in which oppositional action is possible. *Rehearsal* might be understood, indeed, as Harwood's attempt to 'ride technology before it rides us' (Witheford, 1994: 110–115).

Finally, there is in *Rehearsal* a sense of narration occurring within a space and time produced in accordance with the rhythm of new digital machines. As part of this, *Rehearsal* inscribes a play with form itself: the *poesis* here that comes from the drawing up of the real that Jameson describes is in the *medium*, in the dynamics of use; the image of the body is only one part of this economy. In claiming that tellability is the tale, Cavarero is saying more than she might realize about narrative at a particular point in history.

Notes

1 Derrida, 1995: 2.
2 'Imminentdomain.com, exploiting cyberspace for the sale of cyberdeath' (at '$9.95 and upwards') emblazons its virtual gravestone plots: 'This Area Is Available' (J. Berry, 1999).
3 As *Screen Digest* noted as far back as 1997: 'the Internet is becoming clogged with jetsam: outdated sites which haven't been changed since launch. AltaVista estimates that 16 per cent of sites referenced on its search engines haven't been updated since early 1996 and at least 74,000 pages of material haven't been refreshed since 1995' (*Screen Digest*, 1997: 2). There is no evidence to suggest the situation has changed; although new forms of traffic auditing have produced some changes in more commercial sites. Those who do not produce or interact are *reaped* increasingly rapidly.
4 'Recalling a Reclaim the Streets demonstration . . . Naomi Klein tells of a policeman monitoring the action who said into his radio: "this is not a protest. Over. *This is some kind of artistic expression*" ' (Street, 2000: 210, my italics).
5 Cavarero, 1997: 140.
6 To clarify Cavarero's argument, we might compare her sense of the narratable self with Butler's account of subjectivation. Paul Kottman, also in pursuit of this difference, distinguishes between Judith Butler's sense of performatively produced subject, where any possibility for resignification

occurs in the space *between* the discourse that speaks the subject and the individual's life – hence Butler's claim that 'discourse is not life, its time is not yours' – and Cavarero's sense of politics as they cohere around narrative identity when narration is always entrusted to another. As Kottman points out, in part this distinction turns on the question of the nature of that other. There is a difference between what Cavarero understands as the 'necessary other' in narration and Butler's sense of the constitutive outside, the *exclusionary* matrix that produces the subject (Butler, 1993). Kottman understands this in terms of a contrast between Butler's abject other, who is never more than a third person *perspective*, and Cavareo's insistence on 'an other who is really an other' (Kottman, 2000: xii–xiv). The reality of this other is intrinsic to Cavarero's account of narrative identity as based on a *reciprocal* economy of narrative relations which includes a discursive moment but which also exceeds it.

7   Given the widespread association of the Internet with pornography, terrorism and illegal downloading, this connection would not be made in the same way today.

8   There have been many tabloid scandals over events at Ashworth.

9   This term is somewhat inexact, but seems to be the only way to describe those in charge at Ashworth on the ground and at the Home Office.

10   Harwood used tattoos on the image body because he had read US reports current around that time, suggesting the subcutaneous – and lifelong – tagging of offenders (1997a).

4

Annihilating all that's made?
Legends of virtual community

The thin film of writing becomes a movement of strata, a play of spaces.
(De Certeau, 1984: xxi)

Stories . . . traverse and organize places; they select and link them together;
they make sentences and itineraries out of them. They are spatial trajectories.
(De Certeau, 1984: 115)

Prologue: 'this is not an image space'
A world now arose that could not be grasped by looking. (Dagognet, 1992:
110)

'This is not an image space', but as I type these few words, describing a
virtual community and its transformation, appear on my screen. I view
them as an image as well as read them as a text. This textual visual display
thus seems to confirm and confound the assertion it articulates. Clearly
any claim that cyberspace, the interactive world that appears on the screen
but that also reaches behind it to other screens in other places through a
network staggering in scale and astonishing in its material diversity, is not
an image space cannot be an absolute claim, and I don't mean it to be.
W. J. T. Mitchell claims that Foucault's meditation on Magritte's famous
pipe-which-is-not-a-pipe operates as 'an exercise in unlearning . . . it
addresses the relation between pictures and texts and those who believe
they know what that relation is' (Mitchell, 1994: 66–67). A similar
'exercise in unlearning' might be required in the case of virtual space,
which is too often understood as purely an image space, even as the
apotheosis of particular prioritization of the visual (Mirzoeff, 1999: 1)
read as characteristic of modernity (see Jay, 1988) and now also of postmodernity, at least if we take this as 'an epoch of the absorption of all
language into "images" and "simulacra", a semiotic hall of mirrors'
(Mitchell, 1994: 28).

   Cyberspace is as much a textual space as it is a visual one. I am struck
over and over again by the wordiness of websites and blogs, by the skeins

of written speech strung out around the world as e-mail exchanges, by the proliferation of talk spaces which are coalescences of words, by the striking lack of visual cues in many chat-rooms and other virtual communities.[1] The same predominance of the written word is evident in contemporary television news, as a glance at how the screen is divided in services such as Fox and CNN shows. The assumption that digital media accelerate the shift towards a visual economy, predicated on a diminishing sense of the word as text and perhaps therefore accompanied by a turn to orality as an accompaniment to the image, clearly needs to be questioned. The space of the virtual can't be defined purely and simply as *visual* space (and always less purely and simply than might appear, given the intellectual baggage that comes with what Baudrillard characterized as the precession of simulacra [Baudrillard, 1995]) and recourse to the visual therefore isn't an inevitable first move in an attempt to mount a critical appraisal of virtual space.

Of course cyberspace involves forms of visualization, and viewing it as something exclusively textual would therefore also be misplaced. Rather, cyberspace is characterized by a *mutual* bleeding together of the image and the text, and indeed of the spoken and the sung. It is characterized by speaking-writing, by seeing-saying, by the paradoxical use of visual icons to organize word-processing or textual shortcuts to process images, for instance. Cyberspace is an example, not of visual purity but of a thoroughgoing hybridity, extending what Mieke Bal understands as the intrinsically synaesthetic element of the visual and the textual (Bal, 2003: 19). We move as much 'into the word' as 'into the image' when we move into cyberspace.

We also move into a distinctive material space, one that can support particular kinds of fusions and confusions. Paying attention to the material of cyberspace is counterintuitive perhaps, because it displays what François Dagognet would describe as an unusual 'lightness' (Dagognet, 1989),[2] but it is important since cyberspace is not only a visual space or a textual plane, it is a material space that engages with both the visual and the written, that expresses their relationship as space. Remember that the ability to combine and recombine different media types, or even to render them equivalent as media streams to be worked upon, was what gave new media their early nomenclature of *multi*media. Breaking with the instinct to read virtual space as synonymous with the visual image means recognizing the intrinsic impurity of the textual and the visual in new media, but it also entails recognising virtual space *as* a material space, even one that has a particular dimensionality.

If cyberspace is something material, it is also something that is produced through material *practices*. The distinction between virtual space as something *produced* and *reproduced* through material practices and virtual space as an image space is thus another starting point in this chapter. Mike Crang's sense of the 'practices that produce representations' is useful here (Crang, 1997), and I will later suggest that practices not only produce representations, but also narratives.

Crang's formulation suggests the importance of making a distinction between the visual (or textual) record that a practice left and the practice itself, but it also provokes consideration of the role these representations or records play in the ongoing practice of a space, since they may be said to form the historical and ongoing context of this practice, to have *become* space; technologies hold within them memories. There are certainly virtual spaces that extend beyond the evanescent moment of the image on the screen or of the word that scrolls down and is lost, that reach beyond the moment when a particular image is made and beyond the moment it is flattened into a screenshot by the researcher. The question, perhaps, is how these text-image records are used in the ongoing production of a space, something I understand as a process of narrativization. *Not into the image then, but into the space: and finally into the story space.*

This is the history of how an empty space on the Internet became an inhabited place, a virtual community with its own story and with a substantial identity, and how it was then sold on, not like so much real estate, but *as* real estate. It is an example of those processes of commodi-fication that have changed the face of the Internet radically since it emerged into the public eye as a mass system during the 1990s.

Looking back it may appear obvious now that the early hopes for the Internet as a free space were not only misplaced but also naive in the extreme. This chapter challenges the latter perspective to some extent. My intention here is to point to ways in which these early Internet projects caught at possible futures, understood something could be done dif-ferently, and tried it out. It is a measure of their success that virtual community, unlike many other early Internet architectures, didn't fade away, but was restructured and reintegrated into the contemporary Internet, where its values have tended to be redeployed, not in the interests of creativity and social justice but in those of commerce.

Here I explore a virtual community as a history of a particular kind of space, one that is made of words and to a far lesser extent images, but that is more fundamentally to be understood as carved out of code. And finally I understand this spatial construction in narrative terms.

There are commonalities between virtual community and other emerg-ing forms of collaborative narrative production facilitated by new media. These include news stories, which increasingly integrate citizen reports and citizen reporters, sampled video/music projects, where authorship is massively multiple and the collaborative knowledge projects such as Wikipedia. It is no coincidence that questions of ownership, evidenced largely through tussles around intellectual property (I.P.) loom large in all of these arenas (see Berry, 2006), nor that those opposing the extension of I.P rights make their case in the language of the commons, and of the enclosure of the commons (see D. Berry, 2006; Barbrook, 2005).

Henri Lefebvre, the French theorist of everyday life, argues that spaces have symbolic meanings and significance, and that socio-political contradictions can be realized spatially (Massey, 1994: 251).[3] Indeed, for Lefebvre, 'it is only in space that such conflicts come effectively into play, and in doing so they become contradictions of space' (Lefebvre, 1991: 365). For Lefebvre spaces contain and conceal the categories that underpin a particular social order, and a theory of space that stresses space as a social production in this way can (indeed should) be used to make these categories visible (Shields, 1999: 158). In other words, 'an already produced space can be decoded, can be read' (Lefebvre, 1991: 17). Here Lefebvre's injunction to unmask the social dynamics underpinning the production of a space is taken up in relation to GeoCities, a long-standing virtual community. The development of this community space is explored over time, and GeoCities' story is set within the context of the broader history of the privatization and commercialization of virtual community and virtual space.

This chapter falls into three parts. The opening section draws on Lefebvre to explore virtual space as a social production. I then turn to the Internet itself, reading its history, and within that the history of virtual community, as the history of space. It is argued that virtual community is synecdochal for the early Internet and its values, and that these values continue to attach to virtual communities even while discrete productions of community increasingly fail to *instantiate* them. The third section then focuses on the spatial production of GeoCities, which is also understood in narrative terms. I am interested here in drawing out what the sense of virtual community operational in GeoCities takes from earlier models and how the phrase itself might operate as an ideologeme. This may demonstrate the degree to which processes of contradictory integration mean that 'virtual community' has been at once valorized and remade. If the new commercial model of GeoCities is operationalized partly through its appeal to 'virtual community', read as a guarantor of the persistence of human communion within an increasingly automated world, this also tends mask the underlying logic of the Cities, which concerns the production of narrative space as a commodity.

In making a connection between space and narrative I find a starting point in Michael de Certeau's accounts of space and everyday life, which may productively be read in relation to Lefebvre's work on the production of space. For de Certeau, to write a story is to make a space. As he puts it, 'the thin film of writing becomes a movement of strata, a play of spaces' (de Certeau, 1984: xxi); this has always seemed to me extraordinarily suggestive of the dynamics of many online spaces, which grow new dimensions or layers when they are actively inhabited or *lived*. Walking and reading are understood through each other in de Certeau's writing, so that, as he puts it in *Spatial Stories*: 'Stories . . . traverse and organize places; they select and link them together; they make sentences and itineraries out of them. They are spatial trajectories' (de Certeau, 1984: 115). In *Walking in the City*, de Certeau again links walking and writing, so that oppositions between walking as an embedded practice and the scopic view of the city as it can seen viewed from above are partly configured through distinctions made between the transparency of the mapped text and the *opacity* of the narrative woven by the reader as he or she traverses this known space. The opposition thus set out is between the tactical (the walker/reader) and the strategic (the architect or planner viewing the city from above who controls and dominates it). The question of power, the social relation, is thus bound up not only with questions of space and the narrative but with questions of the text-image and its relationship to materiality; these indeed become what Lefebvre would call contradictions in space (1991: 36).

The social production of virtual space

Darkness and obscurity are banished by artificial lighting, and the seasons by air conditioning; night and summer are losing their charm and dawn is disappearing. The man of the cities thinks he has escaped from cosmic reality, but there is no corresponding expansion of his dream life. *The reason is clear: dreams spring from reality and are realized in it.* (Chtcheglov, 1981: 2; italic added)

The cultural history of the Internet is all about the promise of a space. Space is at the core of the rhetoric deployed to describe the potential of the Internet as it emerged into public consciousness from the shadow lands of academe in the late 1980s/early 1990s. There was the fictional terrain of cyberspace opened by William Gibson and his cohorts (see 1991; 1994). There was US Vice President Al Gore, taking up the rhetoric of spatial colonization already evident on the Internet, and making it clear that the information superhighway was also the 'new frontier', whether of the Wild Western or the space-race kind (Gore, 1994). There was a popular rhetoric of virtual space, which read virtual space as free space and emerged at first largely on the Internet, and which understood this new communication system in terms rather different from those of Gore. The promise of endless space the Internet seemed to hold out was thus not only configured around the literal provision of a global 'new frontier' for the USA's globalizing ambitions (see Sardar, 1996), it also had a radical edge – and not only in fiction. Computers, experienced in various forms by citizens and consumers in the advanced countries, had been popularly understood as part of a general extension of control, part of a move towards a more bureaucratic and totally administered society (see Beninger, 1986). The emergence of a space 'between' computers, and above all the unofficial populating of that space, was widely understood as something that might work against that dynamic, and to some virtual space seemed to provide the unexpected new grounds within which increasing levels of control (legal, political, social, moral) might be evaded entirely and new forms of free association and free communication might be developed (see John Perry Barlow, cited in Ross, 1998: 11). Virtual community, arising in the early years of the Internet, encapsulated many of these hopes.

What has happened to those radical hopes and assumptions about virtual space in an era that has seen the rapid commercialization of the Internet? One way to address this question is to explore it by way of another: to ask what happened to the spaces themselves, in particular to those spaces that developed as virtual communities, during this time? Connecting these threads together through the exploration of a change in space as a form of narrative production in the case of one long-standing virtual community, what emerges is a process of 'contradictory reinte-gration' (Osborne, 1995: 162). Complex social bonds, including forms of exchange, present in older forms of virtual community have now been translated into contemporary communities according to the logic of expansion and incorporation. This retention and *detournement* has transformed virtual community but has also tended to mask that transformation.

Geometry, dimensionality

It is striking that many early assumptions that the Internet was and would remain a 'free' space were based either on the material qualities of code (endlessly extensible, infinitely editable) and/or on the morphology of the Internet as a non-hierarchical peer to peer information system founded on a principle of redundancy. The former was understood to provide an endlessly flexible substrate for the free play of identity, while the latter formed basis of the claim that the Internet interprets censorship like damage and simply routes around it. These accounts tended to focus exclusively on what Lefebvre defined as geometrical space (empty area) a form of space that can be contrasted with social space, which is lived practice (1991: 1). In the case of the web the flaws in this approach have become increasingly clear over time; Google[4] was willing and able to route around its democratic principles and rewrite its search algorithms to trade with China, for instance.

Lefebvre himself recognized the geometry of space as part of the social order, but prioritized the practice of space in his work, insisting upon the importance of understanding that '(social) space is a (social) product' (1991: 26). This approach might cope better with the Google example set out above, but where does that leave cyberspace geometries, the famous architectures of freedom?

First, the status of virtual space as a form of space is disputed: some understand it to 'negate geometry' altogether (Mitchell, 1995: 10). More usefully, perhaps, others argue that a particular *kind* of geometry is no longer operational in virtual space (Wertheim, 1999: 228). Most obviously this space is not subject to the Euclidean geometries that have been highly influential in forming a shared space of representation; which is to say, perhaps, that they have given us a certain sense of perspective (see Virilio, 1995; Wertheim, 1999). Virtual space might thus be understood as a new kind of physical space, one that is not yet well understood or well mapped, but one that might provide new perspectives. On this basis Margaret Wertheim claims that, with the advent of cyberspace, 'a new context is coming into being . . . space is evolving' (Wertheim, 1999: 228).

The Internet undoubtedly has a multi-layered physical geography, and atlases now map it from many angles, not only offering views of physical structures as they relate to real world geographies (connections in New York, nodes in Accra), but also mapping traffic flow and density, hits and hyperlink traffic, the latter operating to locate sites as they are positioned in relation to each other virtually (see Dodge, 2000). Virtual space might thus be said to be mappable (in theory at least) and it may also have what Doreen Massey calls a specific 'dimension' (Massey, 1994: 251). That is, virtual space affords particular forms of sensory engagement to users, who experience themselves as both weightless and prostheticized within virtual space in distinctive ways.

The Internet as it exists today *is* in part defined by that concatenation of wires, machines and code which make it up as a physical system, and which might be said to cradle a particular dimensionality, and perhaps to engender a particular geometry. However, it is also more than that, since it is also (always) a social space. Here, then, I turn back to the question of the *social* production of this material social space, and in particular to Lefebvre's contention that social space is defined in contrast to geometrical space and is based on practice. It is through the *practice* of space, organized by Lefebvre into different moments, that spaces come to be realized, finding their form and becoming more than 'empty areas'.

This isn't to say that Lefebvre's sense of space fails to engage with materiality or dimensionality, or that it can handle only the surface of things. Following Lefebvre, the distinction between a form of space as it comes to be sedimented in a highly elaborated virtual community and the kind of social production of space involved in the production of an FTP archive site would not be drawn as an absolute division between 'empty space' and practised space. Lower-level protocols governing connection are as much social productions as higher-level layers such as system software architecture, applications and user 'content'. The divisions that emerge concern questions of how these spaces are organized as social productions – who practises space, and in what conditions and under what constraints, for instance. Conceptualized in this way, a virtual community might be understood as a relatively highly elaborated virtual space, while a storage site or data hotel might be understood as relatively under-elaborated, but neither are to be regarded as 'empty spaces' in the sense Lefebvre means, since they are both forms of space produced as social productions. Thus, while it might be tempting to make divisions between social space and empty space on the grounds of technical distinctions (in particular on the grounds of higher and lower system architecture levels), this isn't tenable – not because these layers support each other (although they do, in fact), but because the social production of space is a material social production all the way down.

Distinguishing different kinds of space, when space is understood as a social production, isn't always easy. Here we may turn back to Lefebvre, who understood (socially produced) space to contain three moments: representations of space (conceived space), representational space (lived space) and spatial practices (perceived space) (Lefebvre, 1991: part I). Conceived space is the dominant space of society and is produced by technocrats and planners, often entailing processes of commodification and bureaucratization. Lived space is the fragile but potentially joyous space of everyday experience as it is lived by inhabitants or users. Perceived space is more difficult to characterize but is perhaps best understood as space *as it appears to us to be organized*. Lefebvre is adamant that these spatial moments do not constitute a spatial geometry, and neither did he wish to consider them as hierarchically arranged, preferring to consider them instead in terms of a triple dialectic (Shields, 1998). However, it might be argued that perceived space *holds* or gathers together both the lived space of everyday experience and the conceived space produced by the work of technocrats, planners and strategists.

The contribution of these different spatial moments to the production of social space as a whole is not equal. For Lefebvre, conceived space, the objective expression of capital, tends to *colonize* the lived space of everyday experience (Lefebvre, 1991: 42; Merrifield, 2000: 174), a process that is more or less visible, that is *perceived* to greater or less degrees; the latter then also influences space as it is socially produced. Understood through Lefebvre's spatial triad, space is a site of conflict and antagonism. A marker of the state of play within this conflict is found in shared perceptions of a space, which may be more or less at odds with space as it is planned or lived by those who inhabit it or control it.

For Lefebvre, the production of space is *necessarily* a communal activity and, given that perception is key to this work of production, it is also clear that the production of space involves a collective work of imagination (see Lefebvre, cited in Wertheim, 1999: 304). In cyberspace this requirement becomes very obvious. William Gibson, for instance, famously defined (fictional) cyberspace not only in terms of data constellations in a shared universe, but also as a 'consensual hallucination' (Gibson, 1991: 67). Cognitive and computer scientists developing early graphical interfaces also understood that acquiring the consent of the user, understood as that process by which the user was persuaded to accept and operate a virtual space through the metaphors offered for use, was essential. For these theorists, inducing a 'willing suspension of disbelief'[5] was a technical question. In contrast, to draw on Lefebvre's argument that the social production of social space is founded on antagonisms between different groups and interests is to read consent as neither purely cognitive nor purely technically achieved, but as a *social* question, one *resolving* into a material social space. In other words, the production of a virtual space over time, involving the joint construction of a shared space through an act of collective imagination, involves a form of consent having been given, having been manufactured, perhaps.

Understanding social space as containing and masking, but also as potentially *revealing*, these different moments of space and their antagonistic relations to each other, is where Lefebvre's understanding of space converges most clearly with his work on everyday life. Indeed, to work with Lefebvre is to understand everyday life partly as that which is projected into space and partly as that which takes place *as space*. Conversely, space as thus produced contains the contradictions and possibilities involved in the practice of everyday life.[6] To emphasize the role of the imagination in the production of space is not to divorce these sites from the 'real world', which would be to posit a division between 'cyberspace and the world we live in', as Kevin Robins once put it (Robins, 1996). On the contrary, even as – *especially as* – a place that is in part imaginary, cyberspace is always an ideological production, and always operates within the horizons of the social totality. The 'consensual hallucination' that is necessary to make cyberspace is always already *earthed* in the real world. Or, as Chtcheglov put it, writing about a different city, under a different sky: 'dreams spring from reality *and are realized in it*' (1981: 2).

'Free cyberspace' and beyond

The bridge . . . aslant through all the intricacy of its secondary construction. The integrity of its span was as rigorous as the modern program itself, yet around this had grown another reality, intent on its own agenda. This had occurred piecemeal, to no set plan, employing every imaginable technique and material. The result was something amorphous, startlingly organic. (Gibson, 1994: 58)

The history of the early years of the Internet has been written many times over and these accounts are not recapitulated here.[7] Rather, de Certeau's sense of narrative activity as a spatial production and Lefebvre's sense of space as a triple dialectic (Shields, 1998), are drawn on to *reread* this history as a spatial history, and to reread it in a particular way. The intention is to reinvoke the context within which virtual community (as a concept, as a blueprint for the future, as the name given to actually existing spatial productions) had a particular meaning, becoming a synecdoche for a series of Internet properties that seemed foundational to many of those commentating at the time, and that may still attach themselves to a series of expectations and understandings about virtual community although, as I've suggested, in contradictory ways. First, then, what were the *strategic* moves that produced the Internet? And who were the players? This is to look at the Internet as a history of conflict between various authorities and bodies controlling it, an exercise which provides a useful partial view of the Internet. I then go on to show that this history is bound up with other spatial practices, less strategic and more tactical, and with the discourses that arose around these practices.

Conflicts of interest: the strategic production of the Internet

Various interest groups have a claim. Business people want the Internet to be put on a sounder financial footing. Government people want the Internet more fully regulated. Academics want it devoted exclusively to scholarly research. Military people want it spy-proof and secure. (Sterling, 1993)

All of this shows how much the government can accomplish when it doesn't put its mind to it. (Wright, 1993)

Telling the story of the Internet as a tale of strategists and planners working for the establishment in the form of the US Government and its allies isn't straightforward, in part because the history of the very early years of the Internet is disputed. Popular mythologizing has produced an 'authorized version' of events that has a certain performative force. This remains attached to claims that the Internet was developed as a cold war information system, explicitly designed to withstand a nuclear attack by routing around damage (Rheingold, 1994; Sterling, 1993). Recently, historians and Internet campaigners have disputed this version of events (see the Electronic Frontier Foundation archives). However, there are areas of consensus, (EFF, 2000) around the central strategic aims of those who first developed the Internet. Firstly, whether or not it was explicitly designed by the US military to withstand a nuclear war, it *is* agreed that the ARPA/Internet was largely funded and built by the US military and was planned as a decentralized communications system based on the principle of redundancy (Dewitt, 1994; Rheingold, 1994; Abbate, 1999). Secondly, the Internet's projected use contexts might have been broader than the nuclear interpretation suggests, but there is general agreement it was *not* envisaged as a publicly available mass communications system.[8] Thirdly, there is consensus that the Internet was not designed to be a medium for interpersonal communication at all. As Janet Abbate, amongst others, points out, in her excellent history, it was intended to facilitate the swapping of *computer programs* between scientists (Abbate, 1999). The transformation of the Internet from a military network for these kinds of transactions into the highly visible public communications medium it had become in mid-1990s was something that occurred *against* the expectations of the Internet's original planners and strategists.

Two explanations offer themselves up here. Bruce Sterling's argument, symptomatic of its time,[9] has some currency. Sterling understood *conflict* between various strategists to be responsible for the 'thrivingly anarchic condition' of the Internet during the early 1990s, after privatization but before large-scale commercialization. Lending some weight to this are a series of developments in 1980s and early 1990s that meant the number of organizations involved in planning for the development of the Internet increased substantially, well before questions of control and ownership amongst these groups could be resolved. Given these developments, Sterling's argument is convincing – the more so since it was made before the advent of the World Wide Web, which resolved this conflict, at least in the sense that it decisively tipped the Internet net towards commercial dominance. As both popular and specialist publications realized almost immediately, the web, which provided a new way to see the Internet and to interact with it, cleared many of the obstacles to popular access and commercial viability. It allowed for multimedia rather than text-only pages, it made authoring relatively simple, and it made it possible to navigate the Internet efficiently and easily (see, for instance, Kelly and Woolf, 1997). A change in *relations* between the different groups involved in the *strategic* development of the Internet, which resulted in shifts in relations between users and producers, was thus inscribed into Internet space itself, since the web, of course, offering itself as a graphical terrain within which interaction took place as much through pointing and clicking as through raw coding or writing, marked a shift in the way in which Internet space was perceived, used and understood *as a space*.

The practice of space from below
Everyday life invents itself by poaching in countless ways on the property of others. (de Certeau, 1984: xii)

Sterling's argument that conflict between the different strategists determined to exploit the flexible and scaleable architecture of the Internet, meant that it developed in ways its originators had not expected, or indeed desired, is part of the story. However, contemporary historians of the Internet also recognize user activity as a significant factor in its transition from the military to the civilian sector and in its development into a mass communications system (Abbate, 1999: 182).

Many insider historians of the Internet go much further, notably those writing within organizations such as the Electronic Frontier Foundation (EFF) and its less ideological successors. These historians argue that user activity not only defined Internet space in ways that were *unforeseen* by the Internet strategists and planners, but also that users effectively *built* the Internet as a space, turning an aspect of the system that had previously been ignored (what is now understood as Internet space then being regarded as a non-space between two physical world spaces) into a vast virtual world or virtual playground (see Rheingold, 1994).

There are caveats to be made here, but it is justifiable to understand the Internet in the early periods (and in particular in the period between privatization and commercialization) to have been produced partly through user activity. The populating of netspace by myriads of users who occupied this space for their own purposes, who built within it and who collectively formed it as a space was something genuinely new. It was unforeseen by the originators of the system (including the US military, governments and the IT technology industries) and was not planned for by those new groups set to inherit it as part of what became the official plan (the commercial interests). I note that this activity was recognized as unauthorized but was not entirely or *necessarily* unwelcome; it would be a mistake to presume that all activity was directly in conflict with the planners' broader agenda, even if it was not part of any of the strategists plans.

To make this point I consider some of the 'irregular' activities that began on the Internet from early in its development (see Rheingold, 1994; EFF, 2000). The range of activity was diverse, but might be briefly categorized here under four headings.

First, it was *users* who initiated the use of the Internet for peer-to-peer communications between humans. This occurred within two years of the inception of the ARAPNET, when scientists using it for research had began to use it to pass personal messages to each other (Rheingold 1994; Goldberg, 1999; Sterling, 1993). Users were also at the forefront of developing the Internet as a mass communication (rather than interpersonal communication) space.

Second, users extended the *types* of peer-to-peer activity the Internet was used for. The first game was played across the Internet in the late 1960s, at around the same time as the first personal messages were sent, for instance.

Third, users developed permanent sites within the Internet. Near the end of the 1970s, Multi User Domains, which were semi-permanent game/ fantasy spaces enrolling users as players with particular characters, were established by UK students.[10] MUDs showed that virtual space could be used for the creation of durable sites to which users could return, and where they might meet with others. It was the sense of place, as much as the sense of connection itself, that MUDs offered, and it was this sense of place that might be said to mark out MUDs from bulletin boards (see Bassett, 1997a).

Fourth, users initiated many of the early experiments in online sociality. For these users, the sense of creating a shared, inhabited space was apparently often exhilarating in itself,[11] and the well-documented shift made by users from game-playing to social MUDS is an example of this (see Bruckman, 1993).[12] Where the spaces in which users gathered together persisted over time and became semi-permanent, they often became defined as specific places – *as virtual communities or virtual cities*. Cix in the UK, the Well in the US, and Xerox Parc's LambdaMOO were all early examples, and each points to a specific mode of development and a specific sense of place (see Rheingold, 1994, for instance).[13]

In sum, these kinds of activities helped create what users understood both as new kinds of online sociality *and* (as a part of that) new kinds of places. It is justified to suggest that, through their explorations of the different use-possibilities of these technologies, end-users[14] created new forms of *inhabitable* space. It is also justifiable to suggest that these spaces were designed to exploit in specific ways the material quality of digitally enabled space, exploring the possibilities of the medium. Many early groups, the Electronic Frontier Foundation amongst them, regarded themselves above all as *builders* on the new frontier, as people building spaces for new forms of interaction and association (see EFF, 2000; Barlow 2000).[15] The general concept of virtual community on the Internet, and specific variations on this concept (for instance virtual cities, 'cities of bits', netizens and netizenry), were not developed *retrospectively* by critical theorists to explain new kinds of Internet sociality or new kinds of Internet spaces (see W. J. Mitchell, 1995); they were *found* on the Internet and on the bulletin boards that pre-empted this kind of scholarship.

It was this popular activity that helped explode the Internet, transforming its official geometries through an unauthorized and seemingly unstoppable accretion of secondary constructions. Like William Gibson's bridge, the Internet architecture was settled, colonized, inhabited, navigated, surfed and linked by the practices of its users. The labyrinth of ad hoc sites and hyperlinks, official and unofficial, legal and illegal, which grew up around and through the official structures produced a second geography of the Internet, emerging through the first and to a degree overwriting it. The result was that the Internet became, briefly at least, a piecemeal structure. Indeed, the Internet that emerged into the public eye, after privatization but before commercialization took hold, could also be called a strangely *amorphous* space. This new space, at once planned and spontaneously organized, emerging in the slippage between privatization and commercialization, diverged from planners' expectations in many ways. Indeed, it seemed to offer evidence of a distinctive built culture of its own.

Virtual community as free community

Virtual community became a term synonymous with this new culture. Howard Rheingold's famous definition of virtual community might be invoked here, encapsulating a general sense of optimism and a series of qualities that virtual communities might be supposed to offer. On a general level, the rhetoric of virtual community emerged through a shared belief that the populating of the Internet represented a form of humanization of technology, perhaps indeed a resistant rehumanization (Jones, 1999) of technological space, a new way in which a life lived with, and even within, technology could be positive. To the extent that it reached back to the values of a mythical form of authentic community, now presumed lost, virtual community also had a nostalgic element from the start, as Jones also points out.

More specifically, the values of virtual community, as it emerged in these early years, cohered around a commitment to free association, to shared sociality and above all to building shared spaces where these kinds of interactions could prosper. Part of the rhetoric of the early Internet and of virtual community was that they were 'naturally' resistant to both commercialization and censorship; the early Internet catchphrase 'information wants to be free', after all, said something about censorship, but also implied something about commercialization.[16]

All of this was believed guaranteed (or at least made worth playing for) by a particular kind of technologically derived rupture which allowed for the production of spaces where modes of exchange were not dominated by the economic mores of the contemporary market, often regarded as (over)controlled by the State (usually the US State – and here the Libertarian tilt of the Internet activism of the time shows) but rather by the particular social mores and codes of the Internet itself. It was in this sense that virtual communities were said to be 'set apart' from the world.

The widespread parallels drawn between the original virtual communities and various forms of gift economy emerged out of these kinds of discourses, often before they were deployed around the crisis of copyright sparked by illegal downloads (see Barbrook, 2005, for instance). Indeed, the *promise* of a gift economy, understanding this term in the popular sense – where it is inflected by a form of altruism as well as self-interest – is at the heart of the general promise of virtual community: at the heart of what it promised to deliver freely to all who wanted to take part.

Making the claim that some early virtual communities did exhibit some of the characteristics described above, albeit temporarily, I am neither claiming that the original virtual communities were uniform, nor am I claiming that they were informed by a *uniform* sense of what virtual community – or Internet freedom – was, is, or ought to be. There were certainly diverse versions of community – more or less cosmopolitan, more or less parochial, in intent and practice.[17] Nor am I claiming that these spaces were at any time entirely 'out of control', if this implies that technology took them *permanently* beyond the social horizon. I do assert that some of the values later *ascribed* to the original virtual communities were actually in operation *even if*, or with the *proviso* that, these values were often contradictory, that they contained different, even conflicting, hopes or expectations, that they were never fully achieved – even in the sites that proclaimed them not as founding principles, but as descriptors of a real state of affairs. Despite the lack of precision found in these popular rhetorics they could and did operate with some force, often through shared metaphors whose potency we misrecognize today as they have become debased through overuse (see Hartmann, 2004).

Commericalization

Even those proselytizing hardest for free communities on the new frontier recognized that the Internet was vulnerable to exploitation. As Howard Rheingold put it:

The net is still out of control in many fundamental ways, but it may not stay that way for long . . . it is still possible to make sure that this vital new sphere of human discourse remains open to citizens before the political and economic big boys seize it, meter it and sell it back to us. (Rheingold, 1994: 5)

Rheingold's sense of how the Internet might be recuperated was partially accurate. The commercialization of the Internet began in earnest with the advent of graphical browsers and the World Wide Web. These developments facilitated an explosion in popular use. This made the Internet viable as a commercial proposition, and made access more available. It also exploded the hopes of those early users who were committed to the Internet as a new kind of social space. By the late 1990s, as commercialization progressed, a sense of disillusionment with the Internet as a socially progressive prospect was common amongst 'veteran users', who shared a sense that greed had 'soured' the dream (Goldberg, 1999). As one Internet pioneer put it, 'the augmentation of human intelligence has become the expansion of shopping opportunities' (Thomas Scoville, cited in Goldberg, 1999).

It was expected that virtual community would fade in the commercial Internet (contemporary industry magazines lamented this change in values). However, as part of the process of commercialization, virtual community, which was once held up as the apogee of 'free' Internet values, became a buzz-word for developers seeking to produce profitable Internet spaces of all kinds. Reflecting this, articles such as 'It takes a Village to Make a Mall' (Kelly, 1997), extolling the virtues of community as a necessary element of transactional space, proliferated in the specialist press. By late 1997, a *Business Week* article could dedicate a front cover and a leading article to the news that Internet communities were now 'shaping electronic commerce' (Hof *et al.*, 1997). In the 2000s, the production of virtual community remains important for many of the large Internet content vendors, although newer forms of Internet community tend to be offered as one component of a range of services. More, site producers in many otherwise straightforwardly transactional sites tend to offer at least vestigial features of community, or at least operate through a rhetoric of community. Different evidence of the growth and diffusion of virtual community can be found in the growth of portals, essentially gateways into the Internet that aim to persuade users to 'stick around' at their point of entry to the greater Internet, rather than surfing straight on through.[18] And there is a Second Life.

The conscious cultivation of virtual community, as a particular practice of space, has become a key Internet practice. The question is, in what form is this delivered? And in what guise is it offered? I am interested here in considering how the concept of virtual community has been retooled in the interests of commerce, asking in particular how the narrative activities of users, essential to the earlier forms of 'making space', can be understood in relation to initiatives by site producers and owners.

The business case for virtual community rests partly on how it sorts, divides and delivers target groups of potential consumers. Community sites deliver groups of users to advertisers because people tend to stay on community sites for *longer* than on non-community sites and may return regularly, becoming enrolled or invested in the community, officially or unofficially. These regular users (community members) are a better prospect as a group that can be precisely targeted by advertisers than general surfers (see Hegel and Armstrong, 1997).

A second way in which community can be exploited is through self-segmentation. A complex community, particularly one with its own sub-groups, delivers groups of users who are self-segmented. Groups emerge along recognized lines: sharing similar interests, ages or locations, for instance. These groups make efficient targets for advertisers and may actively solicit services or may seek to be visible to relevant product manufacturers or advertisers (Kim, 2000; Hegel and Armstrong, 1997).

Third, the actions of users within the grounds of a community and within its various suburbs, can be tracked. Community is thus an efficient means by which to deliver up detailed profiles for possible targets, covering the tastes, interests, activities and affiliations of users (Hegel and Armstrong, 1997; Gates, 1996; Dyson, 1997).

If the rationale for developing a commercial virtual community for e-businesses is clear as outlined above, this still leaves the question of how the producers of such sites set about cultivating virtual community. In particular, what role do users themselves play in this cultivation? This brings me to the fourth and most fundamental form of exploitation available to those who run virtual communities, which is that they rely on the users of those communities to produce the content for the site or, more fundamentally, to produce the site *as* a site, to tell its story, to provide its characters, to organize it temporally by giving it continuity as well as a history, a present, and a future. This aspect of community production subsumes the others to a large degree, since it is this that makes other forms of revenue production possible. It is also the aspect that is most *portable*.

'The ruses of fishes?'

Beginning to make this comparison between old and new community, I have been careful to avoid developing a retrospectively construed form of entirely 'authentic' cyberspace ready to be placed in opposition to its later commodified form. As Crang points out, this is a hazardous exercise and one which threatens to fail to reveal much about either term in the comparison (Crang, 1997: 359). One obvious risk here is the valorization of early cyberspace as an absolutely 'free' space, or 'temporary autonomous zone' (Bey, 1998) and the concomitant valorization of its inhabitants as social revolutionaries, which they were not. The dominant political ideology of those most vocally involved in the early production of netizen rhetoric, including the rhetoric of virtual community, was a form of right-wing libertarianism/communitarianism, something well documented in the EFF archives, among other places. The early rhetoric of the EFF itself is a case in point here; opposed to control of the Internet by big business and big government, it was by no means hostile to small enterprise and entrepreneurship. The dot.coms (and various flavours of the Open Software Movement) have their virtual ancestors.

A second hazard, however, is of swinging too far in the other direction and dismissing the early promise of cyberspace, and within that the potential of virtual community. While the early accounts of cyberspace were optimistic, and indeed unrealistic in many ways, and early cyberspace users were less radical than might at first appear, these users did articulate a belief, genuinely felt at that time and *acted* upon, that new media networks opened up real possibilities. Exploring the early settlements unmasks a desire among significant numbers of people for a different kind of space – even if, as it turned out, technology alone (the dimensionality of virtual space, the supposed indestructibility of the Internet, the virtualization of bodies) could not fully deliver this form of space, and certainly could not maintain it. To make this claim is to break with an understanding of the early years of the Internet as an entirely foolish time when obviously Utopian dreams were quite simply taken for reality.

Read through the lens of de Certeau's conception of strategic and dominant space, envisaged here partly as a contest between writing (narrative) and planning (the scopic or architectural vision), the early activities of the netizens might be understood to represent a temporary domination of lived space over conceived space. User activity on the early Internet could be viewed as a 'tactical' production of space which various official bodies tail-ended as much as controlled; at least for a time. The *ad hoc* early settlements of the internet might in this way be understood as examples of the temporary deformation of what de Certeau calls the proper (1984: 103) through the emergence of a 'second geography': a form of space simultaneous with the architecture of the city, but one produced through user activity. In so far as the user or 'screener' (Rosello, 1994: 135) makes *sense* of these text/spaces, of these cities or virtual communities, through this activity, he or she might be said to be producing narratives, *and in that act of mapping meaning to be producing space.*

This account is alluring, but also problematic in certain ways. Notably, within de Certeau's economy all writing becomes resistant and all mapping is viewed as a mode of domination. This does not mesh with the dynamics operating in early virtual communities, since many of the early users made building more *durable* spaces a key part of their activity, understanding this both as an intrinsic part of 'doing' virtual community in a particular 'place' and in some cases as their contribution to the Internet as a whole, as their architectural *legacy* to the future Internet (see the EFF archives). As Matt Hills has rightly pointed out, de Certeau's sense of resistance as *temporally* based (a momentary appropriation of space by the space-less), doesn't quite fit here (see Hills, 2001b). Nor, indeed, does Certeau's reading of the division between the visual and the written fit with the complexities of the Internet as a space where the visual and the textual, bound up in code, interconnect in new ways.

Complicit with this is a doubt about the legacy of the original virtual community as a legacy of *resistance*. Can the original forms of the virtual city or virtual community, understood as cyberspaces produced by early users, be seen as *resistant* productions of space, precisely? Working within de Certeau's register this conclusion is hard to avoid since, for de Certeau, all kinds of activity from below, from the 'ruses of fishes' to the narrativizing practices of those walking in the city, are classified as resistant, and are to be celebrated. Within this spatial economy it is difficult to make distinctions between action as considered resistance, and action as involuntary movement – Brownian motion, a form of circulation *produced* or provoked by the system or in response to the system and entirely contained by it.

The notion of space de Certeau provides might thus be said to model ideological ambiguities inherent in the concept of virtual community itself, and to raise questions about how its legacy has been delivered to later users and also to what effect. If virtual community, as a legacy concept, also confuses conscious resistance with activity intrinsic to the system, then it is possible to see how virtual community users, subscribing to its mores, might both be exploited and believe themselves to be 'free'. This might suggest one way in which the legacy of 'virtual community' might function ideologically, one way that it might be an ambiguous legacy.

To consider how this ideological construction figures within the spatial dynamic requires stepping beyond de Certeau. Lefebvre's tripartite model of the production of space, where space *as it appears to us* is one element in a tripartite spatial dynamic, is useful here, and I return to it below, noting here that it also produces a rather different understanding of the relationship between narrative and space as a social production. These themes are explored in relation to GeoCities: an heir to older forms of community, an heir to the ambiguous legacy they left behind – but now embarked on a trajectory distancing it from these origins.

Lefebvre suggested that in investigating space as a social production 'the [problem] is to get back from the object [the present space] to the activity that produced or created it' (Lefebvre, 1991: 113). My resolution of this difficulty has been to look the space of GeoCities longitudinally – to see how it has changed over time – and to explore in some detail how the space of the Cities was and is made. In pursuit of this, the changing spatial dynamics of GeoCities are examined at close range below, with the intention of asking how agonistic and collaborative practices of space have shaped that community over time. This exploration reveals something about the complex process of commercialization of a virtual community. It shows how far and how much user practices (lived practices) have been dominated or colonized by the planners and strategists who own the space, and also begins to reveal how this space is seen and understood (perceived). This process is read as it is inscribed in the history of the space itself. It is a means by which to 'reconstitute the process of [a site's] genesis and the development of its meaning' (Merrifield, 2000: 171). As part of this I also explore how ideas of virtual community influence the ways in which contemporary virtual communities are produced; their legacies, which are discursive as well as material, operate as an element within the formation of later virtual communities; in other words, what begins as discourse may here later be expressed as a contradiction within material social space: a contradiction in code.

'Megabytes of creativity': GeoCities

We appreciate your interest and support of GeoCities and pledge to you our continued support in building the Societies of the New Frontier. (GeoCities, 1998a)

GeoCities is a long-standing commercial virtual community founded in 1994 by David Bohnett, listed on NASDAQ in 1998, and taken over by the giant Internet pureplay Yahoo! in 1999. GeoCities was one the first commercial Internet sites to recuperate the original logic of virtual community, and is interesting since it began by deferring not only to the traditional building models for virtual community, but also in various ways to the *values* of original virtual community. The Cities' 'authentic' netizen ethos was one of its main attractions, at least in the beginning. Many of its earlier members joined it to escape the process of rampant commercialization perceived as going on elsewhere on the Internet (Henig,

Red Herring, 1998). This adherence, however, was strained as the company came under increasing pressure to deliver revenues on the back of its service; bluntly, to make virtual community pay. In pursuit of this goal, the development of the site moved away from formal adhesion to the early ideals of virtual community, so that although the production of space explored here has much to do with older models of virtual community, it also breaks with, or rewrites, the traditions of virtual community in increasing numbers of ways. The question of how that break was managed and produced is considered below.

The early history of GeoCities runs from its launch to the takeover, a second stage begins with the takeover and the consequent integration of GeoCities into Yahoo! The Cities were explicitly launched in the spirit of the early Internet, and Bohnett, whose computer industry background was supplemented by his gay activism, claimed that the intention of the site was not to make money but to promote a free and open discussion forum (ZDNET, 1998; Hansell, 1998; Henig, *Red Herring*, 1998; Bohnett, cited in GeoCities, 1998e). In an address to users, Bohnett/GeoCities claimed that 'building Societies of the New Frontier' could be a mutual endeavour (David Bohnett, in GeoCities, 1998f). However, despite Bohnett's ambiguous attitude to the exploitation of virtual community and his espousal of 'standards consistent with the Internet community' (GeoCities, 1998e) which marked his attachment to 'old' Internet values, GeoCities was organized as a commercial proposition from the start.

The basic covenant between users and owners, established when the site began, makes this commercial logic evident, and deserves a closer look. GeoCities set out to give users 'free' space to 'build their homepage and join the publishing community on the web' (GeoCities, 1998f). Once built, sites were hosted on GeoCities servers located within the virtual community of the Cities, often within a specific neighbourhood. All of this was free at the point of use but gave GeoCities some considerable rights, firstly over the material users produced and secondly over the contexts in which this material was displayed. In fact, the bulk of GeoCities' revenues always came from selling advertising through banner ads sited against members' pages as the company's own report to the Securities and Investment Commission (SEC) makes clear (GeoCities, 1998g). As various users pointed out, this covenant meant that the GeoCities service was never actually free at all, but involved an exchange, at best, since it was *users* who created the vast majority of the content against which the ads were sold (See, 1998).

Having built their websites and chosen their locations, the early homesteaders uploaded these sites and advertised them in various ways around GeoCities. At this point, the users got their 'eleven megabytes' of creative presence on the web, and simultaneously the real estate of GeoCities increased by the same proportion. Each new site therefore constituted a new asset, one that was additional to the simple inclusion of the name of the new member on a database of site users (who could be sold to). More, this was an increase in real terms: GeoCities has always declared that it *owned* the content of these sites, even while its Guidelines firmly located *responsibility* for content with users (GeoCities, 1998d).[19] This, non-coincidentally, constitutes a very neat inversion of the division between moral rights and copyright that is intended to protect the rights of authors in UK copyright law.

GeoCities itself was clear that the basis of its operation was the content its users produced. In a report to the SEC, as far back as the late 1990s, it declared that its business model relied on members and community leader volunteers, user content generation, grass roots promotional efforts by GeoCities users, and voluntary involvement of members in attracting users to the GeoCities site (GeoCities, 1998g). User generated 'content' in this sense means not only material produced by users inside their homepages, but also activities within the wider virtual community itself, since this also emerges through user work of all kinds. In the case of GeoCities it encompassed not only traditional 'content', in the shape of the tagged words or images that form the content of a homepage or even of a neighbourhood, but also those interactions through which the Cities were *invested* with feeling; the emotional labour of construction, either through authoring or interaction, might also be understood as a form of content. It was through such interactions and such authoring actions that community came to be felt, or that community became a *meaningful* term to use to describe these sites. To this extent the 'traditional' model of virtual community, involving the elaboration of a second geography over a formal architecture, still pertains here; user activity made this a *lived* space.

This activity took different forms but was centrally concerned with various kinds of construction. Joining GeoCities involved giving some fairly basic demographic details, and waiting a few minutes for confirmation. The way was then open to become a GeoCities homesteader – and the latter label is apt: GeoCities has its side attractions but it has always promoted itself above all as a building community, offering members hosted space and software building tools, the digital equivalent of bricks and mortar and a plot of land. Over the years of its operation vast numbers of sites have been produced by people taking up the offer to host personal homepages for free. These pages often do little more than echo the name, sex, age check of chat sites, but supplement this with various forms of authenticating data – pet pictures, spouse pictures, off-screen interests; more importantly they give users a durable or semi-permanent identity online. Simple biographical homepages aside, other popular 'genres' of site on GeoCities included specialized resource sites, more-or-less permanent tribute sites, and fan sites (famous early sites included one about Monty Python and one about Hollywood), these last gaining by far the most hits. Many thousands of GeoCities pages remain entirely unedited after construction, and to this extent are one-offs. Others, however, are more or less continuously upgraded. In addition, new sites did and do spring up very quickly in relation to specific events. The work of building content and updating content, which is *work carried out by users,* has always been a permanent feature within the GeoCities' environment. Although GeoCities bans unfinished pages from a listing of exemplary sites, the site as a whole is actually always 'under construction'.

During the early years of GeoCities websites could be located within one of the forty or so GeoCities neighbourhoods, each one relating to a particular preoccupation, activity or interest. Many neighbourhoods were named with reference to real-life places: Bourbon Street for jazz lovers, Capitol Hill for politics, for instance. Other sites in GeoCities skipped any reference to physical world location (or real world metaphorical nexus) and simply named the interests they represented. The 'family' community, with its suburbs including 'heartland' and 'religion', was an example of this. Some of the early neighbourhood spaces were highly elaborated, and the most popular were also very crowded so that later entrants had to find residencies off the main streets. Some inhabitants of these neighbourhoods produced newsletters, or managed other aspects of neighbourhood business. Some became community leaders or volunteers, helping to organize community sites, or offering their building skills to newcomers. This kind of volunteer programme, which was also very evident in other online services, grew very quickly in GeoCities' early years. It too amounted to a form of narrative construction, this time not of a single site but a neighbourhood.

Neighbourhoods were one of the ways in which the GeoCities collection of websites were linked together, both by users themselves and through various initiatives organized by GeoCities' owners. These pages were also linked through various forms of branding. The links, the branding and the semi-permanent neighbourhoods provided some coherence, so the GeoCities site gained a meaningful geography and could be mapped – at least in theory. Certainly from very early on GeoCities was a *navigable* space. Early users could confine their surfing to their own neighbourhoods and/or to particular sites or they could choose to surf the GeoCities space more extensively, dropping into different neighbourhoods, using different services, finding chat sites or joining discussion groups. Finally, users were always free, although never encouraged, to exit GeoCities into the rest of the Internet. In surfing, users made the site as a whole live.

Appropriation or production?

The homesteading and surfing practices of users within GeoCities allowed users to make 'maps of meaning' in this new form of everyday life (Squires, 1994: 2). In so far as they produced their own spaces and used their own routes and pathways to explore the wider space of the Cities, the conditions and activities of users in the commercial space of GeoCities might be understood as indistinguishable from those of the original cyberspace 'settlers'. Following de Certeau these everyday user practices in virtual space might be understood as narrative practices, as stories that traverse and organize (de Certeau, 1984: 115), and that might also be productive of a space of some kind. De Certeau, however, understood these other spaces to inhabit time, unlike the built city which inhabits space. A difference here is that in virtual space these tracks *persist* beyond the moment of their being walked. The GeoCities site indeed might be seen as being largely constructed as a mesh of such user stories, whether these are narratives consisting of topographic perambulations or narratives expressed in the biographical homepages. As a consequence, GeoCities *as a whole*, lived city emerged through the embodied and affective practices of users who committed to this space and who made it *mean* something. The *narrative* activity of users, the actions they took and the community they envisioned, was thus very directly recuperated, *and was taken up into the enduring fabric of the community itself.*

GeoCities as a programmed space

All Bourbon Street homesteaders must comply with the above statement. If you do not comply, your page will be put on our 'page alert' and might be referred to GeoCities for proper examination. (Bourbon Street, 1998)

The only code we require to be on ALL of your .html pages (including pages with frames) is a reference back to GeoCities. (GeoCities, 1998e)

If the users of GeoCities practised space, so did its owners, who were not content simply to capture users and to recuperate their assets (their content), but sought to maximize these assets. As a result, GeoCities was from the beginning a cultivated space, one that was both variegated and branded. While the terrain was given its *substance* largely by users, it was *architected* and *conformed* by the site owners in various ways, some of which are addressed below.

GeoCities was shaped through a series of operations that marked out the terrain, mapping it and encouraging internal circulation, and marking the outer walls. Indeed, a wall of words has always buttressed GeoCities in the form of a series of user codes and regulations (GeoCities, 1998e). The codes set out GeoCities policy on child safety, on bigoted and obscene writings, on use of sites for business. They also included the GeoCities policy on trust and commerce, and on privacy (1998c),[20] extensive FAQs (Frequently Asked Question files) and other documents concerning acceptable conduct. These codes functioned as performative declarations, clearly intended to cultivate growth on the site in particular ways. GeoCities set out quite consciously to be a 'well lit space'; there were 'zones for tourism' in the early days of GeoCities, but there were never 'zones for love' in this new kind of city space. Pornography and nudity were banned on member pages, and so was hate speech and other content deemed objectionable.

The subdivision of the forty or so themed communities mentioned was another operation designed to regulate the city space. These communities provided a varied terrain within a vast overarching environment, too big to grasp as something with a single identity. Many neighbourhoods had their own main streets and their less desirable suburbs, where newcomers often had to find housing. Some of these environments had co-opted leaders, some had their own newsletters, and all developed a specific feel. All of this neighbourhood activity was actively promoted in the early days of GeoCities. Other tropes were also adopted to variegate the virtual space of GeoCities: an example was the 'Landmark Sites' programme (GeoCities, 1998b), designed to make a series of well-produced or interesting sites more visible to users. These landmarks landscaped what would otherwise have been a largely empty terrain, since user sites did not routinely appear in overviews of GeoCities. Here user-produced *substance* was used to make the GeoCities terrain as a whole more dense.

Finally, attempts were made not only to encourage the building of particular kinds of environments, but also to generate and direct user traffic around them. In GeoCities many possible routes and pathways were made available and visible, whilst other routes and forms of circulation were circumscribed or unsigned; although this was not the plotted possibility of game space (Solnit, 1995), where free moment is illusory, it was *cued* in particular ways. In particular, surfing was directed within the Cities partly through the rule that all GeoCities sites include a coded pointer back to the GeoCities homepage (GeoCities, 1998e).

Among other initiatives designed to programme how users moved through and around the cities was the GeoTickets system, which was designed to encourage users to display advertising banners from other users, from GeoCities itself and from commercial sponsors on their homepages (see GeoCities, 1998j). GeoTickets was partly a bid to exploit the user's space as marketable space (a standard practice with free e-mail services such as Hotmail), but it was also designed to produce a cross-pollination of GeoCities pages and services by encouraging user movement around the site and *circumscribing* this movement within the GeoCities orbit. Developing (or buying in) internal search engines, so that users had no need to leave the Cities to search, was a similar strategy (see ZDNet, 1998b) and also an example of the priority given to increasing as well as directing surfing.

These kinds of activities became increasingly elaborate as GeoCities developed, and eventually they produced some conflicts with users. Typical of this trajectory was the watermark programme[21] that allowed the company to stamp its visual mark on every sidewalk and every home space in GeoCities *as this space was built* (see GeoCities, 1998j). The controversy over watermarks began in 1998 when GeoCities declared that as part of the contract between the user and GeoCities, a watermark would appear on all user pages, constantly reforming itself to appear at the bottom right hand of the screen as the screener scrolled. The owned environment would now wrap itself around the browsing user, and interpenetrate the work of the homesteader at all points. This seemed to mark a real change in space, since the watermark meant that, while there were thousands of ostensibly private as opposed to public spaces within GeoCities, *nowhere* were there spaces that were unbranded, and there never would be, since GeoCities would be branded as it grew. The kind of online living offered by GeoCities might thus be characterized as a form of branded residency, far from the kinds of community living envisaged by the early cyberspace settlers, and indeed from the De Certeau's sense of a form of inhabitation that involved *ad hoc* settlements within a 'universe of rented spaces' (de Certeau, 1984: 103) of a form of living beneath the notice of strategists, although still within their city. There was considerable dissent over the Watermarks programme. Some users felt that the spirit of the agreement between GeoCities and its users, whereby users donated content and GeoCities hosted space was distorted by what they viewed as GeoCities' attempts to take over the design of 'their' pages (See, 1998).

In all of the ways discussed above, GeoCities' owner's activities were focused on recuperating the activities of users, redirecting their energy into the production of a virtual space conceived of as likely to be commercially successful. Further, it is clear that this process did not by any means stop short at the entrance to the user's 'home'. On the contrary, the process of branding and shaping – of *cultivating* – penetrates down into users' own pages in increasingly aggressive ways. Read in this light, the *explicit* offer GeoCities made to users, which is that they would get their 'own' web space 'for free' is certainly not delivered upon; as users pointed out, space in GeoCities was never free. However, the *implicit* contract which said that users would get their own 'private' hosted web space in exchange for producing content and for building a community space, was also delivered in a less than consistent way. Indeed, it was a promise delivered upon less and less, as the watermarks controversy, which represented a tussle over the ownership and control of the users' space, and even over their identity, suggests.[22]

A final consideration here is why so many users accepted the bargain as offered, and accepted it willingly enough not simply to take their space, but actively to build community within it, by offering up their stories, by accepting the narrative of virtual community and realizing it by 'walking' or navigating in this city. One answer here might be that even while GeoCities operated the virtual community model along commercial lines, it deferred fairly closely to the rhetoric which declared virtual community a free space of exchange and a site for affinity and connection. On the other hand, a commercial logic meant that, in the end, netizen values, or the values 'traditionally' understood to pertain to virtual community as it had grown up in the free Internet, were increasingly subordinated to the logic of commerce.

Mainstream integration: GeoCities and Yahoo!

By 1997 GeoCities had claimed its first million members, and in early 1999 was cited as one the four most trafficked sites on the web, with over two million web pages listed in its domain. The watermarks programme was introduced in 1998, in the run-up to GeoCities' listing as a public company, and around about the time that beginnings of disquiet in the business world over GeoCities' prospects as a commercial entity began to be voiced (see Goodwins, 1999). In these contexts, GeoCities' business model came under scrutiny, and the pressure to deliver revenue from user content grew since, while the strategy of GeoCities owners evidentially worked as a model for attracting members, it was not so successful as a model for making money. By 1999, when the company went public and floated on NASDAQ, it was already having to work hard to convince an increasingly sceptical stock market of the advantages of the low overheads involved in publishing a site which was created 'by millions of volunteers' (Hansell, 1998). The stock markets'/analysts' understanding of GeoCities, indeed, underscores the fact that user activity created this community, as it created other earlier ones. The 'bottom line' was that the original virtual community paradigm, with its reliance on 'free' user activity *remained* in GeoCities in its early years, and it was this that was potentially problematic to the market since analysts at once recognized the power of the user within this model and feared this power as a factor producing uncertainty.

A contemporary news report summed up GeoCities' dilemma when it suggested that 'it is not clear whether the service [GeoCities] can build its business without alienating its members' (Hansell, 1998). Bohnett himself expressed this dilemma at around about the same time in a response to unease around the watermarks programme, commenting that, 'We [at GeoCities] have to balance freedom of expression with commercial viability. Otherwise all of this will go away' (GeoCities, 1998k).

Increasingly, analysts agreed that the business model was difficult (see Peter F. Fitzgibbon, Chris Byron and Francis Gaskin, cited in Henig, *Red Herring*, 1998). In May 1999 GeoCities was bought by another Internet pureplay, Yahoo!, for $2.67bn (Reuters, 1999; Lash, 1999). The link between Yahoo!, with its vast indexes, and GeoCities, with its active population of users, is itself an indication of the priority accorded to various forms of community by the commercial interests seeking to exploit cyberspace. This acquisition was part of a general shift at the time. Other sites specializing in free web space were also bought up in the same period, Tripod and AngelFire,[23] for instance, being acquired by Lycos (See 1998).

In June 1999, Yahoo! announced integration of the two services, opening Yahoo!Geocities and welcoming 'the GeoCommunity' to its fold. At the same time Yahoo!, which had always said it would integrate GeoCities tightly inside its own operations, rolled out a fairly radical restructuring of the site (ZDNET, 1999b). By 2001, the space of GeoCities had changed greatly. The integration into Yahoo! led to the abolition of the old spatial metaphor of streets, operating as a form of *visual* mapping. The top level of the Yahoo!GeoCities interface became consistent with Yahoo!, working squarely on the concept of the page or the directory. Second, many of the old neighbourhoods were killed off or reorganized. Old addresses stopped working and former users or former visitors, returning to the site and using the old addresses, were summarily directed back to the Yahoo!GeoCities homepage. Third, as part of this reorganization many community programmes were restructured and some community leader programmes closed.

Some of the community and neighbourhood leaders revolted when GeoCities declared them no longer necessary and a skirmish, if not a war, in cyberspace went on, as some of these former leaders headed off into exile.[24] The ambiguity over who owned these neighbourhood spaces, which were built through the emotional and physical labour of their residents on GeoCities' grounds was thus rather brutally resolved. GeoCities owned the disputed 'hoods – and therefore its new owners had the right to abolish them.

After integration, GeoCities' front end looked and felt far more like a two-dimensional search engine than like a multi-dimensional community space. The rhetoric of community, and indeed the kind of rhetoric that more easily attaches itself to a space with more than two dimensions, remained in the textual address that GeoCities made to its users, but this textual allusion to community itself often became skeuomorphic, something once practical but now decorative, maintained through tradition rather than having a meaningful function in its changed environment.[25] In this sense the space of GeoCities has not only been extensively redefined and reorganized as it has been integrated into Yahoo!, it has in some sense been *contracted*, perhaps *streamlined*. Certainly the strategic view of the Cities now belongs indubitably to Yahoo! And at the same time ground-level residency and navigation in GeoCities is now obviously performed on Yahoo's terms and in full view. There are few of the idiosyncrasies, the informal groupings or the *ad hoc* spaces of the early years. Clearly there is a new economy of space operating in GeoCities. Today GeoCities is advertised as a free web-hosting site with the catch-line 'share your personality with the world, for free'.

Two ways to read these developments offer themselves up. The first focuses on the change in the visible economy, the second on a change in the practice of space that produces this shift (the practice that produced representations, as Crang put it), but both are bound up together and also relate to the changing ways in which user action can be conceived of within these spaces. The changes in this virtual community might recapitulate on a small scale more general shifts occurring across the Internet as it developed. In the early days of the Internet, as I have shown, users seemed at times entirely to overwhelm the strategists' and planners' conceptions of Internet space, imposing upon it their own sense of geography. At this point the productions of users were unusually visible; this was an economy characterized by architectural exuberance on the part of users as well as by surveillance on the part of Internet strategists. In the new Internet, as exemplified by the new GeoCities, user activity is bound increasingly tightly into a spatial dynamic dominated and organized by the new planners and strategists, so that visibility is organized to produce a form of efficient control.

This development might be understood to deactivate users. Paul Virlio has argued that deactivation is a feature of all virtual spaces, since these spaces are produced through increasingly absolute environmental control as non-spaces, constantly re-forming in real time around the expressed needs and wants of their inhabitants (Virilio, 1997: 25). Those who use these spaces can no longer be viewed as walkers, and can no longer trace out their narrative of the city across its grounds. Rather they are immobilized, or, as Virilio has it, 'prostheticized to the eyeballs'. Not *even* the most fleeting tactical gesture, one made in the temporal interstices of an entirely owned space, is possible here, since there is no possibility of any meaningful response to any imaginative interpretation of an environment from which one is not differentiated (or rather into which one is continually reinserted). Virilio's suggestion is that the *pleasures*[26] of cyberspace are to be understood precisely in terms of this kind of immobility, being based around a model of disability and attenuation. This account of the digital in terms of an aesthetic of disability (Volkhart, 1999) certainly has its resonances with some digital forms, particularly games (see *Wired*, 1998), where the prosthetic perspective is offered up as a way of increasing control. A *Wired* 'Fetish' column once went as far as to include the UR Gear headset 'invented for the physically challenged as an alternative to the mouse' as a piece of equipment offering 'no-hand control over the PC' (*Wired*, 1998).

It is the case that in the new more tightly controlled GeoCities space users no longer navigate in the same way, are no longer invited to explore and tour, and are no longer free to build a collective narrative of their community in the way that they were. However, the account of virtual community developed above makes it clear that user *activity* of some kind is integral to virtual community, not only as this space is perceived, but as it is planned and lived. GeoCities increasing extended its control over its users, often through environmental 'improvements' such as the branding programme and later the shift to directory structures, but that extension of control required user action, since it was users who operationalized those changes in architecture, making spaces through the production of forms of content that gave those spaces both substance and shape. User activity not only persists in GeoCities (early and late) but it remains *essential* to the construction of these spaces.

At issue, then, is not whether action has become inaction, precisely. Rather, we need to ask how 'action' is to be understood, and how it might have changed. Julian Stallabrass's apt description of computer games as providing not only an illusion of scene, but also of action (Stallabrass, 1996: 101) is suggestive here since, in so far as GeoCities became a space operating high levels of environmental control, it might be said to begin to come closer to a configured games environment than to a 'free' terrain. It certainly comes far closer to this than it might at first sight. On the other hand, as we have said, action is key here, and this action is real in the sense that it is productive of space. However, Stallabrass's formulation could be reworked in the case of GeoCities, which might viewed as a space that produces an illusion of informality and free action, even while it operates as an ever more highly organized site for structured consumption.

The shift from early to late GeoCities, typical of shifts in the Internet as a whole, can then be understood to cohere around the move from 'free' action to 'conformed' action, rather than marking a move from action to inaction.

Remaining focused on action rather than inaction makes sense in relation to GeoCities. This is so since the narrativization of space, in homepages, and through hyperlinks, continues to give substance, and with substance to give *meaning*, to GeoCities as a spatial production. The practice of the user thus remains integral to the production of the space, since in the Cities actions by the user, observed and understood through techniques of surveillance, promote a concomitant response from the environment, so that the built space of the city increasingly responds directly to the users' solicited practices, the users thereby being offered more of what they want or need. To understand the GeoCities space as one in which the more the user does, the better the fit between user and space, has some implications. It suggests, first, that the production of space 'there' *does* remain configurable in terms of a dynamic between the practices of user and those of producers, so what is configured can be understood as a form of narrativization, that is promoted and directly recuperated partly through the use of surveillance techniques. Secondly, it is clear that the scopic view is deployed here not only for control purposes, but also in the interests of recuperating this activity from below.

Paradoxically, this dynamic both reintroduces the possibility of meaningful resistance to commercialization, as something that is separate from or distinct from action in and of itself, and invites reconsideration of what such a resistance would amount to. Setting aside Virilio's frozen pessimism, but also the romance of tactical resistance and de Certeau's sense of space as a closed game of strategy and tactics in which one side has all the vision and the other only a form of subterranean writing, I here turn back to recap Lefebvre's rather different sense of the social production of space.

For Lefebvre, space is symbolic of social relations as a whole and the dominance of particular forms of space over others encapsulates the dynamics and the contradictions of a particular social system. The analogies between Lefebvre's sense of space as containing and expressing (secreting) social contradictions, and Jameson's sense of narrative as a socially symbolic act can be linked together here. For Jameson, narratives carry with them the conditions in which they come to be produced – as he says, like a map, or a dream, or a prayer (1981: 81), while for Lefebvre:

> Socio-political contradictions are realized spatially. The contradictions of space thus make the contradictions of social relations operative. In other words, spatial contradictions 'express' conflicts between socio-political

interests and forces; it is only in space that such conflicts come effectively into play, and in doing so they become contradictions of space. (Lefebvre, 1991: 365)

This moves us on from the narrative space de Certeau offers, in which narrative emerges as a practice of space from below within an endless game between the tactical and the strategic, where the ground-rules are always already fixed. Locating the narrativization of space within Lefebvre's tripartite framework of lived space, conceived space and perceived space or spatial practices opens the way to rethinking the relationship between the narrative the user constructs and the shape of the space itself. In other words, the narrative practice of the user is drawn into the spatial production as a whole, becoming part of a larger narrative span which is intrinsically collective. Narratives are thus not only to be found in the trails produced through lived practices of users, although these narratives do help make the city. Rather it is the city as it is produced from moment to moment *which offers itself to us a narrative to be read.*

Bringing narrative back into the frame here allows a return to consideration of the city as *imagined* as well as real space. Regarding the virtual city as an imaginary city (as other cities are also imaginary) we can understand it as a kind of resolution in *poesis*, containing and exceeding all the interactions between humans and other agents and/in virtual space. The key term here, the term that allows us to move between imaginary conceptions of a space and the real operations of a space, and that connects us also to various ideological connotations related to community and technology, is virtual community; which might be understood in this way as an ideologeme. I mean by this that it operates to connect a certain material organization of narrative (in this case a spatial organization), with a certain ideological formation. Thus the relationship between early and later forms of virtual community can be read in terms of a promise 'about' virtual community, already present, but also developing in the early history and inscribed in contemporary spatial productions. The new Cities is an example here since it maintains a formal commitment to community while in fact offering users private spaces in which to produce public faces of themselves, a move which produces these private spaces as also public. This formal adhesion to community, operational within an increasingly public private life, but one that is also increasingly privatized, operates also in other parts of everyday life. We are looking therefore at the reworking of a material practice, and at an ideological construction.

Contradictory reintegration
The history of virtual community so far is a history not primarily of technological advance, nor of user resistance to specific advances or to

specific strategic developments. Rather it is a history of the reintegration
and alignment of a particular form of space. GeoCities has been progressively more tightly integrated into the mainstream through the process of
commercialization but, however far the new GeoCities moved from the
old mores of cyberspace, it was integrated into Yahoo! *as a space that
still involves complex social bonds* (see Osborne, 1995: 165), because
it still set out to deliver (or work with the rhetoric of) 'community', and
was never stripped down to become merely a transactional space. On
the contrary, the promise of virtual community was centred (1) on the
reinvigoration of discourse (on technology providing a new way to
connect, or perhaps to reconnect), and (2) on the creation of a space in
which particularity can be celebrated, and these promises still inform
GeoCities. Users are still offered a community space and the chance to
develop a home site of their own, a site to express 'megabytes of creativity',
(more and more megabytes, in fact). Commercial virtual community
remains recognizable *as* a virtual community, and indeed delivers on the
early rhetoric in some ways.

In sum, GeoCities provides evidence that the early hopes for the Internet
as a different kind of communications space, one that is more free, have
been reinscribed. On the one hand virtual reality, now conceived as a
'brand' of cyberspace, still promises a space in which individual creativity
and free association are possible on tap and are celebrated. On the other
hand, the political economy of Yahoo!GeoCities as a commercial leisure
operation offering 'chat and build' facilities 'free of charge' at the point
of use means that these promises are *delivered* in particular ways.

This is a process of contradictory reintegration. Peter Osborne, whose
work on everyday life I am drawing on here, cites Etienne Balibar on the
operation of this process and the latter's account is useful in underscoring
how the reintegration of virtual community (or of other social forms) can
be understood to hinge on the *expansion* of the value form (by contrast
the gift economy arguments might imply its contraction). Balibar is
concerned with explaining the history of the particular forms of
development of capitalist societies as '[the] history of the reactions of the
complex of "non economic" social relations, which are the binding agent
of a historical collectivity of individuals, to the destructuring with which
the expansion of the value form threatens them' (Balibar, cited in Osborne,
1995: 165). This is the process we can observe in GeoCities.

In the new economy of virtual community, the consumer becomes part
of an exchange, getting a 'well lit' community space alongside a space to
build. This free space increasingly becomes a means by which the user is
individuated, rather than, or as well as, a means of individual expression.
More than that, it is the user's work that is corralled into the general effort

to build the space. And this returns us to space and narrativization since it is this narrative practice, the practice of making meaning itself, that is also increasingly recuperated and commodified. Finally, it is important to note here that users understand very well that this is what they are getting. To discuss the evolution of virtual community, as it is finally delivered to many more people, is to talk of a process to which users *consent*.

The evolution of virtual community can thus be understood as a process characterized by the *commodification* of the *prospect* of the free economy that the Internet seemed at one time to hold out. What is unmasked if the role of the promise of virtual community, read here as the promise of free space, in constructing GeoCities is considered, is that virtual community is quite simply a commodity. The myth of the virtual city (of the early free Internet) and the myth of originary community (which originally fuelled this metaphor), redeployed in different ways in early and late GeoCities, both conceal, in a 'fantastic form', the relations of production which underpin them: inscribed in material technology, produced through a space with a particular dimensionality, but essentially *social* relations.

Conclusion

To know how and what space internalizes is to learn how to produce something better, how to produce another city . . . (Merrifield, 2000: 173)

Lefebvre defines a kind of space he calls differential space (1991). It is different from other kinds of space, not because it has a particular dimensionality or because it operates a particular textual or visual economy, but because it is not a commodity. As such it is, as Merrifield has it, different to the core. 'It is different because it celebrates particularity – both bodily and experiential . . . true differential space is a burden . . . it places unacceptable demands on accumulation and growth' (Merrifield, 2000: 176). We might find here the nub of what the respatialization of the Internet has entailed. It has entailed the repression of the hope that the Internet might be a zone where 'true differential space' might be practised. In the place of this hope, what we see is an increasingly commodified form of space in with particularity is ironed out in favour of an increasingly detailed and quantifiable, but ultimately depersonalizing and dehumanizing, environment; and by dehumanizing here I refer to alienation rather than cyborgization per se.

GeoCities shows how capital can be understood to produce space, even in conditions of virtuality. In GeoCities it is evident that the morphology of form which is supposed to override social action is itself produced in response to the market. In other words, this is a space morphologized by a process of exchange in which users create a space following the call to order issued by a particular organization of space, a particular set of

162 The arc and the machine

conditions, some of which are historical, all of which are ideological. If the meat of Castells's claim for the networked society is that the morphology of networks takes precedence over social action (1996), my claim is that the morphology of networks is not explainable in terms of a technical logic, but is produced through the social totality. The 'network logic', which Castells read as semi-autonomous, is actually a social logic. It is only if one is clear-headed about this, that one can find in everyday life in virtual spaces the 'starting point for the realization of the possible'. Thus, where de Certeau valorizes a certain form of invisibility, a certain form of writing that can always be pitted against the vision machine, whatever its structure, Lefebvre, in the end, seeks a more radical unmasking of the whole.

Notes

1 It is this 'written-wordiness' that the web has already bequeathed to its predecessor forms; see for instance close captioning, the multi-windowed screens of CNN or Fox, or the design of the *Independent*.
2 I am reminded here of Dagognet's sense that weight is elaborated visually as a necessary feint in a world where technology is characterized by its lightness. As Dagognet puts it: 'man is uneasy about living in lightness because he has lived for so long amidst heaviness and horizontality. The architect is therefore forced to feign heavy pillars of load-bearing surfaces in order to reassure man. The imagination lags behind and resists the transition' (1989: 16). This might produce virtual communities in which the visual or textual elaboration of geography is no longer necessary at all. These would not be spaces without geographies nor spaces without stories.
3 Massey contrasts this position with that of Laclau, who declares politics and space to be antinomic terms (see Massey, 1994: 250).
4 Internal corporate motto: 'don't do evil' . . .
5 Coleridge's phrase was widely adopted by the early graphical user-interface developers (see Kay, 1990).
6 As Merrifield puts this, 'everyday life . . . internalizes all three moments of Lefebvre's spatial triad' (2000: 176).
7 I am explicitly comparing the old and new Internets and I do believe a basic division between the 'free' and commercial Internets can still justifiably be made, and indeed is important to make. However, I note that any chronological division between a 'late' and 'early' Internet is somewhat ragged. Early exploiters of the Internet recuperated the rhetoric of the 'free' Internet, and the logic of virtual community, very rapidly, and incorporated it into their sales plans and their marketing well ahead of the mainstream. The second factor here concerns online services. Although they were later somewhat eclipsed in histories of the net, the presence and influence on the early net culture of commercial online services such as CompuServe (which initially resisted virtual community and social chat) and AOL (which made a virtue of it from the start) (Bulkeley, 1996), were considerable.

8 Arguably it was the technologically engineered 'equilibrium' of the Cold War that left the space for communication to begin to disengage from its military niche and be inserted (also) into the commercial sphere. At any rate, as Druckery points out, these processes were occurring simultaneously (Druckery, 1999: 16).

9 See also for instance the strapline to 'The Battle for the Internet' in *Time* magazine in 1994, which asks 'is there room for everyone?' The article goes to suggest that the Internet is being 'pulled from all sides: by commercial interests . . . governments . . . veteran users . . .'.

10 Abbate puts this as 1995 (1999: 200). This indicates the difficulties in documenting the Internet precisely. Some of these problems with dating emerge because parallel networks operated with limited connections before being fully integrated.

11 As an example, we could turn to the words of John Perry Barlow, Internet activist, who wrote a declaration of freedom of cyberspace beginning, 'I come from cyberspace new home of the mind . . .' (EFF, 2000).

12 This might explain the popularity of chat-rooms, which could be defined as spaces where nothing happens *except* connection in a shared space.

13 Cix began as a UK bulletin-board system with a largely technical population, mostly centred on London. The WELL, a US virtual community, was aptly described by *Business Week* as an example of an attempt 'to take the counter-culture to the digerati' (Hof *et al.* 1997). LambdaMOO is a social MUD which began as a formal experiment in computer mediated communication, but moved far beyond the expectations of its founder, Pavel Curtis, and its owner, Xerox (Curtis, 1993), becoming a site renowned for social experimentation, gender switching, digital activism – and visited by academic researchers of all kinds.

14 As Abbate points out, the distinction was extremely hard to draw in the early days of the Internet when the developers were the users. The point, perhaps, is that use practices as much as producer practices gave rise to these sites.

15 Discussions of 'netizenry' are ubiquitous in popular accounts of the Internet designed for new users and published in the early- to mid-1990s. These accounts tend to focus on the minutiae of net-etiquette (see Dewitt, 1994, and also *.Net* magazine, 1998: 43), but Internet citizenry or netizenry is useful here because it was informed by, indeed is in a sense a distillation of, the more general covenant assumed to be operating at the time between users in online spaces. Netizenry was always honoured at least as much in the breach as in the observance. However, it remains an indicator of a particular set of expectations that could realistically be maintained and that might partially have been delivered upon at the time, if not today. In so far as they are centred on the Internet in general, the promises involved in this covenant are focused around free speech, freedom from censorship and free association. However, they also focus on mutual assistance and mutual support within a shared environment (see Rheingold, 1994, and early descriptions of the sharing of knowledge across the web).

16   Kevin Kelly pointed out that corporations want to make money (Kelly, 1997).
17   Scholars have pointed out the rather different connotations of the expressions 'virtual community' and 'virtual city'. McBeath and Webb read the city against the community, arguing that the virtual city points to an environment offering creative disorder, anonymity and a lack of accountability, while community points to orderliness (1997). Steve Jones suggests that, unlike the city, the community is based on an imaginary past, on 'what we thought we once had but lost' (Jones 1998). These distinctions are valid but do not map onto particular formations on the ground. Here the two terms are used arbitrarily and/or conflated, so that a site declares itself at once a virtual city, village, community (see eWorld, Lambda, GeoCities). The point, however, which is that the promise of virtual community is not a *unified* promise, stands. In other words, there are contradictions contained within a general rhetoric of Internet space.
18   The production of artificial friction was always an integral part of 'friction free' capital (see Gates *et al.*, 1996).
19   'By submitting content to any chat-room or forum, you automatically grant – or warrant that the owner of such content has expressly granted – GeoCities the royalty-free, perpetual, irrevocable, non-exlusive right and license to use, reproduce, modify, adapt, publish, translate, create derivative works from, distribute, perform and display such content (in whole or part) worldwide and/or to incorporate it in other works in any form, media or technology now known or later developed for the full term of any rights that may exist in such content.' There then follows a standard legal disclaimer pointing out to users they are responsible for this content – not now apparently their own.
20   GeoCities was subject to a complaint that it sold information about users without their knowledge. GeoCities eventually settled with the FTC (see ZDNet, 1999).
21   Declared as such by the company (GeoCities, 1998j).
22   See Margonelli (1999). AOL volunteers found they did not necessarily even own the screen names by which they were known. In this sense, not only content, but also identity, is apparently the property of GeoCities.
23   These companies were recognized by GeoCities in its SEC report as major competitors (GeoCities, 1998g).
24   Leaders in the Bourbon Street neighbourhood, for instance, set up a parallel service, hosted by Radaka Hosting, offering advice across the web in general (Radaka Hosting, 2001). This has happened before: when Apple closed e-World, its proprietary e-community, some of its residents refused to leave, eventually producing an e-World in exile on the Internet which survived for some time.
25   GeoCities now asks users directly to choose a community to determine the kind of advertising that will appear on their pages.
26   These are not pleasures Virilio seeks to share in.

5

'Just because' stories: on *Elephant*[1]

The order of narrative [can] now be routinely countermanded. (Burgin, 2004: 8)

Flash mobs gather 'just because'. (Spinner, 2003)

Preface

With some trepidation, this chapter explores a film called *Elephant*.[2] This is Gus Van Sant's 2003 account of the shootings at Columbine High School and is at once an experiment with non-linear narrative and an exploration of interactivity as a cultural logic, one emerging within specific historical horizons: those of the United States at war with itself and with the world.

Columbine raised a series of questions that *Elephant* refuses absolutely to answer: why those students, why that school, why that day? Indeed, while many possible triggers or motivations are presented in the film, none of them is presented as commensurate with the events they might have provoked, and none of them is presented as likely to be determining. Rather, possible motivations, reasons, and causal factors pile up as so much useless information, or as so much significant information – the point is that we don't know and are given no clue. The killings happen, and so an ordinary day turns into an extraordinary one, apparently randomly or 'just because'. It is this sense of the 'just because' that is explored in *Elephant*, where it becomes a symptom, something expressing – thematically and structurally – the dilemma of the condition of (apparent) freedom and (real) powerlessness. Working largely through innovations in narrative form, and with conscious reference to inter-activity, *Elephant* asks in a strangely tender way, not why things happened 'just because', but why things happened *just so*. It does so through a complex non-linear narrative that loops and repeats, scorching the spaces it traverses and retraverses with a peculiar intensity. If this narrative was made of celluloid, there would be smoke curling from the projector as the same intersection point was passed through over and over again. It is still held on film stock, of course, but in physical substrate only, and the implications of this ontology are no longer read as they once were.

So my trepidation is not about the film itself, since it falls beautifully within the purview of an account of the logics of new media as a material cultural form. It is, rather, that a certain strand of film studies has held itself rather aloof from new media scholars as the latter have grappled with digital media, convergence and remediation. Perhaps the established tradition of studying cinema as a closed – and often ultimately textually determined – space (the screen, the apparatus, the closures of structural narratology, and/or those of psychoanalytic views of cinematic interpellation) has produced a form of resistance to exploration of the continuities that begin to pertain between cinema and other screen-based media forms as these undergo transformation, particularly when those logics might disturb cinema's favourite *verities*. (Out there, they even have a different Deleuze . . .).[3]

Standoffishness in the realm of theory sometimes becomes real hostility 'on the ground' where it is directed against processes of digital remediation, although many also recognise that resistance is futile. Full digital production, distribution and projection will come to be standard soon. There are film theorists who argue that contemporary developments mean that the 150-year history of cinema has now reached its end (see Elsaesser, 2005), that there can be no productive convergence or exchange between cinema and other media forms brought about through digitalization, and no digital redefinition of cinema itself.

The contexts of this uncertainty are processes of digital convergence, which have proceeded at a markedly uneven pace in the film sector. Notably there has been a disjuncture between, on the one hand, the long-established and rapidly accelerating convergence of the film, software and traditional media industries at the level of acquisitions and through collaborative activity, both of which go back to at least the dot.com boom and arguably further – Silicon Valley lunched with Hollywood in the 1980s, as Robert Cringely noted in 1996 – and on the other, processes of digitalization within film itself. This latter has been a slow process (relative to other media technologies and other industries) so that it is only now that fully digital shooting is becoming widespread. Digital projection remains in the future for most cinemas, and new forms of individuated and/or on-demand distribution through computer networks is in its infancy and much of it remains in the informal economy (notably through services such as Bit-Torrent). These uneven processes of convergence have conditioned the terms of the participation (and non-participation) of film in developing new media ecologies.

Film has remained discrete as a medium, at least until very recently. I mean by this not only that celluloid is not silicon, but also that analogue is not digital so that there is no easy transferability between media. This is changing, of course. DVDs and DVD players that indifferently handle digital films, digital games and digital storage begin to erode this difference from the front end, as do video download services, while all-digital production changes it from the back. For now, though, some distance remains, which means that of necessity (and for other reasons also) films are also discrete not only as cultural artefacts, but also in relation to their formal symbolic economies. This too may seem obvious, yet it is something that can no longer be taken for granted for many other media. The contrast here is with radio or TV shows where web content is solicited in real time and invoked within the broadcast to *alter the programme itself, mid-stream*. Users thus increasingly come to make these shows, but the point here is that they are increasingly to be understood as multimedia productions – integrating multiple media forms *within* the formal composition of the work – and if these examples seem to invert McLuhan's dictum that the content of new media is old media (McLuhan, 1994), this might be a measure of the extent to which older forms are now remediated, so that both are now 'new media'. Similar formations can be observed in relation to the integration of citizen reporting into mainstream newspapers (or online versions thereof), and in relation to gaming and other forms of fully converged media, where the wires between different media types are made visible in order to naturalize certain forms of cross-media interaction. (This last has been very successful: the idea of building a game involving mobile phones, the Internet, GPS and RFID already begins to seem like one of those projects that declares itself original but is wearily predictable even before it is made.) Oddly enough, where cinema deals with digital special effects (CGI), it might be said to operate a form of digital realism that has its parallels with this formation.

Beyond film studies, and particularly in media and cultural studies, it is unfashionable to stress cinema's (even relative) autonomy. I recognize that contemporary films are buttressed by vast amounts of epiphenomenal material (star material, production material, cross-marketed products, fan productions), particularly on the web, and that they may be defined as productions (designed as productions) in relation to this material as much as to the film itself (the *Blair Witch* effect). However, the fundamental division remains; it is, perhaps, one of the contradictions of partial convergence. As a consequence, while it is necessary (and useful) to regard films as 'dispersed *texts*' (see Austin, 2002), we also need to distinguish between this form of media integration and more thoroughgoing processes of convergence, between what is usually defined as the closed formal economy of the film and the open web of texts and other semiotic objects that contribute to its broader economy (which may well also be a narrative economy). This distinction becomes more important, but is also harder to draw, in the case of new media ecologies, and is also raised in relation not only to texts but also to their activation. Notably, there are ways that a text may be set in motion through uses that lie beyond the screen space, but that might still lie within the proximate temporal horizon of a tale. In other words, they may lie within the arc of a narrative as it is told and/or made, *rather than as it might be recollected at a later point*. Parallels here may be found on-screen in the distinction between diegetic and extra-diegetic material, perhaps, since this material confounds and confirms the boundaries between the integral and the epiphenomenal, although it does so from another point in the narrative arc.

Not yet multimedia, film still stands largely apart, physically, from many other forms of screen-based media, and from the forms of integration digital equivalence might allow. On the other hand, it is already a part of an increasingly integrated economy in which a media artefact may well have a presence on multiple media platforms. This places it in conflicted relation to an emerging new media aesthetic of convergence that at once foregrounds the multiple media used in the construction of a particular media programme and blurs the distinctions between what were previously discrete media forms founded on specific technologies. In sum, film might be said to be a part of the processes of the remediation of culture at the hands of information, but to partake of its logics, to some extent at least, obliquely and at some distance.

Elephant is one of a series of films being made as this distance begins to be closed. Rethinking film narrative, it underscores the degree to which processes of remediation (Bolter and Grusin, 1999: 343) involving the *refashioning* of old media in digital spaces can be understood as processes of recombination rather than replacement. As a consequence, older media, coming into contact with new media, remake the latter one more time, not in their own image, nor as they were before, but as something new once again. The forms of interactivity that *Elephant* plays with are thus innovative partly *because* they are *filmic*, as are the narrative possibilities the film explores. So, *Elephant* is a production that (avowedly) deals with and in the logic of interactivity. This becomes the form through which the film speaks, how its tale is activated, but it is also the form whose ideological operations are challenged.

In relation to this, I note that while *Elephant*'s deployment of the interactive form is experimental, certainly art house, even avant garde, it deals with the mainstream, with the cultural forms of everyday life. The assimilation of the interactive principle into mass culture is, after all, at the root of reality television and celebrity culture, both of which are realms where our stand-ins might become 'real' enough, or 'live' enough, or enough 'like us' to work a particular form of identification and involvement. In the case of reality TV, for instance, it is very obvious that while 'we' control 'their' fates with our votes, our own buttons are being pressed in all kinds of ways. More, it is clear that the red *button* that gives us interactive television and freedom to choose as a technical capability might be beside the point if, unlike Neo in *The Matrix*, who chose pink and the revelation of real relations, we have already taken the blue *pill* and gone back to dreamful sleep. Which raises the question of how control operates in these multi-way, but at the same time highly asymmetrical, forms of interaction: is there an elephant in the house?

Re: narrative
The decomposition of narrative films, once subversive, is now normal. (Burgin, 2004: 8)

Exploring film memory, Victor Burgin claims that linear narrative has had its day. The 'decomposition' that he describes tends to release film fragments, so that we no longer remember the tale, but the sequence image, the iconic moment (and if we always have, we do so more than ever). Now, there are growing numbers of films in which linear narrative is *un*done; *Elephant* is one of them. However, narrative within these films is also *re*done, in many and various ways. So that, while decomposition, or a certain unravelling, of narrative is intrinsic to this type of film, it may not be the final word, or the last moment, in a process that might include various forms of narrative recomposition, not only beyond the film but *within* its grounds, both as these are technically discrete, textually defined, and through use or activation. Here, then, I will explore not narrative decomposition per se, but what I call narrative disturbance, taking this to include decomposition and forms of recomposition.

Burgin's assessment is perhaps slightly ahead of its time. Narrative decomposition/recomposition/disturbance is not yet entirely routine, which may be why attempts at definition and classification continue. Bringing some of these accounts together we can assemble a rough map of this field along with a partial history of its emergence. Collections such as Ed Harries's are useful here, making it clear that a non-linear canon and a shared theory of origins have already emerged (Harries, 2002). *Rashomon* is thus repeatedly invoked as an immediate forerunner of non-linear films, while amongst the more-or-less contemporary crop of films, *TimeCode* is celebrated for breaking the spatial unity of the screen, *Memento* for its looped narrative and *Run Lola Run* for its 'forking path' narrative structure. These structural distinctions are useful, but there are also other ways to understand these developments, and filmic locations other than the art house, to be explored here. One other route focuses on consideration of the impact of digital forms on questions of realism as they pertain in documentary (see Bruzzi, 2000). Andrew Jarecki's *Capturing the Freedmans* plays on this through its deployment of retro-video aesthetics and its exploitation of naturalized connections between 'amateurism' and realism or authenticity (see Austin, 2007, forthcoming); and *Elephant* itself is a documentary of a kind, although Van Sant also describes it as a drama (Hattenstone, 2004).[4] Parallel issues concerning the renegotiation of cinematic claims to realism arising in relation to digital technologies as vehicles for narration emerge in relation to CGI in special-effects blockbusters, perhaps less focused on narrative disturbance than on a renegotiation of the relationship between narrative and spectacle: *The Lord of the Rings* is an example here.

The origins of contemporary non-linear film are variously drawn. In his account of new media, Lev Manovich reaches back to early montage cinema, finding there a precursor to the database logic he discerns in a series of contemporary films. The argument here concerns the basic building blocks of cinema and in pursuit of them Manovich moves from Vertov's *Man with a Movie Camera*, filmed in 1929, towards a view of digital cinema as animation with live action footage as one of its elements (Manovich, 2001: 302). This trajectory also takes him out of cinema towards other forms of new media, notably gaming. Coming from the other direction, Jim Bizzocchi's work on the growth of non-linear narrative (as database narrative) connects with his parallel explorations of *future* platforms for home screening in intriguing ways (Bizzocchi, 2005).

New media theorists such as Manovich and Bizzocchi work on the supposition that new media technologies are integral to processes of narrative decomposition seen in cinema. Whatever their take on how various forms of determination spin out (essentially their reading of history and theory), this is quite simply their point of intervention, as it is my own. It means that a particular reading of technology influences the construction of the typology they are developing and vice versa. However, as a counterbalance it is useful to remember that other considerations of narrative disturbance do not begin with technology, and even sidestep it. Geoff King, for instance, has argued that narrative disturbance is a marker of an art house film, and is promoted through this sector (King, 2005).

In fact, narrative disturbance already appears well beyond the (blurred) boundaries of the independent or art house film. (This is also Burgin's starting point, and in a different way, Manovich's.) Nonetheless, King's comments, made partly with reference to *Gerry*, another Van Sant film, are salutary since they raise the question of genre and/in its relationship to the narrative transformations under investigation. Genre articulates a link between audiences, political economies of film and the 'text', and is influenced by what can be done and/in relation to technology, but it doesn't specifically explore *how* this influence might operate: at the level of culture, or ontology, or technology, for instance. If there is a genre of films based around narrative disturbance that does not invoke the technological centrally, then what has to be satisfied, and in what way, for a film to fit into this genre? What do we expect from these kinds of films? And is *Elephant* one them?

This is interesting in relation to *Elephant* because the film does not offer many of the traditional satisfactions of new media, particularly those cohering around interactivity, or not if this is adumbrated as the right to make active choices between given alternatives or routes through a text. *Elephant* is thus not a new media artefact that is easily recognizable as such. There are no buttons to push, no mouse to click, no decisions to make, and no matter how many times the film is viewed, there is no way to change the already known outcome, or even to reach it in a new way. Death comes at the end for many of the film's characters, as we knew it would from before the beginning. Van Sant, however, declares (rightly in my view) that this is an interactive narrative, conforming to a particular logic, *textually* if not technologically; the film was cut by hand and is almost a craftwork (Hattenstone, 2004).

Van Sant's film, in fact, happily tramples across many genres, and might indeed provoke reconsideration of the relationship not only between technology and genre (and the degree to which one tends to determine aspects of the other) but also between genre formation and technological *innovation*. Genre is suggestive here because it invites consideration of the degree to which cued expectations based on new media technologies can exist relatively independently of their technological instantiation, so that interactivity may be offered and accepted in different ways. From which it follows that it may be possible to presume a shared understanding of a digital logic in advance of its proximate arrival. This can then be worked with not only thematically (for example through figures such as Lara Croft) but also by working a transformation in form, by changing the form narrative takes, how it is organized temporally and spatially, and finally through this work with form, invoking as a question, at least, the possibilities of new forms of interactive engagement from the spectator/user/activator.

Consideration of genre thus opens up ways to think about distinctions *between* various forms of non-linear film, one of which is based on the degree to which, and the manner in which, interaction (rather than narrative per se) is organized, textually and/or technologically, to make this distinction rather crudely.

With these different taxonomies, possibilities, definitions and modes of articulation in mind, I now turn back to look more closely at narrative itself. If the breaking of the narrative line is now commonplace, if this is an order that can now be routinely countermanded, then what is coming to replace it? What form of narrative is this, if it is narrative at all? Let me offer three examples of different kinds of visual media each of which deals with the question of narrative and information technology in a particular way, but only two of which are non-linear.

Reaching back, the exception is Ridley Scott's *Blade Runner*, which famously explores a particular kind of technological insertion into a near future form of everyday life. This is not an interactive narrative, but it does take up themes of automation and control diegetically and, in particular, though the production of a street aesthetic in which impossible tangles of architecture and various forms of low life come together to produce a screen version of what Jameson termed 'dirty realism' (1994: 145), a form of lived intensity forged within a techno-social totality too vast to be grasped or reached, that begins to overreach linear narrative as a cultural logic.

The second example is *Elephant*, which tells the tale of Columbine through a series of narrative loops rather than following a linear path, producing dislocated temporal and spatial returns that organize and then reorganize the viewers' relationship to the tale, taking them through various narrative pathways, but not handing the work of assembly over to them. The thematics of *Elephant* are tightly bound up with this innovative narrative structure, as I'll argue below. If *Elephant* is not interactive in technical fact, it is an 'interactive' cultural form, one that *recomposes/decomposes* narrative in ways that both break with and redefine the medium of cinema. *Elephant* is also interesting as an interactive movie because this is done on the grounds of form, on a play with form, rather than solely through a play with content. Thus it might be said to an interactive movie, rather than a film *about* interaction. This doesn't mean it is the same as other interactive artefacts (like a game for instance). It does mean that drawing out the differences between the game and the interactive film may not simply be a question of technical difference or technical advancement. Nor is it precisely about the form of puzzle: I don't believe there is a ludological versus a representational logic on offer here.

The third example is not a film but a game series. Here I am referring to Sid Meier's *Civilization* series, in which the game or narrative (letting this ride for the moment) is constructed by being played in response to the moves offered. This is very linear in fact, but it is also highly interactive, both in the sense that much is demanded of the user (particular kinds of action being necessary for the game to move forwards at all), and in the sense that interaction is not only with the tale (which can be constructed in various ways) but also with the code. Indeed, arguably it is through constructing the right code that the player builds the right story. The end of the game comes when rules (the algorithm governing play) have been discovered and executed. Arguing that there is an absolute coincidence between the game content and (successful) game play, Alex Galloway suggests that gaming is algorithmic rather than 'allegorithmic': the way to world domination (*Civilization*'s aim) is to find its algorithm, its executable rule (Galloway, 2004b). My sense is that this also depends on embodied use (perhaps on *habitus* as a form of emplotment) that may well cross-cut such isomorphism. However, for Galloway narrative too is completely coincident with game play (and therefore, presumably, fundamentally not just non-linear, but non-continuous, *in potentia*) which, Galloway argues, produces a lack of depth that militates against ideological critique, although he is far from saying that these cultural products are non-political. This constitutes a strong argument for database and against narrative, couched in terms of immanence. Here the thematics of the game are once again bound up with the formal economy of the work, but this time not only in relation to what goes on on-screen, but also in relation to the execution of code.

It would be possible to read this list as a trajectory mapping out a progression from *Blade Runner*, a traditional narrative in which informatics can only be considered internally, to *Elephant*, in which forms of non-linearity constitute a text, to *Civilization*, in which a fundamentally non-linear interactive structure and form are coded possibilities. Taking this as a progression, user activity in this last case might be viewed as integral to the formal constitution of the work, which cannot be understood except as a technological constitution. In this sense it reflects a particular way of understanding the status of information as a cultural logic.

I am nervous about accepting this trajectory. Or, at least, I want to think what *kind* of trajectory is implied here (what powers it, perhaps). I believe that it can too easily begin to slide towards a form of revealed ontology for new media that would inevitably lose sight of the different factors that operate to condition narrative here, factors that sometimes operate in concert, but often only partially in unison, and sometimes indeed in conflicting ways. What I am driving at here is that narrative possibilities do not map directly onto questions of technological capacity (technological progress, however this is read), although they are obviously influenced by these questions. *Elephant*, I think, begins to show how this might be so. Another brief example might be found in generative narrative involving cellular automata (A-Life algorithms) since, although a necessary condition for generative narrative might be a fully digital platform, turning to this platform would not by any means guarantee that what was produced was narrative.

These questions of trajectory are of course old ones, relating to debates around essentialism and determination raised earlier in this book, and connect also to the 'history' versus 'theory' debates within the study of cinema itself (see Krutnik, 1991). These debates concern the distinction between narrative cinema as revealed ontology (the Bazin tradition) and cinema as a historically contingent construction which can be understood to have developed as 'a series of surprises', through incidents and accidents of all kinds. Those advocating this latter tradition argue that there is 'no primitive groping for story film' (Bordwell, 1997: 121); the advent of cinema as a 'narrative machine' is accidental (rather than providential, as Metz viewed it, perhaps), in which case logically there can be no inevitable trajectory towards gaming and away from narrative either (Bassett, 2007). At any rate, if there is no revealed ontology for narrative, neither is there one for technology. In the place of the double determination that worried the apparatus theorists, the fear of a clash of ontologies (see Rosen, 1986 and Chapter 1 above), the world-view of the history scholars offers us a redoubled and rather radical contingency.

Not entirely surprisingly, there are ways to route around this somewhat arbitrarily laid out division between history and theory. One way is to ask 'which theory?' Bordwell's answer to this is encapsulated in his battle against structural excess, which is also a critique of ideological analysis in favour of cognitivism (see Ryan, 2004: 196). Other forms of theory relevant to contemporary transformations in film which intersect with these debates include the confluence of the influence of Deleuze/Guattari's schizoid politics within cultural studies and the vogue for the Deleuze of *Cinema2* and the movement-image in cinema studies, although here a division is reformed rather than dissolved perhaps, since this turn might reinscribe Bordwell's original complaint.

A way between the system of surprises and the groping for an underlying form begins to be found if we consider what might connect historical developments and theoretical formations. Frank Krutnik can thus argue that there is 'no polarisation of history and theory' since 'culture speaks to itself and of itself through its art and its cultural and representational artefacts – that is, through its *activities* of representation' (Krutnik, 1991: 1 my italics). These cultural logics operate within the realm of history as it is broadly defined and they relate to material technological innovation, to the making of things. To me, at least, Williams's description of television as a technology that was foreseen and desired in the social world before it was 'invented' as a technology remains a beautiful account of how a complex process of innovation can be understood as a form of material cultural production (Williams, 1990: 129). I return to a theory centred on historical materialism to explore developments in narrative film as it decomposes and recomposes.

This still leaves some thorny problems, notably cohering around the distinction between different narrative materials: those that are textual and those that are technological; those that are internal to the formal system of narrative and those that are external. The point here is that these two sets of oppositions do not match up, are indeed not purely oppositional but are also imbricated in each other. Considerations of the materiality of technology are implicated within debates around the ontology of cinema, but not necessarily in ways that line up with the form the history/theory debates have taken.

At this point I return to the three examples cited above, whose forms we can now view as neither inevitable (ontologically) nor as purely accidental, but as having a cultural and historical logic that is itself not entirely linear, and that is bound up in logics of technology and of narrative, which latter do not have to be viewed as collapsing into each other. In particular, we do not have to view gaming, or the supremacy of the database model, as film's inevitable destination. This is also true in reverse; that is, the presumption that all forms of visualization emerging from the computer inevitably move towards film-style realism (Sobchack, 1999) is, if not misplaced, historically contingent (Bassett, 2007).

The edge of narrative (recursion and mediation)

So far I have argued this new kind of film narrative might have arrived, not ontologically nor accidentally, but contingently and/in relation to historical constellations. I have also suggested that different determinations are involved here, so that if there is a trajectory involved in the move towards interactive narrative in film, and one towards gaming, then this trajectory is to be understood as complex and non-linear. These interpretations condition how various limits to the tale might be set: temporally (in terms of continuity or coherence), technologically (in relation to discrete materials) and algorithmically (in terms of what codes narrative). But this question also needs to be extended to include questions of ideology and power. What, in other words, is the diffuse purchase of this kind of narrative as an informing cultural logic, and how do the cultural/historical horizons within which it is formed in turn tend to shape this form or give it purchase?

One way into these issues can be found through a return to Burgin, whose argument is that in conditions of decomposition, in times when narrative is fast fraying, the value of the film fragment grows, in part because it detaches itself differently from the body of the work after the viewing event itself. His account therefore deals largely, not with film memory as something contiguous with the event, but with remembrance after the act. This memory, a fragment of narrative, is discrete from the real event, from the first activation of the narrative: *'The film we saw is never the film I remember'* (Burgin, 2004: 110).

Burgin does not say, but George Perec's work implies, that these film memories may come together to produce new narratives; that these free-floating fragments are part of that detritus of everyday life, 'our life's treasure', which we may recall into a tale through a form of inventorizing (Bassett, 2003; Perec, 1997). We live in an unending rainfall of images, as Calvino once put it, and amongst those that land and take root, those that hybridize, are fragments of film. An inquiry not pursued here, but one that interests me, is how these memory tales, these narrative reconfigurations of memory traces, may themselves be more fragmented, more partial, more ephemeral, more non-linear, as narrative itself mutates (Burgin's own sense of what happens to the fragment of narrative does not quite tend this way).

A further extension of narrative takes us into a new narrative cycle; perhaps that of narrative life lived through the overlaying activation and deactivation of multiple tales, through investigation (or neglect) of the memory traces they leave behind. This form of narrative identity also demands narration or activation to be understood in its fullest extent, in turn. Thinking about this process of the 'after the act' it might be said that if gaming simply repeats, narrative *fructifies*.

At any rate, Burgin's cut is clear. His film memories are not part of a single arc of narrative but are cut free of the original film (something made easier because, as he sees it, film is decomposing). A more difficult case can be found in relation to gaming, where proponents of ludology argue that it is 'the fall into narrativity' (Espen Aarseth, cited in Ryan, 2004) that ends the game, because it means the death of simulation. Ryan thus compares the 'live, real-time experience' of the game to the 'retrospective availability of meaning' (Ryan, 2004: 334), often the only justification for describing games as narratives, she feels. This comes fairly close to Manovich's line here, since for him too, the contention that a new media artefact may be counted as narrative only through retrospective construction, that is, after the act, is not justifiable (see Ryan, 2004: 332). I too am uneasy about defining something as a continuous narrative, or even as narrative, if narrative emerges *only* after the act. However, I also want to note that when narrative itself is regarded as a form of active emplotment it is far more closely integrated into new media artefacts than this account suggests, even within a highly interactive game, perhaps *especially* in a highly interactive game – at least if gaming itself is viewed as a form of doing narrative. This has implications for the way in which game playing is understood as paradigmatic of interactive content. Certainly there are other ways to deal with interactive forms of content than to solve them as a puzzle.

Finally, these questions may operate in relation to what falls in advance of the tale as well as behind it. Burgin's distinction between the memory and the tale might find a physical – and more prosaic counterpart – in the film website or the marketing campaign, which also remain in important ways external to the frame of the work, not only within formalist analysis but more generally (the cult of celebrity, audience studies and convergence as an industrial process involving cross-marketing all make bridges across the gap, but it remains nonetheless). One difference here is that where Burgin is exploring an 'after the act' in temporal terms (through memory), much epiphenomenal material involved in the cultural production, but not in the film itself, operates simultaneously with the film or in advance of it, where it may cue particular responses (which is why it has so much to do with genre). This might reframe the gaming question, since narrative thematics also stand in advance of the game and may cue a narrative response to it. There may be interactions that are central to the way in which the work as a whole finds its significance, but that are discrete from the tale.

Drawing lines between the tale and the epiphenomena around the tale, and/or between the tale and the memory of the tale, is relatively straightforward, although it still produces different accounts of the cultural form under investigation. A different set of questions about narrative continuity and cohesion versus a database logic of discrete interrogation emerges if we explore the parameters of the tale itself – and in that last phrase hangs the question.

Here we might return to Manovich's argument that the principle of new media is one that looks back towards a tradition of montage, swallowed up by the dominance of traditional narrative film but now refound, and that looks forwards towards a reinstantiation of that tradition in animation. For Manovich, the montage tradition is now retooled through the formalist logic of assembly provided by the algorithm and the database. This begins to provide us with glimpses of a form of film in which narrative is irrelevant within the terms of the act, this act consisting of the operation of the algorithm on the database. This position moves Manovich logically enough towards gaming, since it is here that the database (arguably at least) operates in its purest form, pleasure emerging as the user finds the algorithm that cracks open the database: this is essentially to be understood as a ludic activity. For Manovich, narrative's decomposition at the hands of new media thus results in its decline rather than its reassembly. This produces as a new genre the database film, a form of non-narrative (fiction) film (Manovich, 2000).

Jim Bizzocchi's elaboration of the database argument is focused tightly on film (rather than moving towards games and other new media forms). His detailed breakdowns of *Run Lola Run*, for instance, set out a case for a form of database narrative. He thus entertains an accommodation with Manovich, but produces a distinct position (Bizzocchi, 2005). This stresses recombination alongside diagrammatic modelling: Bizzocchi's argument is that narrative is composed of a series of discrete database extractions. Viewing or using is a form of data-mining, in other words. However, he also accepts that these extractions are recombined in forms and patterns that are not entirely derived algorithmically. Manovich's account shares with Bizzocchi's a particular kind of formalism, the latter operating through diagrammatical models of database and data extraction and recombination from which the user is excluded.

Something striking about these accounts is that, in different ways, they work with a tightly constricted sense of narrative's limits. Working with a more extensive sense of narrative's arc, some elements that Burgin, Manovich and Ryan regard as beyond the tale might be taken back into its arc. Expanding outwards from Manovich's restricted (formalist) analysis opens up the question of how use plays out, not only in the constitution of the text 'itself', but also in the constitution of the tale. This concerns both the way in which a text might be activated (formally constituted), and ways in which it might be understood *in process*. This begins to suggest ways in which databases are taken up into narrative, not so that narrative comes at the end, or as the end, but *integrally*, as part of what it means to 'read' a text. Paradoxically, when the arc of narrative is extended to include the horizon of reception in this way, it becomes easier to think about narrative continuity (the making of some form of temporal coherence) as continuous with the activation of a text, rather than as something increasingly occuring after the event. More, understanding narrative continuity to be located not only in the core of the tale, but also in configuration (the desire for the story) and refiguration (its reopening or activation in a particular horizon) means that narrative can more easily be understood to be newly formed, to be non-linear. A new time of the tale might emerge between different moments of this narrative arc, a resolution of the time of the tale measured out both as the time offered in the tale and as the time of its full traversal, the time of its activation.

Assuming some connection between the cultural forms we produce and those we wish and desire to consume, narrative's mutability should spread this far. Assuming an extensive arc of narrative, within the grounds of narrative itself the pleasures of the reception of the tale also might begin to be thought about in non-linear terms.

There are ways of conceptualizing interactive narrative (and of building it) that reject forms of thinking about interactivity that only see in it a desire to reassemble fragments according to a preordained law, or to play with them in this way. The purified gaming logic of puzzle-solving and mastery does not automatically become embedded in all forms of interactive narrative (is not narrative's new and fatal destiny). Indeed, at this point a comparison presents itself between non-linear interactive narrative, which might be explored in terms of the temporal resolution it offers, and a game, in which the logic of the puzzle pertains so that the key term is not resolution but solution. In relation to narrative this produces something rather open-ended (many children have wondered what *happens* 'ever after'); in relation to the game it produces a repeat: more of the same, although probably a little bit different.

Elephant stands as an example of this. It is one of a growing number of films, many of them interactive or non-linear, in which we are aware of the plot in advance so that the puzzle cannot be viewed as central (obviously there are exceptions to this). And as I will suggest below, it does not operate according to the logic of the game. We are not invited to solve the mystery. On the contrary, the elephant is in the room.

Arcs and mirrors

Ricoeur argues that narrative is constituted by that broad arc that includes prefiguration or the call to story (*Mimesis*1), configuration (*Mimesis*2), and refiguration as reception (*Mimesis*3), which reopens the text into the horizons of the reader (see earlier chapters). Narrative is only understandable 'at its fullest extent' when it is articulated across this arc.

Taken on its own, each of these elements can offer only a partial account of narrative. At the same time however, Ricoeur is clear that *Mimesis*2, the central element, itself constitutes a tale. At issue here is whether this most internal moment of the tale itself recapitulates in miniature those other elements of the tale, either in form or content. If it does not it cannot be called complete. If it does, then other problems arise: either those of infinite recursion, in which the narrative arc becomes a hall of mirrors, or those of terminal closure, in which each element of narrative maps back precisely onto the other, leaving no space for innovation.

Bakhtin resolves this in relation to the novel in his account of dialogics, where different voices come to take particular parts, producing a form of internal reception (see Chapter 1). In Ricoeur's case it is the process of mutual informing between different elements of the narrative arc that makes this an open rather than a closed recursive process; there is no hall of mirrors. Changes in narrative preconfiguration (the way in which a call to story is understood) and reconfiguration (the reactivation of the tale into new horizons) may thus inform a shift in a general understanding of, even perception of, narrative form. In this way the outer wings of the arc may inform the central element of narrative, *mimesis*2. Even as they do so, however, new forms of narrative may flower from this central element outwards, new forms of fictionalizing informing the call to story and the ways in which it comes to be reopened. This constant flow between narrative's inward and outward faces might both produce a reconfiguration of narrative itself, and reconfigure or reconstitute our narrative sense of our world.

Elephant, consciously an experiment with interactive narrative, seems to inscribe this process within its own dynamics, since here the apparently resolved temporality and the spatiality of a series of events is endlessly unresolved, written and rewritten so that the first version of a particular space-time intersection is scratched out, added to, continuously overlaid. And each time space and time are bound up in new ways. In the end, if what is inscribed is the tale, it is also the case that what is inscribed is partly the *pattern* of that change, which itself *produces a changed narrative and a changed narrative form*. Inside *Elephant*, the space-time segment we revisit again and again is the one we remembered from the first time around, but it is also different. Burgin's sense that 'the film we saw is never the film I remember' (Burgin, 2004: 110), which concerns memory after the event, might be rethought in this way, since the segments he notices outside film space (in the general media environment) are also found *within* the interactive film, and there too they may mutate.

The tale end of the elephant[5]
An ordinary high school day. Except that it's not. (Catch-line for *Elephant*)

The final sections of this chapter turn on questions of mediation and begin with a return to the figure of the elephant. *Elephant* explores the 1999 killings at Columbine High School, but was also made with reference to Alan Clarke's (1989) film of the same name which documents murders in Belfast during the Troubles, a time of civil strife and armed struggle. Van Sant reputedly understood the naming of the original film to refer to an old tale in which a group of blind men meet an elephant, each man connecting with one part of the beast, feeling its ears, its trunk, its legs, or its tusks. The result of this partial contact is that each of them comprehends the elephant in their own way. In fact, Clarke's film took its name from the elephant in the living room, the one that everybody walks around. This elephant becomes, if not invisible, then unnoticed by collective agreement, and needs to be renamed to be brought back into view before it can be turfed out. This is the elephant in the house: the Troubles as the huge but unremarked-upon backdrop to everyday life in Ireland at that time.

In fact, Van Sant's *Elephant* resonates with both of these two elephant stories. First, the violence of America's global and domestic policies forms the looming but unacknowledged context within which a form of local, even intimate, violence is played out. Second, the film plays on many levels with partial perspectives (this is *how* the elephant is hidden) so that users are enjoined to take up the perilous game of taking of parts for a whole, a game that in this case is coupled with various forms of redundancy and repetition which may intensify the effect. *Elephant* was shot in Van Sant's home state of Oregon using non-professional actors recruited from a local school, supplemented by professionals playing mostly adult roles. The claims to realism this produces add another layer to the complex temporal economy of the film.

Elephant traces the tale of this ordinary/extraordinary day at Columbine, following the movements of a small group of students including the two student killers. In the first half of the film the story of the day as it is paced out by the two shooters thus shades into the quotidian details of other everyday school lives: desperate unhappiness, love, classroom arguments, student societies, sexuality, changing rooms, a film about Hitler, guns, canteens, store rooms, death. A peculiar equivalence pertains between the murderous preparations of the shooters and the routine anxieties, tensions and obsessions, of the others, as they live their lives with at an intensity that would be the more remarkable were it not simply teenage. It is clear from the start that these are the lives at risk, that these intertwined lives are about to be ripped apart, and some of them ripped to pieces. Since the audience knows that some of these characters will not come through, the repeated trajectories and insistent returns to the same points of intersection begin to take on a certain cruelty.

It might be possible to take *Elephant* apart, to build a database of its characters, events, actions, intersections, and to see how its assets are worked upon (to find the algorithm governing the action), to map its forks and intersections. But a more compelling way to see the film is to explore the force and logic of the narrative assembly operating here. At the level of prefiguration, Columbine is understandable as a story to be told rather than a series of database assets to be drawn upon and the drawing up of the events into the tale is not one that seems to depend on a database sort (an algorithm). This isn't to say there aren't database resonances within

Elephant. The sheer redundancy of the data available, and its apparently interchangeable qualities have something to do with database selection and reselection, and with the database sort – which is itself a response to a world shot through with information. Redundancy means choosing the explanation desired (fifty-seven kinds of coffee, fifty ways to leave your lover, any number of ways to understand the reasons why two teenagers killed their classmates); this is the artificial paradise of mass consumer society, after all (see Moretti, 1983: 231 and Chapter 1).

Elephant, in the end, as it appears on screen, both offers choices (multiple ways around the site, multiple reasons for the killings) and withdraws them, through a form of interactivity that finds multiple pathways but refuses to offer anybody a choice about which of them to take, and perhaps through a refusal to say, ultimately, if the explanation chosen was right.

In tracking these tales through long shots, exposing these fragments, and in returning over and over again to these spaces and interactions, each time through somebody else's eyes, *Elephant* moves space and time apart. The effect is something like a Spirograph pen tracing a new parabola with each full traversal around a loop, but in doing so crossing through the same point so that it becomes over-used, even breaks the surface of the paper, destroys it. Ripping into space in this way by crushing too much time into it, Van Sant in the end exhausts the viewer, and even the film itself. Somehow it would not be entirely surprising if at a cinema somewhere the projector began to smoke as the film loop returned again to that same spot of corridor.

In the first half of the film this produces a peculiarly poetic landscape, the school corridors holding the remembered tracks of students moving through the space, stopping, talking, ignoring each other, and holding also the same students who figure again and again in their own and others *derives*. This landscape becomes partly familiar to us through these slow repetitions that operate 'as if' we had taken on the perspective of a particular character, but it is also made strange by this unaccustomed time-space organization. Thus it is a landscape at once intimate and remote that becomes a killing field, a plane of action for the two killers taking their final turn through the school, in the second half of the film. Here the film speeds up somewhat, although it continues to oscillate between the aesthetic of a dream and the sudden clarity of a nightmare, between tense inaction and sudden bursts of fire. The viewpoint is also narrowed. The film follows the final preparations and then tracks the separate killing trajectories of the two students and their own fatal final meeting; in doing so, it also begins to take on the *aesthetic* of the game.

The focus in *Elephant* as it launches the viewer on these trajectories is at once intimate and totalizing. Each move is observed closely; through the detail offered by the replay function, we come to know a space from many angles, but this knowledge comes from a remote we do not hold in our hands. This is a play on surveillance and control. It is also obliquely a comment on what de Certeau understood as the subterranean or opaque quality of everyday life. We are seen 300 times a day (this is true in Britian at least) but something is still withheld. At the end of this examination, we still do not know.

The repetitions, the shifts in viewpoint and perspective, the redundancy of pathways through this space, the temporal loops and re-use of spaces, are what make this an interactive landscape. Taken on forking pathways through this landscape, we largely feel our way through it from the inside. And I want to insist: this *is* the tale. Narrative here is not retrospectively applied after the event, applied if you like to the database or the gaming action (nor is it something that can be understood only in terms of the trajectory of the students as their life stories). Narrative *is* the twists, distensions, switchbacks, the straight lines, the curves, the parabolas and the repetitions of the tale.

It is notable that gathered up inside this interactive narrative, intrinsic to its form but also part of its thematic, are themes of surveillance, intimacy, redundancy, control and information or explanation – even in a sense the game space. It would be hard *not* to account for this film – and for this narrative form – in terms of its thorough embedding in the information age. What is gathered up here into the texture of the film is not only a commentary on content, the United States today, but also on form, on *how* we live and experience these remediated lives.

Afterword: ideology, control, modulation

So what does *Elephant* do? And what does this form of narrative do? Or what can it do? Four points are made here. Perm them any way you like but remember that the elephant, although not the algorithm, is capitalism.

First, while this interactive narrative refuses explanation at one level (the killings happened 'just because'), it clearly offers it at another. There is in the film an injunction – 'only have fun' – given by one of the killers to his companion, just before the shooting game begins. It seems apposite here, since *Elephant* might be read as a film about the contemporary USA, the pursuit of happiness and the cost of that pursuit – and of course Columbine was widely read as a symptom. Here, then, the elephant stalking through the film concerns the knowledge that that this day was, despite its unusualness, not an aberration, but only a stronger than usual response to a form of everyday alienation within a system that says you can have everything but may have nothing. This is everyday life in the US, but not as it usually allows itself to be understood. *Elephant* tells us that, beyond the irrationality of the proximate moment, there are any number of reasons why Columbine happened; as one web reviewer put it, seeing *Elephant*, the astonishing thing is that there are not more Columbines.

In this way *Elephant* becomes a meditation on violence itself. The questions the USA asked about the Columbine killers parallel many of those asked in the UK as it confronted home-grown terror in London. Those acts too were meaningless, but all too understandable. Which is not to say that they were justified. There is no *grace* to be found in the violence at Columbine as it comes to be understood in *Elephant* and none in the bombings in London, either. And these spaces are nearer than they once were. Indeed, we outsiders to the US increasingly have little choice about being propelled through the landscapes America creates, even if we have multiple perspectives on these spaces, seeing them over and over again, through different camera eyes.

First, the form of narrative that is recomposed through *Elephant* is recognizably narrative, but changed. Narrative disturbance produces a new narrative form. This form is tricky with time, but is not a game-play. There is a form of temporal resolution on offer here (rather than the promise of solution offered by the game). More, this resolution is temporal, but it is complex and non-linear, rather than operating through a sense of recombinant linearity. *Elephant*, in other words, is an example of how narrative can be mutable and innovative: it might gather up into its newly woven fabric, through the form that fabric takes, something of the conditions under which it was made, of which it is a part. Among those conditions is an awareness of the medium itself, so that *Elephant* is a meditation on the possibilities for a particular (emerging) form of material cultural expression, one that arises within and as a part of a particular political, economic, social constellation.

What is the force of this form? Clearly the narrative structure of *Elephant* does not set out to soothe or reassure, as Doane argued (presciently, since she wrote in relation to the Challenger space-shuttle disaster, but might have been writing about 9/11) that narrative and repetition might in relation to TV news. Here what is offered through narrative is an explanation of events that allows them to be grasped within existing frameworks (Doane, 1990). This stands in contrast to *Elephant's* withholding of information. *Elephant*, at any rate, is not a soothing narrative that distances the viewer from the event by making it comprehensible, but one that takes you in into the mundane, the quotidian, where horror flies out of the sun unexpectedly. And it is not so much that your viewpoint is intimate, but that your form of seeing is *both* dislocated and 'real-time'. This begins to tie up with the documentary claims that circulate around the film and that pose questions about the forms of realism interactivity supports. *Elephant* at least engages with that desire for 'real' connection that is seen in reality TV – but also in disasters – where each of us reaches for our link to the tale, to make it our tale. In the case of the London bombings everybody, it seems, was 'almost there' or knew somebody who was, or had been there, on that same bus route, *before*.

First, Elephant is an avant garde production that sets out to experiment with a form and perhaps to challenge its usual operations, to challenge the uses to which it is put. Here I fragment still further. (a) *Elephant* is a response in form to the meaninglessness of the empty flash-mob gathering that happens 'just because', particularly when it is viewed as a mode of activism. It renders this form of collective action back, not as activism, but as a picture of alienation. (b) *Elephant* underscores the extension of control that particular kinds of automation provide. Interactive computing intensifies control (takes us from discipline to control, if you want to read it in terms of the Foucault/Deleuze apposition), because it reaches further and more deeply into everyday life and everyday life processes. The interactive narrative of *Elephant* reconstructs the space and time of experience, slow-motions it, puts it under the control of the repeat button, so that at a granular, flexible, intimate level, this experience is *captured* and in a form of 'real time', although not one we would recognize as such before our own 'real time' became fundamentally mediated. And it is never the viewer here who chooses what to see.

First, to me at least *Elephant* remains a film that can be explored in ideological terms. For theorists such as Galloway, writing fantastic accounts of gaming and protocol, this isn't any longer the case (or is not the case in terms of fully converged or 'uniquely informatic' objects). Code recapitulates the tale too exactly in all its depths and its surfaces (no allegorithm because all is algorithm); there is no sublimation (Galloway, 2004b: 34). Against this (a) *Elephant* shows us that the narrative logics can gather up the forms of information and can precisely sublimate them, but in ways that are profoundly *informational*. Gaming has a 'faulty logic', not as a form of play, but because it makes a claim that the world is automated, can be expressed algorithmically. *Elephant* does not express the logic of code, but the logic of a highly informated *society*. And the form of expression? This is not an ideological unveiling of a traditional kind, perhaps, but the flaunting of the missing centre which is mediation, which is what sits between or in-between depth and surface. Now finally revealed as the figure for a new form of control.

Notes

1 This chapter is for Denise Albanese, who is very good at seeing elephants.
2 *Elephant*'s budget was $3,000,000. For other commercial information see IMBd business data.
3 Here Deleuze is harbinger of the modernist film as the fulfilment of a particular kind of temporal metaphysics rather than the bearer of a schizoid politics, as Christian Kerslake points out (2005: 17).
4 'I knew there would be no dramatic coverage of the event because of the way we think of drama as entertainment and not as investigative . . . My reaction was, why not? Why don't we use drama to look into something like this?' (Van Sant, cited in Grierson, 2005).
5 'No expression characterized the California gold rush more than the words "seeing the elephant". Those planning to travel west announced they were "going to see the elephant". Those turning back claimed they had seen the "elephant's tracks" or the "elephant's tail" . . . The expression predated the gold rush, arising from a tale current when circus parades first featured elephants . . . A farmer . . . encountered the circus parade, led by an elephant. The farmer was thrilled, but his horses were not. Terrified, they bolted . . . "I don't give a hang", the farmer said, "for I have seen the elephant". (Levy, 1992: xvi).

Bibliography

Aarseth, Espen, 1999. 'Aporia and Epiphany in Doom and The Speaking Clock: the Temporality of Ergodic Art', in Marie-Laure Ryan (ed.), *Cyberspace Textuality, Computer Technology and Literary Theory*. Bloomington and Indianapolis: Indiana University Press. pp. 31–41.

Abbate, Janet, 1999. *Inventing the Internet*. London: MIT Press.

Abram, David, 1995. 'Merleau–Ponty and the voice of the earth', in Max Oelschlaege (ed.), *Postmodern Environmental Ethics*. New York: Suny Press, pp. 57–77.

Alaimo, Stacey, 1994. 'Cyborg and Ecofeminist Interventions: Challenges for Environmental Feminism', *Feminist Studies*, 20:1 (Spring), 133–152.

Alshejni, Lamis, 1999. 'Unveiling the Arab Woman's Voice through the Net', in Wendy Harcourt (ed.), *Woman @ Internet*. London: Zed Books, pp. 214–219.

Amsterdamski, Olga, 1997. 'Surely You Are Joking, Monsieur Latour!', *Science, Technology and Human Values*, 15:4, 495–504.

Anderson, Benedict, 1991. *Imagined Communities*. London: Verso.

Andrejevic, Mark, 2005. 'The Work of Watching One Another: Lateral Surveillance, Risk and Governance', *Surveillance and Society*, 2:4, 479–497.

Andrejevic, Mark, 2002. 'The Work of Being Watched: Interactive Media and the Exploitation of Self-Disclosue', *Critical Studies in Media Communication*, 19:2, 230–248.

Ansell Pearson, Keith, 1997. 'Viroid Life', in Keith Ansell Pearson (ed.), *Deleuze and Philosophy – the Difference Engineer*. London: Routledge, pp.180–210.

Appadurai, Arjun, 1990. 'Disjuncture and Difference in the Global Cultural Economy', in *Theory, Culture and Society*, 7, 295–310.

Apple Computer, 1984. Advertisement for the first Macintosh, directed by Ridley Scott, Quicktime version viewable on-line at www.apple-history.com/quickgallery.html.

Arendt, Hannah, 1989. *The Human Condition*. Chicago: Chicago University Press.

Arendt, Hannah, 1979. *Dageurreotypes*. Chicago: Chicago University Press.

Armitage, John, 1999. 'Resisting the NeoLiberal Discourse of Technology', *C-Theory*, 22:1–2, www.ctheory.com/a68.htm.

Armstrong, Isobel, 1996. 'Transparency', in Frances Spufford and Jenny Uglow (eds.), *Cultural Babbage: Technology, Time and Invention*. London: Faber and Faber, pp. 123–148.

Auge, Marc, 1995. *Non-Places: An Introduction to an Anthropology of Supermodernity*. London: Verso.

Augustine, 1991. *Confessions*. Oxford: Oxford University Press.

Auster, Paul, 2003. *Oracle Night*. New York: Henry Holt.

Austin, Thomas, 2007. *Watching the World: Screen Documentary and Audiences*. Manchester: Manchester University Press (forthcoming).

Austin, Thomas, 2002. *Hollywood Hype and Audiences: Selling and Watching Popular Film in the 1990s*. Manchester: Manchester University Press.

Bakardjieva, Maria and Richard Smith, 2001. 'The Internet In Everyday Life', *New Media & Society*, 3:1, 67–83.

Bal, Mieke, 2003. 'Visual Essentialism', *Journal of Visual Culture*, 2:1, 5–31.

Barbrook, Richard, 2005. 'Internet Banking, E-Money, and Internet Gift Economies', in *First Monday*, special issue 3, 'The High Tech Gift Economy', www.firstmonday.dk/issues/issue3–12/barbrook/.

Barbrook, Richard, 2000. 'Cyber-Communism', *Science as Culture*, 9:1, 5–39.

Barbrook, Richard and Andy Cameron, 1996. 'The Californian Ideology', *Science as Culture*, 26:6/1, 44–72, http://ma.hrc.wmin.ac.uk/ma.theory.4.2.db.

Barlow, John Perry, 1994. *The Information Railroad*, www.eff/org/pub/infrastruc/info/railroad.

Barry, Aisla, 1996. 'Who Gets to Play: Art, Access and the Margin', in John Dovey (ed.), *Fractal Dreams: New Media in Social Context*. London: Lawrence and Wishart, pp.136–153.

Barry, John, 1991. *Technobabble*. London: MIT PRESS.

Barthes, Roland, 1983. *Mythologies*. London: Paladin.

Barthes, Roland,1982. *Image, Music, Text*. London: Flamingo.

Bassett, Caroline, 2003. 'How Many Movements?', in Michael Bull and Les Back (eds), *The Auditory Culture Reader*. Oxford: Berg, pp. 343–355.

Bassett, Caroline, 1997a. 'Virtually Gendered, Life in an Online World', in Sarah Thornton and Ken Gelder (eds), *The Subcultures Reader*. London: Routledge, pp. 537–550.

Bassett, Caroline, 1997b. 'With a Little Help from Our (New) Friends', *Mute*, 8, 46–50.

Bassett, Caroline and Chris Wilbert, 1999. 'Where You Want to Go Today (Like It or Not): Leisure Practices in Cyberspaces', in Dave Crouch (ed.), *Leisure/Tourism Geographies: Practices and Geographical Knowledge*. London: Routledge, pp. 181–194.

Baudrillard, Jean, 1995. *Simulacra and Simulation*. Michigan: University of Michigan Press.

Baym, Nancy K., 1999. *Tune In, Log On: Soaps, Fandom and the Online*. London: Sage.

Belloc, Hilaire, 1907. 'Matilda', from *Cautionary Tales*, www.poetry-archive.com/b/matilda.html.

Belt, Vicki, Richard Ronald and Juliet Webster, 2000. 'Women's Work in the Information Economy', *Information, Communication and Society*, 3:3 (Autumn), www.infosoc.co.uk/0001/ab8.htm.

Beninger, James, 1986. *The Control Revolution: Technological and Economic Origins of the Information Society*. Cambridge, MA: Harvard University Press.

Benjamin, Walter, 1992. 'The Storyteller', in *Illuminations*. London: Fontana, pp. 83–101.

Bennett, Matt, 2000. 'Beautiful Patterns of Bits', *New Media and Society*, 2:1, 115–119.

Bennett, Tony, 1988. 'The Exhibitionary Complex', *New Formations*, 4 (Winter), 73–103.

Berg, Anne-Jorunn, 1996. 'Karoline and the Cyborgs: The Naturalization of a Technical Object', conference paper, CostA4 and GRANITE workshop, The Shaping of Information in Everyday Life, Amsterdam, 8–11 February.

Bergman, Simone, 1995. 'Communication Technologies in the Household: The Gendering of Artefacts and User Practices', Cost A4 and GRANITE workshop, Amsterdam, 8–11 February.

Berkeley, Edmund, 1949. *Giant Brains, Machines that Think*. New York: Wiley, www.scs.fsu.edu/~burkardt/fun/misc/giant_brains.html.

Berry, Dave M., 2006. 'A Contribution to a Political Economy of Open Source and Free Culture', in Fiona Macmillan (ed.), *New Directions in Copyright Law*, IV. London: Edward Elgar, pp. 193–223.

Berry, Josephine, 1999. 'Defying Eternity', *Mute*, 15, 15–16.

Bey, Hakim, 1999. 'La Red como Crisis Epistemologica', panel discussion, IV Muestra Internacional de Nuevas Tecnologias Arte y Communicacaión, University of Alicante, November.

Bey, Hakim, 1998. 'The Information War', in Joan Broadhurst Dixon and Eric Cassidy (eds.), *Virtual Futures*. London: Routledge, pp. 3–11.

Bey, Hakim, 1991. *The Temporary Autonomous Zone: Ontological Anarchy, Poetic Terrorism*. London: Autonomedia.

Biocca, Frank, 1995. 'Virtual Reality', in Robert Aston and Joyce Schwarz (eds), *Multimedia Gateway to the Next Millennium*. London: AP, pp. 12–24.

Birch, David, 2000. 'Second Sight', *The Guardian* (17 August), www.guardianunlimited.co.uk/Archive.

Bizzocchi, Jim, 2005. '*Run Lola Run* – Film as Narrative Database', MIT4, http://web.mit.edu/comm-forum/mit4/papers/bizzocchi.pdf.

Bloch, Ernst, 1992. 'Something's Missing: A Discussion between Ernst Bloch and Theodor W. Adorno on the Contradictions of Utopian Longing,' in Ernst Bloch (ed.), *The Utopian Function of Art and Literature: Selected Essays*. Cambridge, MA: MIT Press, pp. 12–30.

Boczkowski, Pablo, 1999. 'Understanding the Development of Online Newspapers', *New Media and Society*, 1:1, 101–127.

Bogard, William, 1996. *The Simulation of Surveillance*. Cambridge: Cambridge University Press.

Bolter, David Jay, 1991. *Writing Space: The Computer, Hypertext, and the History of Writing*. New Jersey: Lawrence Erlbaum.

Bolter, David Jay, 1989. 'The Computer as Defining Technology', in Tom Forester (ed.), *Computers in the Human Context*. Oxford: Blackwell, pp. 33–45.

Bolter, David Jay and Richard Grusin, 1999. *Remediation: Understanding New Media*. Cambridge, MA: MIT Press.

Bordwell, David 2004. 'Neo-Structuralist Narratology and the Functions of Filmic Storytelling', in Marie-Laure Ryan (ed.), *Narrative across Media: The Languages of Storytelling*. London: University of Nebraska Press, pp. 203–220.

Bordwell, David 1997. *On the History of Film Style*. Cambridge, MA: Harvard University Press.

Bordwell, David, 1985. *Narration in the Fiction Film*. London: Routledge.

Borgmann, Albert, 1984. *Technology and the Character of Contemporary Life*. Chicago: University of Chicago Press.

Bourdieu, Pierre, 1984. *Distinctions: A Social Critique of the Judgement of Taste*. London: Routledge.

Bowie, Andrew, 1995. 'Romanticism and technology', *Radical Philosphy*, 72 (July/August), 5–11.

Braidotti, Rosie, 1996. 'Cyberfeminism with a Difference', *New Formations*, 29 (Summer), 9–25.

Braman, Sandra, 2000. 'From Vertu, to Virtue, to the Virtual', in Stephanie B. Gibson and Ollie Oveido (eds), *The Emerging Cyberculture*. New Jersey: Hampton Press, pp. 307–324.

Brand, Stuart, 1987. *The Media Lab: Inventing the Future at MIT*. New York: Viking.

Bruckman, Amy, 1993. 'Gender Swapping on the Internet', conference paper EFC–1, The Internet Society, San Francisco, August.

Brunsdon, Charlotte, 1991. 'Satellite Dishes and the Landscapes of Taste' *New Formations*, 15 (Winter), 23–43.

Bruzzi, Stella, 2000. *New Documentary: A Critical Introduction*. London: Routledge.

Bryld, Mette and Nina Lykke, 2000. *CosmoDolphins: Feminist Cultural Studies of Technology, Animals and the Sacred*. London: Zed Books.

Bulkeley, Jonathan, 1996. Interview in *MacUser UK*, 12:4, 24–28.

Burgin, Victor. 2004. *The Remembered Film*. London: Reaktion Books.

Buse, Peter, 1996. 'Nintendo and Telos, Will You Ever Reach the End?', *Cultural Critique*, (Fall), 163–185.

Bush, Vannevar, 1945. *As We May Think*, www.theatlantic.com/doc/194507/bush.

Butler, Judith, 1993. *Bodies that Matter*. London: Routledge.

Caffentzis, George, 1997. 'Why Machines Cannot Create Value', in Michael Stack, Jim Davis and Thomas Hirschel (eds), *Cutting Edge*. London: Verso, pp. 29–56.

Cairncross, Frances, 1997. *The Death of Distance: How the Communications Revolution Will Change our Lives*. London: Orion Business Books.

Callinicos, Alex, 1999. *Social Theory: A Historical Introduction*. London: Polity.

Callinicos, Alex, 1995. *Theories and Narratives*. London: Polity.

Callon, Michel and Bruno Latour, 1992. 'Don't Throw the Baby Out with the Bath Water', in Andrew Pickering (ed.), *Science as Practice and Culture*. Chicago: University of Chicago Press, pp. 343–367.

Callon, Michel and Law, John, 1995. 'Agency and the Hybrid Collectif', in *South Atlantic Quarterly*, 94:2, 480–507.

Calvino, Italo, 1996. *Six Memos for the Next Millennium*. London: Vintage.

Cameron, Andy, 1995. 'Dissimulations, the Illusion of Interactivity', in *Millennium Film Journal*, 'Interactivities', 28 (Spring), 32–48, http:// wmin.ac.uk./ media/vb/dissim.html.

Caputo, John D., 1987. *Radical hermeneutics: Repetition, Deconstruction and the Hermeneutic Project*. Bloomington: Indiana University Press.

Carey, James, 2002. 'A Cultural Approach to Communication', in Denis McQuail (ed.), *McQuail's Reader in Mass Communication*. London: Sage. pp. 36–45.

Castells, Manuel, 1999. 'An Introduction to the Information Age', in Hugh Mackay and Tim O'Sullivan (eds), *The Media Reader: Continuity and Transformation*. London: Sage/The Open University, pp. 398–410.

Castells, Manuel, 1996. *The Information Age: Economy, Society and Culture, The Rise of the Network Society*, I. Oxford: Blackwell.

Cavarero, Adriana, 1997. *Relating Narratives: Storytelling and Selfhood*. London: Routledge.

Ceruzzi, Paul, 1999. 'Inventing Personal Computing', in Donald MacKenzie and Judy Wajcman (eds), *The Social Shaping of Technology*. Buckingham: Open University, pp. 64–86.

Cheney, Jim, 1995. 'Postmodern Environmental Ethics: Ethics as Bioregional Narrative', in Max Oelschlaeger (ed.), *Postmodern Environmental Ethics*. New York: SUNY Press, pp. 23–42.

Chtcheglov, Ivan, 1997. 'Formulary for a New Urbanism', in Ken Knabb (ed.), *Situationist International Anthology*. Berkeley: Bureau of Public Secrets, pp. 2–4, www.uncarved.org/turb/articles/formulary.html.

Clucas, Stephen, 2000. 'Cultural Phenomenology and the Everyday', *Critical Quarterly*, 42:1, 8–34.

Cockburn, Cynthia, 1992. 'The Circuit of Technology: Gender Identity and Power', in Roger Silverstone and Eric Hirsch (eds), *Consuming Technologies*. London: Routledge, pp. 33–42.

Cohen, Tom, 1996. 'The Ideology of Dialogue: the Bakhtin/De Man Disconnection', *Cultural Critique*, Spring, 33–45.

Collins, Harry and Steven Yearly, 1992. 'Epistemological Chicken', in Andrew Pickering (ed.), *Science as Practice and Culture*. Chicago: University of Chicago Press, pp. 301–326.

Copjec, Joan, 1989. 'The Orthopsychic Subject, Film Theory and the Reception of Lacan', *October*, 49, 53–72.

Coward, Ros and John Ellis, 1978. *Language and Materialism*. London: RKP Press.

Coyne, Richard, 1999. *Technoromanticism*. London: MIT Press.

Coyne, Richard, 1995. *Designing Information Technology for the Postmodern Age*. London: MIT Press.

Crang, Mike, 1997. 'Research through the Tourist Gaze', *Progress in Human Geography*, 21:3, 359–373.

Crary, Jonathan, 2000. *Suspensions of Perception*, Cambridge, MA: MIT Press.

Cringely, Robert X., 1992. *Accidental Empires: How the Boys of Silicon Valley Made Their Millions*. London: Penguin.

Crowley, Tony, 1996. *Language in History: Theories and Texts*. London: Routledge.

Culler, Jonanthan, 1976. *Saussure*. London: Fontana.

Currie, Mark, 1998. *Postmodern Narrative Theory*. London: Macmillan.

Curtis, Pavel, 1993. 'MUDS Grow Up: Social Virtual Reality in the Real World', www.eff.org/Net_culture/MOO_MUD_IRC/muds_grow_up.paper.

Dagognet, François, 1992. Preface to *Etienne Jules Marey*. New York: Zone Books.

Dagonet, François, 1989. Preface to *The Material of Invention*. Boston, MA: MIT Press.

Darley, Andrew, 2000. *Visual Digital Culture*. London: Routledge.

Davis, Kathy, 2000. 'Monsters and Family Values: Assisted Reproduction and the Ageing Natural Body', in Janine Marchessault and Kim Sawchuk (eds), *Wild Science: Reading Feminism, Medicine and the Media*. London: Routledge, pp. 105–120.

De Certeau, Michel, 1984. *The Practice of Everyday Life*. California: Berkeley University Press.

De Lauretis, Teresa, 1984. *Alice Doesn't*. London: Macmillan.

De Saussure, Ferdinand, 1983. *Course in General Linguistics*. London: Duckworth.

De Sola Pool, Ithiel, 1983. *Technologies of Freedom*. New York: Cornell University Press.

Deleuze, Gilles, 2005. *Cinema 2: The Time-Image*. London: Continuum.

Deleuze, Gilles, 1992. 'Postscript on the Societies of Control'. *October*, 59 (Winter), 3–7.

Deleuze, Gilles and Félix Guattari, 1987. *A Thousand Plateaus*. London: University of Minnesota Press.

Denning, Peter, *et al.*, 1989. 'Computing as a Discipline', *Communications of the ACM*, 32:1, 9–23.

Derrida, Jacques, 1996. 'As if I Were Dead: An Interview with Jacques Derrida', in John Brannigan, Ruth Robbins, and Julian Wolfreys (eds), *Applying: To Derrida*. London: Macmillan, pp. 212–226.

Derrida, Jacques, 1995. *Archive Fever*. London: University of Chicago Press.

Derrida, Jacques, 1987. *The Post Card: From Socrates to Freud and Beyond*. Chicago: Chicago University Press.

Derrida, Jacques, 1978. *Writing and Difference*. Chicago: University of Chicago Press.

Derrida, Jacques, 1976. *Of Grammatology*. Baltimore: Johns Hopkins University Press.

Derrida, Jacques, 1972. *Margins of Philosophy*. Chicago: University of Chicago Press.

Dewitt, Philip Elmer, 1994. 'Battle for the Internet', *Time Magazine*, 144:4 (25 July), 50–56.

Doane, Mary Anne, 1990. 'Information, Crisis, and Catastrophe', in Patricia Mellancamp (ed.), *Logics of Television: Essays in Cultural Criticism*. Indiana: Indiana University Press, pp. 221–238.

Dodge, Martin and Rob Kitchin, 2000. *Mapping Cyberspace*. London: Routledge.

DoubleClick, 2001. Homepage, www.doubleclick.com.

Druckery, Peter, 1999. 'Ready or Not?', in Tim Druckery (ed.), *Ars Electronica – Facing the Future*. London: MIT Press, pp. 16–19.

Dyson, Esther, 1997. *Release 2.0, a Design for Living in the Digital Age*. London: Peachpit.

Eagleton, Terry, 2003. *After Theory*. Harmondsworth: Penguin.

Edwards, Paul, 1996. *The Closed World: Computers and the Politics of Discourse in Cold War America*. Cambridge, MA: MIT Press.

Edwards, Paul, 1994. 'Hyper Text and Hypertension: Post-Structuralist Critical Theory, Social Studies of Science and Software', *Social Studies of Science*: 24, 229–278.

EFF, 2000. Electronic Frontier Foundation, archive, www.eff/org/archive.html.

Elsaesser, Thomas, 2005. 'The Cinematic Apparatus: Typologies, Affinities, Ontologies', conference paper, Cinema and Technology International Conference, Institute for Cultural Research, Lancaster, 6–9 April.

Etzioni, Amitai, 1999. *The Limits of Privacy*. New York: Basic Books.

Fairclough, Norman, 2000. *Language and Power*. London: Routledge.

Farquahar, Dion, 2000. '(M)other Discourses', in Gill Kirkup, Linda Janes, Kath Woodward and Fiona Hovenden (eds), *The Gendered Cyborg*. London: Routledge, pp. 209–221.

Feenberg, Andrew, 1999. *Questioning Technology*. London: Routledge.

Felski, Rita, 2000. 'The Invention of Everyday Life', *New Formations*, 'Cool Moves', 39, 15–32.

Ferguson, Marjorie, 1991. 'Marshall McLuhan Revisited: 1960s Zeitgeist Victim or Postmodern Pioneer', *Media Culture and Society*, 13:1, 71–90.

Flaxman, Gregory, 2000. 'The Brain is the Screen', interview with Gilles Deleuze, in *Deleuze and the Philosophy of Cinema*. Minneapolis: University of Minnesota Press, pp. 91–97.

Flusser, Vilem, 2002. *Vilem Flusser, Writings*. London: University of Minnesota Press.

Foucault, Michel, 1975. *Discipline and Punish*. Harmondsworth: Penguin.

Frisson, Valerie, 1995. ' "Decoding" Telecommunications in Everyday Life', CostA4 and GRANITE workshop, Amsterdam, 8–11 February.

Fuller, Matthew, 2003. *Behind the Blip: Essays on the Culture of Software*. London: Autonomedia.

Fuller, Matthew, 1996. 'Daydream Believer', notes on *Rehearsal of Memory*. CD-ROM, London.

Gaggi, Silvio, 1997. *From Text to Hypertext: Decentering the Subject in Fiction, Film, the Visual Arts, and Electronic Media*. Philadelphia: University of Philadelphia Press.

Galloway, Alexander, 2004a. 'Playing the Code, Allegories of Control in *Civilization*', *Radical Philosophy*, 128 (November/December), 33–40.

Galloway, Alexander, 2004b. *Protocol: How Control Exists After Decentralization*. Cambridge MA: MIT Press.

Gandy, Oscar, 1993. *The Panoptic Sort, A Political Economy of Personal Information*. Boulder: Westview Press.

Gates, Bill, Nathan Myhrvold and Peter Rinearson, 1996. *The Road Ahead*. Harmondsworth: Penguin.

Geertz, Clifford, 1993. *The Interpretation of Cultures*. London: Fontana.

GeoCities, 2001. Homepage, http://us.geocities.yahoo.com/v/info.html.

GeoCities, 1998a. GeoCities user guidelines (website, no longer accessible).

GeoCities, 1998b. Landmark sites, information for users (website, no longer accessible).

GeoCities, 1998c. Privacy statement, information for users, (website, no longer accessible).

GeoCities, 1998d. Guidelines on Bourbon Street, www.geocities.com/Bourbon Street/8775/guidelines.html (no longer accessible).

GeoCities, 1998e. Rules and Regulations, www.geocities/com/BourbonStreet/8775/guidelines.html (no longer accessible).

GeoCities, 1998f. Homepage, www.geocities.com, accessed in 1998.

GeoCities, 1998g. Report to the Securities and Investment Commission, form 10–K, www.sec.gov/archives/edgar/data/1062777/000101/062–99–000571.txt.

Geocities, 1998h. 'Rules and Regulations', GeoCities information to users (website, no longer accessible).

GeoCities, 1998i. GeoCities codes (website, no longer accessible).

GeoCities, 1998j. 'What is the Watermark?', notice to homesteaders, (website, no longer acessible).

GeoCities, 1998k. GeoCities Worldreport, http://209.1.233.1//picketfence/1298/newyork-times.html.

Gere, Charlie, 2002. *Digital Culture*. London: Reaktion Books.

Gibson, Andrew, 1996a. *Towards a Postmodern Theory of Narrative*. Edinburgh: Edinburgh University Press.

Gibson, Andrew, 1996b. 'Interactive Fiction and Narrative Space', in Warren Chernaik, Marilyn Deegan, and Andrew Gibson (eds), *Beyond the Book: Theory, Culture and the Politics of Cyberspace*. Oxford: Office for Humanities Communications, pp. 79–91.

Gibson, J. J., 1950. *The Perception of the Visual World*. London: Houghton Mifflin.

Gibson, Stephanie B., 2000. 'Literacy, Paradigm, and Paradox: An Introduction', in Stephanie B. Gibson and Ollie Oviedo (eds), *The Emerging Cyberculture*. New Jersey: Hampton Press, pp. 1–25.

Gibson, William, 1994. *Virtual Light*. Harmondsworth: Penguin.

Gibson, William, 1991. *Neuromancer*. Harmondsworth: Penguin.

Goldberg, Andy, 1999. 'What Happened to the Dream', *Electronic Telegraph Archive*, 'Connection, the Science and Technology Download', 25, 11, 99, www.telegraph.co.uk.

Golzen, Godfrey, 2000. 'Emotional Labour', *First Person Global*, www. firstpersonglobal.com/article/cgi=226.

Goodwins, Rupert, 1999. 'Column', ZDNet News (30 January), 1, zdnet.co.uk/news/1999/4/ns-6823.html).

Gore, Al, 1994. Speech at the Superhighway Summit, Royce Hall, UCLA, 11 January, http://clinton1.nara.gov/White_House/EOP/OVP/other/superhig.html.

Gortz, Andre, 1992. *Farewell to the Working Class*. London: Pluto.

GospelCom, 2001. GospelCom, www.gospelcom.net/realgold/digest.shtml.

Gozzi, Raymond, 1999. *The Power of Metaphor in the Age of Electronic Media*. New Jersey: Hampton Press.

Graham, Beryl, 1997. 'Not a Show about New Technology', in Beryl Graham (ed.), *Serious Games*. London: Barbican Art Gallery, pp. 6–10.

Graham, Philip, 2000. 'Hypercapitalism', *New Media and Society*, 2:2, 131–156.

Graham, Stephen, 2000. 'The Fifth Utility', *Index on Censorship*, 3, Spring, www.indexoncensorship.org/300/ban.html.

Gram Hanssen, Elizabeth, 1996. 'Objectivity in the Description of Nature: Between Social Construction and Essentialism', in Nina Lykke and Rosi Braidotti (eds), *Between Monsters, Goddesses and Cyborgs*. London: Zed Books, pp. 88–105.

Grange, Joseph, 1994. 'Whitehead and Heidegger on Technological Goodness', *Research in Philosophy and Technology*, 'Technology and Everyday Life', 14, 161–173.

Greimas, A. J., 1996. 'Reflections on Actantial Models', in Susan Onega, Jose Angel and Garcia Landa (eds), *Narratology*. Harlow: Longman, pp. 76–93.

Greimas, A. J., 1987. *On Meaning*. London: University of Minnesota Press.

Grierson, Tim, 2005. *Black Table*, www.blacktable.com/index_0411.htm.

Haddon, Leslie, 1995. 'The Home Computer, the Making of a Consumer Electronic', *Science as Culture*, 7, 7–36.

Hall, Stuart, 1992. 'Encoding/Decoding', in *Culture, Media and Language*. London: Routledge, pp 128–138.

Hansell, Saul, 1998. 'GeoCities' Cyberworld Is Vibrant, but Can It Make Money?', *New York Times* (13 July), http://209.1.244.1//picketfence/1298/newyorktimes.html.

Haraway, Donna, 1997. *Modest_Witness@Second Millennium FemaleMan_ Meets_OncoMouse*. London: Routledge.

Haraway, Donna, 1992. 'The Promise of Monsters', in Lawrence Grosberg, Cary Nelson and Paula Treichler (eds), *Cultural Studies*. New York: Routledge, pp. 295–338.

Haraway, Donna, 1991. *Simians, Cyborgs and Women*. London: Routledge.

Hardt, Michael and Antonio Negri, 2000. *Empire*. London: Harvard University Press.

Harries, Ed, 2002. *The New Media Book*. London: BFI.

Hartmann, Maren, *et al.* (eds), 2005. *Domestication of Media and Technology*. Maidenhead: Open University Press.

Hartmann, Maren, 2004. *Technologies and Utopias: The Cyberflâneur and the Experience of 'Being Online'*. Munich: Verlag Reinhard Fischer.

Harwood, Graham, 1998a. Unpublished interview with Caroline Bassett.

Harwood, Graham, 1998b. 'Change of Address', letter to nettime (an online discussion group), posted by Matt Fuller, www.desk.nl/~nettime/.

Harwood, Graham, 1997a. Unpublished interview with Caroline Bassett.

Harwood, Graham, 1997b. *Rehearsal of Memory*, in Graham Beryl, (ed.), *Serious Games*. London: Barbican Art Gallery, pp. 38–41.

Harwood, 1997c. *Rehearsal of Memory*, CD-ROM. Artec and Bookworks: London.

Harwood, Graham, 1995. Text, Next Five Minutes conference, Amsterdam, 11–14 September, www.dds.nl/~m5m/texts/graham.html.

Haskel, Lisa, 1996. 'Rehearsal of Memory, some Notes on Distribution for an Artist's CD-ROM', internal marketing report, Artec.

Hattenstone, Simon, 2004. 'All the World's an Art School', *The Guardian* (24 January).

Hayles, Katherine, 1993. 'The Materiality of Informatics', *Configurations*, 1:1, 147–170, www.muse.jhu.edu/journals/configurations/v001/1/hayles.html.

Hayles, Katherine, 2002. *Writing Machines*. Cambridge, MA: MIT Press.

Hayles, Katherine, 1998. 'The Condition of Virtuality', in *Language Machines*. London: Routledge, pp. 183–208.

Hegel, John III and Arthur Armstrong, 1997. *Net Gain: Expanding Corporate Markets Through Virtual Communities*. Boston: Harvard Business Press.

Heid, Jim, 1991. *MacWorld Complete Mac Handbook*. London: IDG Worldwide.

Heidegger, Martin, 1993. *Basic Writings*. London: Routledge.

Heims, Steve Joshua, 1991. *The Cybernetics Group*. London: MIT Press.

Helmore, Edward, 2000. 'Dangers of the Digital World: Be Very Afraid of the Future', *The Observer*, (19 March), 19.

Henig, Peter, 1998. 'To know GeoCities Is to Love It, but to Know GeoCities' Business Model Is to Be Skeptical of It', *Red Herring*, (11 August), www.tekekomnet.com/.

Herz, J. C., 1995. *Surfing on the Internet*. London: Abacus.

Hillis, Ken, 1999. *Digital Sensations*. Minneapolis: University of Minnesota Press.

Hills, Mathew, 2001a. Review of Nancy K. Baym, *Tune In, Log On: Soaps, Fandom and Online, New Media and Society*, 3:1, 115–119.

Hills, Mathew, 2001b. 'Virtually Out There: Strategies, Tactics and Affective Spaces in Online Fandom', in *Technospaces: Inside the New Media*. London: Continuum, pp.147–160.

Hirschkop, Ken, 1989. 'Bakhtin and Cultural Theory', in Ken Hirschkop and David Shepherd (eds), *Bakhtin and Cultural Theory*. Manchester: Manchester University Press, pp. 1–39.

Hodges, Alan, 1983. *Alan Turing: The Enigma*. New York: Simon and Schuster.

Hof, Robert D. with Seanna Browder and Peter Elstrom, 1997. *Business Week*, 'Internet Communities', European Edition (5 May).

Homer, Sean, 2006. 'Fredric Jameson and the Limits of Postmodern Theory', www.shef.ac.uk/uni/academic/N-Q/psysc/staff/sihomer/limits.html.

Idhe, Don, 1993. *Post-Phenomenology*. Illinois: North Western University Press.

IMDb, 2006. Business data for *Elephant*, The Internet Movie Database, www. IMDb.com.

The Independent, 2000. 'Threats to E-Commerce', leader (13 June), www. fipr.org/rip/.624.

Industry Standard, 1998. 'Home Pages Set to Become Next Commodity' (28 July), www.cnn.com/TECH/computing.

Irigaray, Luce, 1985a. *Speculum of the Other Woman*. Ithaca: Columbia University Press.

Irigaray, Luce, 1985b. *This Sex that Is Not One*. Ithaca: Columbia University Press.

Jameson, Frederic, 1994. *Seeds of Time*. New York: Columbia University Press.

Jameson, Fredric, 1991. *Postmodernism or, The Cultural Logic of Late Capitalism*. Durham, NC: Duke University Press.

Jameson, Fredric, 1987. 'Foreword' in *On Meaning*. London: University of Minnesota Press, pp. vi–xxiii.

Jameson, Fredric, 1984. 'Postmodernism or, The Cultural Logic of Late Capitalism', *New Left Review*, 146 (July–August), 59–92.

Jameson, Fredric, 1981. *The Political Unconscious: Narrative as a Socially Symbolic Act*. London: Methuen.

Jarry, David and Julia, 1991. *Sociology*. London: Harper Collins.

Jay, Martin, 1998. 'Scopic Regimes of Modernity', in Hal Foster (ed.), *Visual and Visuality 2*. Seattle: Bay Press, pp. 3–38.

Johnston, John, 1997. 'Friedrich Kittler: Media Theory After Post–Structuralism', in John Johnston (ed.), *Literature Media Information Systems*. Amsterdam: G+B Arts, pp. 1–27.

Jones, Steve, 1999. 'Understanding Micropolis and Compunity', in *Proceedings of the First International Conference on Cultural Attitudes Towards Technology and Communication*. London: CATaC98, pp. 21–33.

Jones, Steve, 1998. 'Information, Internet, and Community: Notes Towards an Understanding of Community in the Information Age', in Steve Jones (ed.), *CyberSociety 2.0*. London: Sage, pp. 1–35.

Kay, Alan, 1990. 'User Interface, a Personal View', in Brenda Laurel (ed.), *The Art of Human Interface Design*. London: Addison Wesley, pp. 191–207.

Kearney, Richard, 1984. *Dialogue with Contemporary Thinkers*. Manchester: Manchester University Press.

Kelly, Kevin, 1997. 'It takes a Village to Make a Mall', *Wired*, 5:8 (August), www.wired.com/wired/archive/5.08/hagel.html.

Kelly, Kevin, 1994. *Out of Control*. London: Fourth Estate.

Kelly, Kevin and Gary Wolf, 1997. 'Push: The Radical Future of media', *Wired UK*, 3:3, 69–81.

Kember, Sarah, 1995. 'Surveillance, Technology and Crime', in Martin Lister (ed.), *The Photographic Image in Digital Culture*. London: Routledge, pp. 115–126.

Kennedy, Barbara, 1996. 'Cyberfeminisms: Introduction', in David Bell and Barbara Kennedy (eds), *The Cybercultures Reader*. Routledge, London, pp. 283–290.

Kerslake, Christian, 2005. 'Transcendental Cinema, Deleuze, Time and Modernity', *Radical Philosophy*, 130 (March/April), 7–19.

Kim, Amy Jo, 2000. *Community Building On The Web*. London: Peachpit.

Kinder, Marsha, 2002. 'Narrative Equivocations between Movies and Games' in Dan Harries (ed.), *The New Media Book*. London: BFI, pp. 119–132.

King, Geoff, 2005. *American Independent Cinema*. London: I. B. Taurus.

Kirkpatrick, Graeme, 2000. 'Towards a Critical Sociology of the Computer Interface', *Imprints*, 5:1 (Summer), 75–89.

Kittler, Friedrich A., 1997. *Literature Media Information Systems*. Amsterdam: G+B Arts International.

Kline, Roland and Trevor Pinch, 1999. 'The Social Construction of Technology', in Donald MacKenzie and Judy Wacjman (eds), *The Social Shaping of Technology*. Buckingham: Open University Press, pp. 113–115.

Klinger, Barbara, 1989. 'Digression at the Cinema: Reception and Mass Culture', *Cinema Journal*, 28:4 (Summer), 3–19.

Kollock, Peter and Mark Smith, 1999. *Communities in Cyberspace*. London: Routledge.

Kottman, Paul, 2000. 'Introduction', in *Relating Narratives*. London: Routledge, pp. vii–xxxii.

Kramarae, Cheris, 1999. 'The Language and the Nature of the Internet: The Meaning of Global', in *New Media and Society*, 1:1, 47–53.

Kroker, Author, 1996. 'Virtual Capitalism', in Stanley Aronowitz, Barbara Martinsons and Michael Menser (eds), *TechnoScience and CyberCulture*. London: Routledge, pp.167–181.

Krutnik, Frank, 1991. *In a Lonely Street: Genre, Film Noir, Masculinity*. London: Routledge.

Lacan, Jacques, 1991. *The Seminar of Jacques Lacan: Book II: The Ego in Freud's Theory and in the Technique of Psychoanalysis*. London: W. W. Norton.

LaCapra, Dominick, 1983. *Rethinking Intellectual History: Texts, Contexts, Language*. Ithaca: Cornell University Press.

Landow, George, 1994. 'What's a Critic to Do? Critical Theory in the Age of Hypertext', in George Landow (ed.), *Hyper/Text/Theory*. Baltimore: Johns Hopkins University Press, pp. 1–50.

Landsberg, Alison, 2003. 'Prosthetic Memory: The Ethics and Politics of Memory in an Age of Mass Culture', in Paul Grainge (ed.), *Memory and Popular Film*. Manchester: Manchester University Press, pp. 144–201.

Lanham, Richard A., 1993. *The Electronic Word: Democracy, Technology, and the Arts*. Chicago: University of Chicago Press.

Lash, Alex, 1999. 'Yahoo Closes GeoCities Merger, Beats the Bubble', *Industry Standard*, www.thestandard.com.au.

Lash, Scott, 2002. *Critique of Information*. London: Sage.

Latour, Bruno, 2000a. 'How to be Iconophilic in Art, Science and Religion', in Caroline Jones and Peter Gallison (eds), *Picturing Science Producing Art*. London: Routledge, pp. 418–441.

Latour, Bruno, 2000b. 'When Things Strike Back – A Possible Contribution to Science Studies', *British Journal of Sociology*, Millennium Issue, 107–123.

Latour, Bruno, 1999. *Pandora's Hope*. London: Harvard University Press.

Latour, Bruno, 1996. *Aramis, or, The Love of Technology*. London: Harvard University Press.

Latour, Bruno and Steve Woolgar, 1979. *Laboratory Life: The Social Construction of Scientific Fact*. London: Sage.

Laurel, Brenda, 1991. *Computers as Theatre*. London: Addison Wesley.

Laurier, Eric and Chris Philo, 1999. 'X-morphizing', *Environment and Planning*, 31, 1047–1071.

Law, John, 1999. 'After ANT' in John Law and John Hassard (eds), *Actor Network Theory and After*, special issue of *Sociological Review*, pp. 1–14.

Lee, Martyn, 1997. 'Relocating Location: Cultural Geography, the Specificity of Place and the City Habitus', in Jim McGuigan (ed.), *Cultural Methodologies*. London: Sage, pp. 126–341.

Lefebvre, Henri, 1991. *The Production of Space*. Oxford: Blackwell.

Lenoir, Timothy, 1994. 'Was the Last Turn the Right Turn: The Semiotic Turn and A. J. Greimas', *Configurations*, 1, 119–136.

Leonard, Andrew, 2000. 'Do-It-Yourself Giant Brains!', *Salon* (22 June), http://archive.salon.com/tech/fsp/2000/06/22/chapter_2_part_two/print.html.

Lessig, Lawrence, 2002. *The Future of Ideas: The Fate of the Commons in a Connected World*. New York: Vintage.

Levinson, Paul, 1997. *Soft Edge*. London: Routledge.

Levy, Jo Ann, 1992. *They Saw the Elephant: Women in the California Gold Rush*. Norman: University of Oklahoma Press, www.goldrush.com/.

Levy, Stephen, 1995. *Insanely Great*. London: Penguin.

Levy, Steven, 1984. *Hackers' London*. London: Penguin.

Lie, Meret and Knut Sorensen, 1996. 'Introduction', in Meret Lie and Knut Sorensen (eds), *Making Technology Our Own: Domesticating Technology into Everyday Life*. Oslo: Scandinavian University Press, pp. 1–31.

Light, Ann, 1999. Review of 'Invisible Computing' in *New Media and Society*, 1:2, 268–272.

Lister, Martin, 1995. 'Introduction', in Lister (ed.), *The Photographic Image in Digital Culture*. London: Routledge, pp. 1–29.

Luckhurst, Roger, 1996. '(Touching on) Tele-Technology', in John Brannigan, Ruth Robbins and Julian Leonard Wolfreys (eds), *Applying: To Derrida*. Basingstoke: Macmillan, pp. 171–183.

Lury, Celia, 1999. 'Marking Time with Nike, the Illusion of the Durable', in *Public Culture*, 11:3, 499–526.

Lury, Celia, 1998. *Prosthetic Culture: Photography, Memory and Identity*. London: Routledge.

Luxembourg, Rosa, 1970. *Rosa Luxembourg Speaks*. London: Pathfinder.

Lyon, David, 1988. *The Information Society: Issues and Illusions*. Cambridge: Polity Press.

Lyotard, Jean-François, 1984. *The Postmodern Condition: A Report on Knowledge*. Manchester: Manchester University Press.

McBeath, Graham and Stephen Webb, 1997. 'Cities, Subjectivity and Cyberspace', in Sally Westwood and John Williams (eds), *Imagining Cities*. London: Routledge, pp. 249–260.

McCullough, Malcolm, 2004. *Digital Ground*. Cambridge, MA: MIT Press.

McCullough, Malcolm, 1996. *Abstracting Craft: The Practiced Digital Hand*. London: MIT Press.

Mackay, Hugh and Tim O'Sullivan, 1999. *The Media Reader: Continuity and Transformation*. London: Sage.

MacKenzie, Donald, 1984. 'Marx and the Machine', *Technology and Culture*, 25, 473–502.

MacKenzie, Donald and Judy Wacjman, 1999. 'The Technology of Production: Introduction to Second Section', in Donald MacKenzie and Judy Wacjman (eds), *The Social Shaping of Technology*. Buckingham: Open University Press, pp. 141–152.

McLuhan, Marshall, 1994. *Understanding Media: The Extensions of Man*, Cambridge, MA: MIT Press.

McNay, Louis, 2000. *Gender and Agency: Reconfiguring the Subject in Feminist and Social Theory*. Cambridge: Polity.

Malik, Suhail, 1997. 'Is the Internet a Rhizome?', *Mute*, 7 (Winter), xiv.

Malik, Suhail, 1996. 'Is Cyberspace Postmodern?', *Mute*, 6 (Autumn), xv.

Mander, Jenny, 1999. *Circles of Learning, Narratology and the Eighteenth-Century French Novel*. Oxford: Voltaire Foundation.

Manovich, Lev, 2001. *The Language of New Media*. Cambridge, MA: MIT Press.

Manovich, Lev, 2000. 'Database as a Genre of new Media', *AI and Society*, 14:2, 176–183.

Manovich, Lev, 1996. 'The Labor of Perception', in Lyn Hershman Leeson (ed.), *Clicking In, Hot Links to a Digital Culture*. Seattle: Bay Press, pp. 180–190.

Marcuse, Herbert, 1972. *One Dimensional Man*. London: Abacus.

Margonelli, Lisa, 1999. 'Inside AOL's Cyber-Sweatshop – How a Fortune Was Built on the Fingers of Tens of Thousands of Unpaid Volunteers', *Wired* (7 October), www.hotwired.com.

Marvin, Carolyn, 1988. *When Old Technologies Were New*. Oxford: Oxford University Press.

Marx, Karl, 1980. 'Speech at the Anniversary of the People's Paper', in Karl Marx and Friedrich Engels, *Collected Works*, XIV. London: Lawrence and Wishart, pp. 655–656.

Marx, Karl, 1977. *Selected Writings*. Oxford: Oxford University Press.

Marx, Karl, 1973. *Grundrisse*. Harmondsworth: Penguin.

Marx, Karl, 1954. *The Communist Manifesto*. London: Progress Publishing.

Massey, Doreen, 1994. *Space, Place and Gender*. Cambridge: Polity.

Massumi, Brian, 1995a. 'The Autonomy of Affect', *Cultural Critique*, 31 (Autumn), 83–109.

Massumi, Brian, 1995b. 'Interface and Active Space', conference paper, Sixth International Symposium in Electric Art (ISEA), Montreal, 18–22 September, www.anu.edu.au.HRC/first_and_last/works/interface.htf.

Mattelart, Armand and Michelle, 1998. *Theories of Communication*. London: Sage.

Merrifield, Andy, 2000. 'Henri Lefebvre, a Socialist in Space', in Mike Crang and Nigel Thrift (eds), *Thinking Space*. London: Routledge, pp. 167–182.

Metz, Christian, 1974. *Film Language: A Semiotics of Cinema*. New York: Oxford University Press.

Microsoft, 1994. *Computer Dictionary*. Redmond: Microsoft Publishing.

Miller, Daniel and Dan Slater, 2000. *The Internet: An Ethnographic Approach*. Oxford: Berg.

Mirzoeff, Nicholas, 1999. *Visual Cultural Studies: A Reader*. London: Routledge.

Mitchell, William J., 1995. *City of Bits: Space, Place, and the* Infobahn. Cambridge, MA: MIT Press.

Mitchell, W. J. T., 1994. *Picture Theory*. Berkeley: University of California Press.

Moravec, Hans, 1988. *Mind Children: The Future of Robot and Human Intelligence*. Cambridge, MA: Harvard University Press.

Moretti, Franco, 2005. *Signs Taken for Wonders*. London: Verso.

Moretti, Franco, 2003. 'Graphs, Maps, Tree', *New Left Review*, 24 (November–December), www.newleftreview.net/Issue24.shtml.

Morkes, John, Hadyn Kernal and Clifford Nass, 1999. 'Effects of Humor in Task-Oriented Human-Computer Interaction and Computer-Mediated Communication: A Direct Test of SRCT Theory', *Human Computer Interaction*, 14:4, 395–435.

Mumford, Lewis, 1946. *Technics and Civilization*. London: Routledge.

Murray, Janet, 1999. *Hamlet on the Holodeck*. London: MIT Press.

Nelson, Jeff, 1991. 'Lotus Marketplace', *Risk Digest Report*, 10:61, hosted by ACM Committee on Computers and Public Policy, http://catless.ncl.ac.uk/Risks/10.61.html#subj2.

Nelson, Ted, 1987. *Computer Lib: You Can and Must Understand Computers Now/Dream Machines: New Freedoms through Computer Screens – a Minority Report*. Washington: Microsoft Press.

.*Net*, 1998. 'In Depth: Netetiquette', 50 (October), 43–45.

Nielson, Jakob, 1995. *Multimedia and Hypertext: The Internet and Beyond*. London: AP Professional.

Norman, Donald, 1998. *The Invisible Computer*. London: MIT Press.

Norman, Donald, 1990. *The Design of Everyday Things*. New York: Doubleday.

NuaSurveys, 2001. 'How many people use the web?', www.nua.ie/surveys/s.

O'Rorke, Imogen, 2000. 'All-seeing Society', *The Guardian* (11 September).

Onega, Susana, Garcia Landa and Jose Angel, 1996. 'Introduction', in *Narratology*. London: Longman, pp. 1–35.

Ong, Walter, 1998. *Orality and Literacy: The Technologizing of the Word.* London: Routledge.

Orwell, George, 1989. *1984.* Harmondsworth: Penguin, www.kulichki–lat. rambler.ru/moshlow/orwell/r/1984.txt.

Osborne, Peter, 1995. *Politics of Time, Modernity and the Avant Garde.* London: Verso.

Pangaro, Paul, 1994.'Cybernetics', www.pangaro.com/published/cyber-macmillan. html.

Parisi, Luciana, 2004. *Abstract Sex: Philosophy, Bio-technology and the Mutations of Desire.* New York: Continuum

PC Magazine, 2000a. 'GeoCities Report' (September), www.ZDNet/ PCMagazine.

PC Magazine, 2000b. 'ISPs May Move Offshore to Protect Privacy' (October), www.fipr.org/rip/182.

Penley, Constance, 1997. *NASA/TREK: Popular Science and Sex in America.* London: Verso.

Penley, Constance and Andrew Ross, 1991. *Technoculture.* Minneapolis: University of Minnesota Press.

Perec, George, 1997. *Species of Spaces and Other Pieces.* London: Penguin.

Perron, Paul J., 1987. 'Introduction', in *On Meaning.* London: University of Minnesota Press, pp. xxiii–xxiv.

Pickering, Andrew, 1992. 'From Science as Knowledge to Science as Practice', in Andrew Pickering (ed.), *Science as Practice and Culture.* Chicago: Chicago University Press, pp. 1–29.

Pinch, Trevor and Wiebe Bjiker, 1984. 'The Social Construction of Facts and Artifacts', *Social Studies of Science,* 14, 399–441.

Plant, Sadie, 1997. *Zeroes and Ones.* London: Fourth Estate.

Plant, Sadie, 1996. 'On the Matrix, Cyberfeminist Simulations', in Rob Shields (ed.), *Cultures of Internet, Virtual Spaces, Real Histories, Living Bodies.* London: Sage, pp. 170–183.

Plato, 1973. *Phaedrus and Letters VII and VIII.* London: Penguin.

Pollock, Griselda, 2003. 'Responses to Mieke Bal's "Visual Essentialism and the Object of Visual Culture"', *Journal of Visual Culture,* 2:2, 228–267.

Poster, Mark, 2001. *What's the Matter with the Internet?* London: University of Minnesota Press.

Poster, Mark, 1995. *The Second Media Age.* Cambridge: Polity.

Poster, Mark, 1991. *The Mode of Information.* London: Polity.

Preece, Jenny *et al.,* 1994. *Human-Computer Interaction.* Reading: Addison Wesley.

Radaka Hosting, 2001. 'Important News', notice from Bourbon Street community leaders, www.radaka.org.html.

Rajchman, John, 2001. *The Deleuze Connections.* Cambridge MA: MIT Press.

Renand, Sheldon, 1996. 'The net and the Future of Being Fictive', in Lyn Hershman Leeson (ed.), *Clicking In: Hot Links to a Digital Culture.* Seattle: Bay Press, pp. 61–70.

Resnick, David, 1998. 'Politics on the Internet: The Normalization of Cyberspace', in Chris Toulouse and Tim Luke (eds), *The Politics of Cyberspace*. London: Routledge, pp. 48–68.

Reuters, 1999. 'Yahoo, GeoCities Deal Is a Go' (28 January), www.zdnet. co.uk.news.

Rheingold, Howard, 1994. *The Virtual Community*. London: Martin Secker and Warburg.

Ricoeur, Paul, 1992. *Oneself as Another*. London: University of Chicago Press.

Ricoeur, Paul, 1991. 'The Creativity of Language', in Mario Valdes (ed.), *A Ricoeur Reader, Reflection and Imagination*. Toronto: University of Toronto Press, pp. 463–481.

Ricoeur, Paul, 1984. *Time and Narrative*. Chicago: University of Chicago Press.

Riding, Chris, 1995. 'Drowning by MicroGallery', in James Brook and Iain Boal (eds), *Resisting the Virtual Life, the Culture and Politics of Information*. San Francisco: City Lights.

Robins, Kevin, 1996. 'Cyberspace and the World We Live in', in John Dovey (ed.), *Fractal Dreams: New Media in Social Context*. London: Lawrence and Wishart, pp. 1–29.

Robins, Kevin and Frank Webster, 1999. *Times of the Technoculture: From the Information Society to the Virtual Life*. London: Routledge.

Robins, Kevin and Frank Webster, 1987. 'Cybernetic Capitalism: Information Technology, Everyday Life', in Vincent Mosco and Janet Wasco (eds), *The Political Economy of Information*. Madison: University of Wisconsin Press, pp. 44–71.

Robins, Kevin and Frank Webster, 1986. *Information Technology: A Luddite Analysis*. New Jersey: Ablex.

Rodowick, David, 2001. *Reading the Figural, or, Philosophy after the New Media*. London: Duke University Press.

Rollo, Jane, 1996. Interview with Caroline Bassett, Bookworks.

Rosello, Mireille, 1994. 'The Screener's Maps: Michel de Certeau's Wandersmanner and Paul Auster's Hypertextual Detective', in George Landow (ed.), *Hyper/Text/Theory*. London: Johns Hopkins University Press, pp. 121–158.

Rosen, Michael, 1986. 'Introduction', in Michael Rosen (ed.), *Narrative, Apparatus, Ideology: A Film Theory Reader*. New York: Columbia University Press, pp. 3–16.

Ross, Andrew, 1998. *Real Love: In Pursuit of Cultural Justice*. London: Routledge.

Ross, Andrew, 1997. 'Coming to an Office Near You', *Wired*, 3:3 (March), 39–40.

Rossetto, Louis, 1995. 'We Have It in Our Power to Begin the World Over Again', cover story and opening leader, *Wired UK*, 1:1, 14.

Ryan, Marie-Laure, 2004. Introduction to Digital Media section, in Marie-Laure Ryan (ed.), *Narrative across Media: The Languages of Storytelling*. London: University of Nebraska Press, pp. 329–335.

Ryan, Marie-Laure, 2004. 'Will New Media Produce New Narratives?', in Marie-Laure Ryan (ed.), *Narrative across Media: The Languages of Storytelling*. London: University of Nebraska Press, pp. 337–390.

Ryan, Marie-Laure, 1991. *Possible Worlds, Artificial Intelligence and Narrative Theory*. Bloomington and Indianapolis: Indiana University Press.

Sampio, Anna and Janni Aragon, 1998. 'To Boldly Go Where No Man Has Gone Before: Women and Politics in Cyberspace', in Chris Toulouse and Tim Luke (eds), *The Politics of Cyberspace*. London: Routledge, pp. 144–166.

Sandford, Stella, 2004. 'Let's Talk about Sex', *Radical Philosophy*, 127 (September/October), 35–40.

Sardar, Ziauddin, 1996. 'alt.civilisation.faq: Cyberspace as the Darker Side of the West', in Ziauddin Sardar and Jereme R. Ravetz (eds), *Cyberfutures; Culture and Politics on the Information Highway*. London: Pluto, pp. 14–42.

Sassower, Raphael, 1997. *Technoscientific Angst*. London: University of Minnesota Press.

Schiller, Dan, 1997. 'The Information Commodity, a Preliminary View', in Michael Stack, Jim Davis and Thomas Hirschl (eds), *Cutting Edge*. London: Verso, pp. 103–131.

Schmeiser, Lisa, 1995. 'Women on the Web', *CMC Magazine*, 2:3 (March), www.ibiblio.org/cmc/mag/1995/mar/lisa.html.

Schultz, Tanjev, 2000. 'Mass Media and the Concept of Interactivity', *Media Culture and Society*, 22:2–5, 222.

Screen Digest, 1997. 'News Briefs' (2 April), 2.

See, Diane, 1998. 'Homesteaders Threaten to Up Stakes', *Industry Standard* (23 June), www.industrystandard.com.

Sekula, Allan, 1986. 'The Body in the Archive', *October*, 39: 1–64.

Sellers, Don, 1997. *Getting Hits: The Definitive Guide to Promoting Your Website*. London: Peachpit Press.

Sherman Barrie and Phil Judkins, 1992. *Glimpses of Heaven, Visions of Hell – Virtual Reality and Its Implications*. London: Hodder and Stoughton.

Shields, Rob, 1998. *Lefebvre, Love and Struggle: Spatial Dialectics*. London: Routledge.

Silverstone, Roger, 2006. 'Domesticating Domestication. Reflections on the Life of a Concept', in Thomas Berker *et al.* (eds), *Domestication of Media and Technology*. Maidenhead: Open University Press, pp. 229–248.

Silverstone, Roger, 1999. *Why Study the Media?* London: Sage.

Silverstone, Roger, 1994. *Television and Everyday Life*. London: Routledge.

Silverstone, Roger, 1981. *The Message of Television*. Aldershot: Avebury Press.

Silverstone, Roger and Eric Hirsch, 1992. 'Introduction', in Roger Silverstone Eric Hirsch (eds), *Consuming Technologies, Media and Communication in Domestic Spaces*. London: Routledge, pp. 15–31.

Singhal, Arvind and M. Everett Rogers, 2000. *India's Communications Revolution*. London: Sage.

Sobchack, Vivian, 1999. 'Nostalgia for a Digital Object: Regrets on the Quickening of Quicktime'. *Millennium Film Journal*, 34 (Fall), 4–23.

Solnit, Rebecca, 1995. 'The Garden of Merging Paths', in J. Brook and Iain Boal (eds), *Resisting the Virtual Life, the Culture and Politics of Information*. San Francisco: City Lights, pp. 221–234.

Soper, Kate, 1986. *Humanism and Anti-Humanism*. London: Hutchinson.

Spinner, Jackie, 2003. 'A Fast-Moving Fad Comes Slowly to Washington: "Flash Mobs" Gather, Just Because', *Washington Post* (21 August), A01.

Spivak, Gayatri Chakravorty, 1988. 'Can the Subaltern Speak?', in Cary Nelson and Lawrence Grossberg (eds), *Marxism and the Interpretation of Culture*. Urbana and Chicago: University of Illinois Press, pp.271–314.

Squires, Judith, 1996. 'Fabulous Feminist Futures', in Jon Dovey (ed.), *Fractal Dreams: New Media in Social Context*. London: Lawrence and Wishart, pp. 194–216.

Squires, Judith, 1994. 'Introduction', in Erica Carter, James Donald and Judith Squires (eds), *Space and Place: Theories of Identity and Location*. London: Lawrence and Wishart.

Stabile, Carol, 1994. *Feminism and the Technological Fix*. Manchester: Manchester University Press, pp. 2–8.

Stallabrass, Julian, 1999. 'The Ideal City and the Virtual Hive: Modernism and the Emerging Order in Computer Culture', in John Downey and Jim McGuigan (eds), *TechnoCities*. London, Sage, pp. 108–120.

Stallabrass, Julian, 1996. *Gargantua*. London: Verso.

Standage, Tom, 1998. *The Victorian Internet*. London: Weidenfeld and Nicholson.

Stanworth, Celia, 1998. 'Telework and the Information Age', *New Technology and Employment*, 13, 51–62.

Sterling, Bruce, 1993. 'Internet', *Magazine for Fantasy and Science Fiction* (February), http://w3.aces.uiuc.edu/AIM/scale/nethistory.html.

Stern, Megan, 2004. 'Techies: A Review of Kaplan's Readings in Philosophy and Wacjman's Technofeminism', *Radical Philosophy*, 127 (September/October), 44–48.

Stone, Allucquere Rosanne, 1995. *The War of Desire and Technology at the Close of the Mechanical Age*. London: MIT Press.

Strate, Lance, 2000. 'Hypermedia, Space and Dimensionality', in Stephanie Gibson and Ollie Oviedo (eds), *The Emerging Cyberculture*. New Jersey: Hampton Press, pp. 267–285.

Street, John, 2001. 'The Transformation of Political Modernity', in Barrie Axford and Richard Huggins (eds), *New Media and Politics*. London: Sage, pp. 210–225.

Strout, Joe, 2000. 'Uploading by the Moravec Procedure', www.ibiblio.org/jstrout/uploading/moravec.html.

Taylor, Paul, 2000. 'McLuhan's Millennium Message', *New Media and Society*, 2:3, 373–381.

Taylor, Paul, 1999. *Hackers: Crime in the Digital Sublime*. London: Routledge.

Terranova, Tiziana, 2004. *Network Culture*. London: Pluto Press.

Terranova, Tiziana, 2000. 'Infallible Universal Happiness', in Angela Dimitrakaki, Pam Skelton and Mare Tralla (eds), *Private Views: Spaces and Gender: Contemporary Art from Britain and Estonia*. London: Women's Art Library, pp. 110–120.

Thrift, Nigel, 1996. *Spatial Formations*. London: Sage.

Turkle, Sherry, 1996. 'Rethinking Identity through Virtual Community', in Hershman Leeson (ed.), *Clicking In, Hot links to Digital Culture*. Seattle: Bay Press, pp.116–123.

Turkle, Sherry, 1995. *Life on the Screen*. London: Weidenfeld and Nicolson.

Uhlig, Robert, 1995. 'Digital Eve is Brought to Life on the Internet', *Electronic Telegraph*, (30 November), www.telegraph.co.uk/.

Valdes, Mario, 1991. 'Paul Ricoeur's Post-Structuralist Hermeneutics', in Mario Valdes (ed.), *A Ricoeur Reader, Reflection and Imagination*. Toronto: University of Toronto Press, pp. 3–43.

Van Mourik Broekman, Pauline, 1995. 'Video Positive 1995', *Mute*, 12:2 (Summer), xii–xiii.

Vaneigem, Raoul, 1961. 'Comments against Urbanism', *Internationale Situationniste*, 6 (August), 33–37.

Virilio, Paul, 1997. *Open Sky*. London: Verso.

Volkhart, Yvonne, 1999. 'Infobiobodies: Art and Aesthetic Strategies in the New World Order, in the *Next Cyberfeminist International*. Hamburg: Old Boys Network, pp. 61–69.

Voloshinov, Valentin N., 1973. *Marxism and the Philosophy of Language*. New York: Seminar Press.

Wacjman, Judith, 2004. *Technofeminism*. Cambridge: Polity.

Wakeford, Nina, 1997. 'Networking Women and Grrrls with Information/ Communication Technology', in Jennifer Terry and Melanie Calvert (eds), *Processed Lives, Gender and Technology in Everyday Life*. London: Routledge, pp. 51–66.

Waldby, Catherine, 2000. *The Visible Human Project*. London: Routledge.

Wall, Angela, 2000. 'Mothers, Monsters and Family Values: Assisted Reproduction and the Ageing Natural Body', in Janine Marchessault and Kim Sawchuk (eds), *Wild Science, Reading Feminism, Medicine and the Media*. London: Routledge, pp. 167–185.

Watson, Ben, 1998. *Art, Class and Cleavage*. London: Quartet Books.

We, Gladys, 1994. 'Cross-Gender Communication in Cyberspace', in *Arachnet Electronic Journal on Virtual Culture*, 2:3 (July), www.mith2.umd.edu/ WomensStudies/Computing/Articles+ResearchPapers/ArachnetJournal1/ contents.

Weber, Samuel, 1983. 'Capitalizing History: Notes on the Political Unconscious', *Diacritics*, 13:2 (Summer), 14–28.

Webster, Frank, 1995. *Theories of the Information Society*. London: Routledge.

Wertheim, Margaret, 1999. *The Pearly Gates of Cyberspace*. London: Virago.

Wiener, Norbert, 1961. *Cybernetics, or Control and Communication in the Animal and the Machine*. Cambridge MA: MIT Press.

Wilbert, Chris, 1996. 'Anti-This, Against That', conference paper, Geographies of Domination/Resistance, University of Glasgow, 19 September.

Williams, Raymond, 1990. *Television, Technology and Cultural Form*. London: Routledge.

Winner, Langdon, 1999. 'Do Artifacts Have Politics?', in Donald MacKenzie and Judy Wacjman (eds), *The Social Shaping of Technology*. Buckingham: Open University, pp. 28–41.

Winner, Langdon, 1989. 'Mythinformation in the High Tech Era', in Forester Tom (ed.), *Computers in the Human Context*. Oxford: Blackwell, pp. 82–94.

Winner, Langdon, 1977. *Autonomous Technology*. Cambridge, MA: MIT Press.

Winograd, Terry, 1994. Interview with Jenny Preece, in Jenny Preece (ed.), *Human-Computer Interaction*. Reading: Addison-Wesley, pp. 28–29.

Winston, Brian, 1998. *Media Technology and Society*. London: Routledge.

Wired, 1998. 'Fetish Column', *Wired*, 6:5 (May), 32.

Witheford, Nick, 1994. 'Autonomist Marxism and the Information Society', *Capital and Class*, 52 (Spring), 85–125.

Woolgar, Steve, 1985. 'Why Not a Sociology of Machines? The Case of Sociology and Artificial Intelligence', *Sociology*, 19:4 (November), 557–572.

Worthington, Simon, 1996. 'Release to ROM', *Mute*, 5 (Summer), xviii.

Wright, Robert, 1993. 'Voice of America', *New Republic*, www.EFF.org./archive/html.

Yahoo!, 1999a. 'Yahoo Completes GeoCities Acquisition', press release (28 May), http://docs.yahoo.com/docs/pr/release321.html.

Yahoo!, 1999b. 'Yahoo! Opens Yahoo!GeoCities', press release (28 June), http://geocities.yahoo.com/docs/pr/release557.html.

Yahoo!GeoCities, 2001. College Park, www.yahoo!geocities.com.

Yahoo!GeoCities, 2000. Homepage, http://geocities.yahoo.com/main/about.html.

Yoffie, David, 1997. *Competing in the Age of Digital Convergence*. Boston: Havard Busines School Press.

ZDNet, 1999a. 'FTC Will Back Online Privacy Groups', *ZNNet UK News* (28 May), www.zdnet.co.uk.news.

ZDNet, 1999b. 'Yahoo Does It Again', *ZDNet UK News* (8 April), www.zdnet.co.uk.news.

ZDNet, 1998. 'Us Report: GeoCities Looks for Revenues in Searches', UK News (20 October), www.zdnet.co.uk.news.

Index

EU authorised representative for GPSR:
Easy Access System Europe, Mustamäe tee 50,
10621 Tallinn, Estonia
gpsr.requests@easproject.com

www.ingramcontent.com/pod-product-compliance
Lightning Source LLC
Chambersburg PA
CBHW071424050326
40689CB00010B/1973